ORSON WELLES'S LAST MOVIE

ALSO BY JOSH KARP

A Futile and Stupid Gesture:
How Doug Kenney and National Lampoon
Changed Comedy Forever

Straight Down the Middle:
Shivas Irons, Bagger Vance, and How I Learned to
Stop Worrying and Love My Golf Swing

ORSON WELLES'S LAST MOVIE

THE MAKING OF THE OTHER SIDE OF THE WIND

JOSH KARP

ST. MARTIN'S PRESS ≋ NEW YORK

www.stmartins.com

Designed by Steven Seighman

Library of Congress Cataloging-in-Publication Data

Karp, Josh.
    Orson Welles's last movie : the making of The other side of the wind / Josh Karp.—First edition.
        Pages   cm
    ISBN 978-1-250-00708-7 (hardcover)
    ISBN 978-1-250-01608-9 (e-book)
  1. Other side of the wind (Motion picture)   I. Title.
    PN1997.O755K37 2015
    791.43'72—dc23   2015002464

St. Martin's Press books may be purchased for educational, business, or promotional use. For information on bulk purchases, please contact the Macmillan Corporate and Premium Sales Department at 1-800-221-7945, extension 5442, or write to specialmarkets@macmillan.com.

First Edition: April 2015

10   9   8   7   6   5   4   3   2   1

For my father—a lover of the absurd, the eccentric, and the larger-than-life

CONTENTS

A director makes only one movie in his life.
Then he breaks it into pieces
and makes it again.

—Jean Renoir

ORSON ···· ···· WELLES'S LAST MOVIE

PROLOGUE: AFTER "THE END"

O rson would have started here—at the end—with the death of his main character. If this were a movie, and Orson were directing, it might well have begun like this.

First, a new day begins, with an opening shot of a cloudless Dodgers-blue sky and a magnificent sun shining, after which we cut to the familiar palm trees that adorn a mansion-lined Beverly Hills street. Now—Orson's voice:

It is seven thirty A.M., *October 10, 1985, and this is Roxbury Drive in Beverly Hills, California. They call it "the Street of the Stars." It's the kind of place where the hero of our story might live—given that he was a larger-than-life figure of Hollywood's golden era.*

We travel past mansion after mansion, with Orson pointing out that each is someplace where our main character *didn't* live. Places such as Jimmy Stewart's Tudor, Lucille Ball's colonial, and Jack Benny's place with the big bay windows.

No. He didn't live in any of these homes.

We see lawns being watered, men retrieving newspapers, and hedges being clipped by uniformed landscapers. Orson explains that in 1985 nobody is working with a trainer or going to yoga at seven thirty A.M. Instead, the old stars who live in these houses are likely in bed or sitting by their pools, eating soft-boiled eggs, grapefruit, toast with marmalade, and coffee—all served off silver trays by a member of their staff.

Our story, Orson explains, doesn't start here. No, it begins a few short miles (but a world away) northeast at the other end of Sunset Boulevard in West Hollywood. So we leave Beverly Hills, until the camera captures Sunset Boulevard landmarks such as the Chateau Marmont, Sunset Tower, Whiskey a Go Go, and Trocadero. Soon there is a left turn, heading a block or two up above Sunset and Hollywood Boulevards to a less swanky neighborhood made up of smaller mansions, large but ramshackle homes, and the kinds of three-floor apartment buildings where one can imagine fading stars, of the Peter Lorre variety, living in their decline.

Then the camera stops and focuses on a small but beautiful, white-pillared Georgian with a wrought-iron fence.

Well, Orson would say with a sigh, *here we are: a long way from Beverly Hills at this lovely but modest home on North Stanley Avenue, where our subject lives. Though it's hardly Roxbury Drive, it has some trappings of a star's home: a beautiful garden in front, spraying red and pink roses across the white exterior; and out back there is a guesthouse and a lovely pool. But, no, you won't find our hero floating dead in the water like* Sunset Boulevard's *Joe Gillis—the screenwriter who always wanted a pool and finally got one. No, our hero never wanted money, or a mansion, and definitely not a pool. He didn't want any of that. Instead, he was simply a poor slob who just wanted to make pictures.*

And it is here, at this house, on North Stanley Avenue, that our story ends and, thus, it also begins. Let's go in.

The camera leads us in an open front door, down a sunny hallway, through a living room, and into the kitchen, where a white-coated houseman is cleaning up last night's dinner: empty bottles of old wine; a standing rib roast, picked clean; a vast empty salad bowl; a crystal dish smeared with cocktail sauce and filled with shrimp tails; and ashtrays brimming with the wide stubs of fat Cuban cigars.

After exiting the kitchen, we walk up a staircase, soon following a faint ribbon of smoke. As the smoke gets thicker, we follow it upstairs and into a bedroom turned office. There is a bookshelf filled with scripts. A film editing table. A still camera. An easel and some paints. Then there is the source of the smoke: an ashtray sitting on a card table that also holds a typewriter—which the camera closes in on to reveal a silver tag screwed to its side, reading: "Property of Columbia Pictures." Panning up, we see paper in the typewriter, then pull back to see a mane of dark graying hair tossed forward on the page. Farther back still, we see the hair sits on the head of a gigantic man in a purple robe who is facedown on the keyboard. Then, Orson continues:

And so we begin here, at the end, October 10, 1985, at this home on North Stanley Avenue, with the death of our main character. Myself. Your obedient servant: the late Orson Welles.

During my seventy years I said many things. Because I was Orson Welles, many of them were written down by reporters, friends, film students, enemies, worshippers, biographers, cineastes, and critics. I confess that much of it was fiction created to protect myself or burnish my legend by creating an air of mystery. Sometimes it was simply for my own amusement. But if you'll allow me to indulge in the utterly narcissistic act of quoting myself, I want to share something I said in candor and which seems well suited to the moment.

"We are born alone, we live alone, and we die alone. Only through our love and friendship can we create the illusion that for the moment we are not alone."

I suppose I was right. Because there I am—most certainly dead and clearly alone. The irony isn't lost on me. I can assure you of that.

Yet there is also something else important I want you to take away. I made my living as an actor and film director. My career was built on creating illusions for others and myself.

And thus it was fifteen years earlier that I had just begun work on one of my greatest acts of creating such illusions to prove that I was anything but alone. I was making a movie . . .

It was 1970. I'd just returned to Hollywood after more than a decade in Europe, determined to make an innovative comeback movie about a legendary director who returns from a decade of self-imposed exile in Europe, looking for money to complete his innovative comeback movie.

Some will say it was autobiographical. Others will call it an exposé about Hollywood in the early 1970s. There will be those who think it's a big "fuck you" to the studios or revenge against Ernest Hemingway. A few believe it was a way of turning my girlfriend into a movie star, or even some type of Ponzi scheme. Most of all, people will claim it was more than a movie. That it was a final artistic statement; a bookend to Citizen Kane; *and the only thing keeping me alive. Were they right? Well, I suppose that's the question. But, for now, I've told you enough. From here forward, I will let you hear the story of* The Other Side of the Wind—*told through the eyes of those who were there and some who weren't. I will let you listen to those perspectives and viewpoints. Because I've found out that it is the only way to see if we can understand art, behavior, and life. And as the jury, I call upon the best people I can think of—the individual members of the audience. They are the ultimate judge—and always will be.*

BACKSTORY: BEFORE
THE BEGINNING

One of the things you must understand about Orson Welles is that he was a remarkable storyteller: in person, on-screen, at your dinner table, late at night, onstage, over a long lunch, in his living room, and anywhere else he happened to be. His life, work, faults, brilliance, towering achievements, and epic failures were all amazing stories that Orson told masterfully.

The initial inspiration for *The Other Side of the Wind*, actually came from one of those stories—one that Orson liked to tell about the day he had a fistfight with Ernest Hemingway.

It was May 1937: before *War of the Worlds,* before *Citizen Kane,* and more than thirty years before he shot the first frame of *The Other Side of the Wind.*

Hired to narrate Hemingway's script for *The Spanish Earth,* a proleftist Spanish Civil War documentary made by Joris Ivens, Orson entered a Manhattan recording studio and encountered the legendary author.

On the day the two men met, Welles was only twenty-two but had already achieved more than most artists dream of accomplishing in a lifetime. He was a Broadway wunderkind with his own theater company and his own radio show. As a radio performer he was making more than $1,000 a week during the Depression and was the voice of the title character on the wildly popular radio detective show *The Shadow,* meaning he was heard in millions of living rooms each week.

It was a juncture in his life when Welles was so busy that he allegedly hired an ambulance (sirens blaring to avoid traffic) to get him from radio gigs to the theater on time. It wasn't illegal and he was Orson Welles, so why not?

By the time he met Hemingway, Welles had staged an all-black *Macbeth* set in nineteenth-century Haiti and was working on a fascist-themed, modern-dress *Julius Caesar.* Within a year he'd appear on the cover of *Time* magazine. Then that Halloween there was the broadcast of *The War of the Worlds,* and if anyone hadn't heard of Orson Welles by November 1938, they were either living in a cave or dead.

Now famous, he went to Hollywood, where by the age of twenty-six he'd co-written, directed, and starred in his first full-length film: *Citizen Kane.* It was a time, said one friend, where "anything seemed possible" when you were working with Orson.

Anything was possible. Everything was possible. And the day he met Hemingway, Orson was on the cusp of exploding as an artist and a star.

Hemingway, meanwhile, was thirty-seven and had already written *A Farewell to Arms* and *The Sun Also Rises.* He'd driven an ambulance in World War I, where he'd been injured by mortar fire and witnessed violent death firsthand while still in his early twenties. Hemingway knew life in the most physical sense. He was a man's man who stalked big game, reeled in gigantic marlins, and chased adventure to such an extreme that years later he survived two plane crashes in the same day while hunting in Africa. It fit perfectly with the image he cultivated—one crash simply wasn't enough. It had been a life consciously marked by death and violence, things that were in his blood and affirmed his existence.

They didn't know it, but Welles and Hemingway shared more than artistry and big personalities. Both men had a deep love for Spain and the art of bullfighting, and each was friendly with legendary torero Antonio Ordóñez. But in May 1937, their shared passions were of no consequence. What mattered was what Orson did after entering the studio.

Having reworked Shakespeare, Welles likely didn't think twice about trying to improve Hemingway's script. Orson claimed he'd tried only to make it more Hemingwayesque, cutting the words back to their essence and letting images on-screen speak for themselves. Perhaps they could do away with lines such as "Here are the faces of men who are close to death" and just show the faces themselves.

Shocked by Welles's audacity, Hemingway immediately went after the softest spot he could find and used Orson's theater background to infer that he was gay and didn't know a thing about war or other manly pursuits. More than a decade later, Hemingway would tell John Huston that every time Welles said "infantry" it "was like a cocksucker swallowing."

Not yet fat, young Orson Welles was still a big man, tall and sturdy, with large feet. Despite his size, however, Welles wasn't prone to violence. But, having dealt with bullies since his youth, he knew just how to retaliate. If the hairy-chested author wanted a faggot, Orson would give him one. So, great actor that he was, Welles camped it up and drove Hemingway over the edge.

"Mister Hemingway," Welles lisped in the swishiest voice he could muster, "how strong you are and how big you are!"

The counterpunch hit Hemingway exactly where Orson intended, and the novelist exploded, allegedly picking up a chair and attacking Welles, who grabbed a chair of his own. The aftermath, as Orson described it, was a cartoonish sound booth brawl played out while bloody images of the Spanish Civil War flickered behind them.

Eventually, however, both men concluded that the fight was insane, collapsed to the floor in laughter, and shared a bottle of whiskey. Thus began a friendship that lasted until Hemingway shot himself in the head on July 2, 1961.

Welles told this tale time and again: the epic day that two of the great creative geniuses of the twentieth century duked it out while men died for freedom on the screen in the background. And when *The Spanish Earth* premiered that August, the narration had been rerecorded by Hemingway himself.

While visiting writer Peter Viertel in Klosters, Switzerland, in 1958, Welles mentioned that he'd been working on a script about a ridiculously masculine novelist who has lost his creative powers and is now trailed across Spain by a collection of sycophantic biographers, worshipful grad students, and others who reassure him of his greatness.

Married to actress Deborah Kerr, Viertel was close friends with both Hemingway and John Huston, having fictionalized the latter as an adventure-seeking filmmaker in his novel *White Hunter Black Heart*, an account of making *The African Queen* on location in Uganda and the Congo.

As Welles described how his character is suffering the plight of middle-aged artists who "get to be like Hemingway, nothing but people writing about you," and his ensuing obsession with a young male toreador, Viertel asked Orson if the movie was about Hemingway or himself.

"It's about both of us," Welles said with a deep, wheezy laugh.

With a few exceptions, Welles would spend the rest of his life insisting the film wasn't autobiographical, including in an interview in 1962, a year after Hemingway died.

"I will play the part," Orson said. "But don't look for a self-portrait in it."

Welles explained that unlike Hemingway and F. Scott Fitzgerald, he didn't believe that genius disappeared with age.

"At the end of his life, Hemingway always tried to prove that he was still young. Fitzgerald, even before he turned forty, was rotted with the same anguish," said the forty-seven-year-old Welles. "That attitude is death. It's not something that bothers me."

His film, Welles told the reporter, was ultimately "about death, the portrait of decadence, a ruin."

He was calling it *The Sacred Beasts*.

Documentary filmmakers Albert and David Maysles (the eventual creators of *Grey Gardens* and *Gimme Shelter*) were at Cannes in 1966 when they were told Orson Welles wanted to meet them at a bar about twenty minutes from town. When the pair arrived, Orson said he was impressed by their work and asked where they'd be going after the festival.

"Back to New York," they said.

"Why don't you come spend a week with me in Madrid?" Welles said, and received the only response people gave when he asked that question.

"We spent day after day with him," Albert Maysles said. "And on the first or second day, he began talking about a movie we'd make together about people who go to bullfights. So we picked up our cameras and started filming him."

The result was *Orson Welles in Spain*, a ten-minute documentary in three segments. In the first, Orson speaks Spanish as he walks toward a bullfight arena. Part two, shot in the stadium, shows a jowly, clean-shaven Welles describing the ritual of the corrida, which he considers "a tragedy in three acts," with noble bulls as heroes who await "their death in the afternoon." The tragedy, Orson explains, is based on the pure, innocent virtue of the bulls, who are truly the sacred beasts.

A longtime lover of bullfighting, Welles told Peter Bogdanovich that he'd been a matador in his late teens while he lived in Seville and briefly made good money writing pulp novels, which allowed him to buy his own bulls and get in the ring a few times, billed as "El Americano." Working as "a pro," Welles said, he was "scared to death . . . but having the time of [his] life" inside the ring.

By 1966, his feelings had changed. Bullfighting now seemed a voyeuristic act, as he told Michael Parkinson in 1974, where fans were "living and dying second hand" through the toreadors.

The third section shows Welles in a light-filled outdoor restaurant in the atrium of a Madrid hotel, where he's addressing a group of Americans who have been described as potential investors or producers but whom Maysles recalls as being curious hotel guests. It's an apt description of a group that resembles a collection of midwestern attorneys and their wives, in town for a conference, who realize Orson Welles is at their hotel. So they stand, drinks in hand, as Welles lays out the film, its protagonist, and the novel manner in which he intends to shoot it.

Calling it a picture "about the love of death," Welles describes the main character, who is no longer a novelist but is instead a "pseudo-Hemingway, a movie director, a fellow that you can hardly see through the bush of hair on his chest."

The plot, he explains, contains "a confrontation between my hero, an aging American romantic who is having trouble supporting himself, and an anti-romantic young man of the 'new generation' who ends up subscribing to romanticism and defending the bullfight."

Then he drops the bomb.

"We're going to shoot it without a script," Welles says, excitement lighting up his face. "I've written the script, I know the whole story. I know everything that happens. . . . [But] what I'm going to do is get the actors in every situation, tell them what has happened up to this moment, who they are, and I believe they will find what is true and inevitable from what I've said. . . ."

Then a man in horn-rimmed glasses asks a question worthy of any producer:

"Have you ever done that with other films?"

"Nobody's ever done it," Welles responds proudly.

Later, Welles says, the shoot will be short. Eight weeks—at most.

In the years since his confrontation with Hemingway, Welles converted a brief encounter into the seed of a story that morphed into *The Sacred*

Beasts and, then, *The Other Side of the Wind,* which he began shooting in August 1970.

By then he'd changed the bullfighting angle into a symbolic piece of backdrop and changed the locus from Spain to Hollywood. Compressing the action into a single day, he used a seventieth birthday party for the main character that would end with his death. The day he chose was July 2, the date on which Hemingway took his own life.

Imbuing it with brilliance, magic, mystery, chaos, and the search for identity that seems to be at the heart of nearly all his movies, Welles embarked on directing a film whose making would prove to be one of the greatest Orson Welles stories of them all.

ORSONOLOGY:
WHAT YOU MUST KNOW

Orson 101: Genius—1915–1941

What he hated was the responsibility of his own genius.
—Orson Welles on John Barrymore

Another story Welles liked to tell was about his childhood and the claim that the first word his mother ever spoke to him was "genius." And true or not, Orson Welles was indeed born a genius—or literally, and successfully, raised to be one.

Taking on a mythic quality, the genius within Orson was supported by the contention of his future guardian, Dr. Maurice Bernstein, that an eighteen-month-old Orson told him that "the desire to take medicine is one of the greatest features that distinguishes men from the animals."

As a child of such brilliance, he was profiled in the Madison,

Wisconsin, *Capital Times* under the headline CARTOONIST, ACTOR, POET AND ONLY 10.

Describing him as a voracious reader of books about "the old masters," with a facility for language comparable to that of an adult, the article also illustrates Orson's almost manic desire for creative expression:

> *At times when Orson is in the midst of a story and becomes particularly interested in one of the characters he is seized with the inspiration to paint the character and forthwith takes up his box of oil paints, making a study that, though amateurish in technique, shows a keen insight and interpretation.*

The simple, absolute fact of young Orson's genius (first encouraged by his mother, Beatrice, and then by everyone else) was so thoroughly ingrained that Welles later joked that "it had never occurred to me that I wasn't [a genius] until middle age."

Being declared a genius from birth leads life in many directions. A normal childhood, however, is rarely one of them. And such was the case with George Orson Welles, who took his first breath on May 6, 1915, in Kenosha, Wisconsin.

Orson was the second child for Richard and Beatrice Welles; another son, Richard ("Dickie"), was ten years older and had already failed to live up to his parents' expectations. Later diagnosed with schizophrenia, Dickie was unable to exude charm or brilliance, thus causing his parents to imbue Orson with all of their hopes and dreams. This was made all the more urgent by the faltering nature of their marriage, which would end while Orson was still a small child.

His father, Richard, was the kind of man with his own brand of cigar and a racehorse named after him. Born into a well-to-do family, he'd made a small fortune from a bicycle headlamp he'd invented, but he was also a charming alcoholic who liked to live the high life.

Strong-willed and a talented pianist filled with artistic aspirations, Beatrice left Richard and took Orson with her to Chicago. There, in her apartment, she hosted salons and other cultural gatherings, which Orson was allowed to attend as long as he behaved and conversed like an adult.

In 1924, Beatrice contracted hepatitis and died just days after Orson's ninth birthday. Shortly before passing, she had Orson come into her darkened bedroom and gave him a birthday cake. Told to blow out the candles and make a wish, Orson blew them out, but never made a wish. In his later years, he would say that not making that wish was one of his great regrets.

Upon Beatrice's death, Orson was left in the care of Richard and Dr. Bernstein, his mother's loyal suitor, who had a penchant for love triangles and had played some part in the destruction of the Welles marriage. Bernstein, however, was in love with more than Beatrice. He was utterly enthralled (though not romantically) with Orson, who called him "Dadda Bernstein."

Despite the unsavory way he'd entered the Welles family, Bernstein was more responsible than Richard, who dedicated much of his post-married life to drowning his sorrows in alcohol, opium, women, and gambling.

When it was decided that he should attend the Todd School for Boys in Woodstock, Illinois, Orson picked up a third father figure in the form of its energetic young headmaster, Roger "Skipper" Hill. With Todd as his second home, Orson became a central figure on campus, where Hill allowed him to indulge any interest and avoid anything that didn't capture his imagination. Sports and math fell by the wayside, replaced by writing, acting, and directing campus productions.

The power Orson exuded was so extraordinary that Hill's wife felt in genuine competition with the eleven-year-old who came to their home and soliloquized about writers and artists. Eventually, Hortense Hill gave in to Orson's charms. The Hill children, however, didn't acquiesce quite so easily.

Richard Welles, Maurice Bernstein, and Roger Hill shared Orson's and Beatrice's conviction that he wasn't like other children. The boy was extraordinary and deserved every bit of attention that he received. Orson Welles had been born to greatness, and nothing would disabuse these men of the belief that his destiny was to be a larger-than-life genius.

This resulted in a remarkable, and remarkably strange, upbringing, in which Orson was encouraged incessantly, given few boundaries, and rarely heard the word *no* from anyone in authority. And when limitations were created, Orson undoubtedly charmed or talked his way around them them.

Richard Welles was the weak link in the uneasy alliance that was raising Orson. Though it was his father who'd allowed Orson the rare opportunity to act like a real child during summers at a hotel he owned in Grand Detour, Illinois, Richard's drinking, jealousy of Orson, and bitterness over his failed marriage were problematic. This became all too apparent when he showed up drunk to a play Orson directed at Todd. Afterward, Orson was encouraged to cut off communication with Richard until his drinking was under control.

For that reason, Orson was estranged from his father on December 28, 1930, when Richard Welles died at fifty-eight, alone in a Chicago hotel room, of alcohol-related kidney and heart disease. As a result, his fifteen-year-old son inherited a massive well of guilt that stayed with him forever. It was a guilt so deeply felt that Orson eventually told others he was present at his "father's suicide," despite the actual facts of Richard's death. Even when he edited an issue of *Vogue Paris* in 1982, Welles wrote that as both a child and an adult, he was "convinced . . . that I had killed my father."

Now orphaned, Orson graduated from Todd the next year and seized even greater freedom to do as he pleased. Encouraged to accept a Harvard scholarship, Welles persuaded Bernstein (now his legal guardian) to first let him take a painting tour of Europe, funded by his inheritance.

On his own, Welles found his way to Dublin, where he walked into the Gate Theatre smoking a cigar and claiming he was both older and a Broadway actor.

Hilton Edwards and Micheál MacLiammóir, the gay couple who ran the Gate, didn't believe him. But it didn't matter. Listening to his deep voice, taking in the gigantic body, arched brows, and narrow eyes, they saw more than a teenager trying to be an adult. They saw *the* Orson Welles.

"He knew that he was precisely what he himself would have been had God consulted him on the subject at birth," MacLiammóir said. "He fully appreciated and approved of what had been bestowed and realized that he couldn't have done a better job himself. In fact, he would not have changed a single item."

Cast as Duke Karl Alexander in *The Jew Süss*, Welles stole the show and received a rave in *The New York Times*. Then, after a season at the Gate, Welles went to New York, where he ultimately became a famous creative wunderkind who was not only making a sizable living in the Broadway theater, but was also a young man, not yet twenty-five, who had the audacity to reimagine Shakespeare in ways that seemed to bring new significance to a pair of the great playwright's best-known works. He was more than talented or destined for stardom. Orson Welles was a tidal wave of restless creativity, spontaneous brilliance, unflagging energy, remarkable productivity, and magnetic personality, wound together in a vessel whose immense capacity to attract attention and publicity seemed just another component of his all-encompassing, all-devouring personality.

This was the Orson who conquered two mediums (radio and stage) and was preparing to transform a third. Married for the first time, he was a man who seemed to have named his daughter Christopher simply because it allowed him to send out a birth announcement that read: "Christopher—she is here."

There was fame, family, and affairs with several actresses and ballerinas. Orson acted, directed, and produced in a stormy but symbiotic partnership with John Houseman, whose own talents took a backseat when he saw that his role was to make sure everything was arranged so that Orson could show up and do nothing but be his brilliant Orsonian self.

It is hard to imagine that he ever slept.

That was Orson Welles up until 1941. He was spectacular.

ORSON 102: SENSATIONAL CATASTROPHES—1942–1970

At a 1979 American Film Institute (AFI) seminar covering his career, Welles lamented, in good humor, that it was "hard to imagine a movie career more littered with sensational catastrophes than mine."

Now almost sixty-four, Orson had started working on *The Other Side of the Wind* nearly a decade earlier. Every time things seemed to be going well, something would screw it all up. At the time of the seminar, as he claimed to be nearing resolution of a dispute with his chief financial backer—the brother-in-law of the shah of Iran—that same backer's assets (ostensibly including the film's negative) were allegedly being seized by Ayatollah Khomeini's regime, which had toppled the shah only weeks before.

If Welles circa 1941 couldn't be stopped, Orson in 1979 just couldn't catch a break. All that had come so easily now seemed as if it had somehow become cursed.

It actually started with *Citizen Kane,* over which he was given something unprecedented in Hollywood: nearly total artistic control. The fact that the final cut was being given to an outsider (in his early twenties, no less) who'd never even directed a feature film made him a less than popular figure in late thirties/early forties Hollywood.

Though it came to be regarded as arguably the greatest film ever made, *Kane* only broke even at the box office, due in part to threats and attacks suffered at the hands of William Randolph Hearst and his newspaper empire. But given his thirst to create, Orson was undeterred.

His next film was *The Magnificent Ambersons,* the story of a wealthy

ector for hire, in order to convince executives he was still fit to make
ns for their studios. Between 1946 and 1948, he directed *The Stranger,*
e Lady from Shanghai, and *Macbeth*—the last made for Republic,
'overty Row studio that occasionally cranked out higher-end fare such
The Quiet Man.

By the late 1940s, Welles gave up and headed for Europe, where
acted in other people's films and became a truly independent film-
ker. During this time, he made *Othello* and *Mr. Arkadin,* both shot
der duress with money Orson raised from financiers who ultimately
ved problematic for a variety of reasons.

When he returned to Hollywood in the late 1950s, Universal hired
elles to direct *Touch of Evil* (1958), a potboiler about corrupt cops in
Mexican border town. Orson converted it into a noir classic. Given a
all paint box, he produced art. But old problems reemerged, and a
pute over final cut found Welles skipping his eldest daughter's wed-
ig to write a passionate fifty-eight-page memo to Universal execs me-
ulously detailing ideas he hoped would provide a solution for both
m and the studio. His ideas were largely ignored.

After that, Orson concluded that he was incapable of operating within
ystem where studios had "no madness in their method." The feeling
s mutual. Welles was fine as an actor, but as a director he was a
in-in-the-ass perfectionist who cared only about fulfilling his creative
ion.

So it was back to Europe, where he adapted Franz Kafka's *The Trial,*
rked on his never-completed *Don Quixote* (as well as other unfin-
ed projects), and made *Chimes at Midnight*—which some believe
s his greatest creation: a triumphant weaving together of Falstaff's
ry line from several of Shakespeare's plays. The result was a film about
character he admired and to whom he related:

"[Falstaff] is the greatest conception of a good man, the most com-
etely good man in all drama," Welles said. "His faults [laziness, ex-
ssive joviality, and the inability to control his appetites] are so
all . . . But his goodness is like bread, like wine."

turn-of-the-century midwestern family that loses ev
fails to acknowledge the changes in society represen
mobile. A bittersweet and nostalgic look at a lost era,
one in which his father thrived, *Ambersons* was a rich
terpiece that some thought was better than *Kane*. If
been allowed to finish it. Instead, after faring poorly
in Pomona (at which many audience members said it v
film), spooked RKO executives decided to cut an hour
while Orson was in South America, at the governmen
ing *It's All True*.

A documentary-like series of vignettes intended to s
Latin American relations during the war, *It's All Tru*
off from Hollywood and *Ambersons*. Though he begge
machine in order to recut the film while in Brazil, We
and the studio released its own version of *Ambersons* w
"happy ending," making it the first in a series of might-l
plagued Welles for the next thirty years.

Based on a somewhat amorphous idea, *It's All True*
ficult shoot that Orson believed was under a curse after
doo needle stuck through its screenplay. And in keepin
that some form of spell had been cast over the producti
zilian hero drowned while filming one of his scenes.

Were that not enough, Welles's relationship with RK
management changes and delays on *It's All True* cause
up on the picture and leave Orson holding the bag. Back
Welles was now a former genius who'd allegedly aband
tures since *Kane*.

Ultimately, Orson would come to see *Ambersons* ar
as the foundation of his destruction. And years later,
Welles confidant would tell a story in which they found
Ambersons late one night while shooting *The Other Sid*
In every version, the storyteller opens the door and see
and weeping, then leaves before Welles realizes he is be
For the next several years, Orson tried working in H

Playing Falstaff himself, Welles created vivid, chaotic battle scenes on a shoestring, capturing the brutality and horror of war without romance or glamour. In return he received a lengthy standing ovation at Cannes in 1966, but in the United States the film did poorly, even in art houses, and disappeared quickly.

Though so many are now considered masterpieces, every Welles film after *Kane* came with a backstory explaining what *might have* happened if Orson had been given adequate funding and support. Each delay or failure to make a profit, it seemed, had been caused by some exterior force, often bad luck or a scamming producer; each challenge was just another mountain he needed to scale in order to achieve a compromised version of his art.

With this backdrop, the Orson Welles who returned to Hollywood in 1970 was more than one man. He was a mix of personae and reputations that were as complicated as a Picasso and as simple as a caricature on the wall at Sardi's.

To executives he was an undisciplined, irresponsible spendthrift who defied any reasonable form of restraint. Meanwhile, many critics, scholars, and young filmmakers perceived him to be a certifiable genius, and his work became the subject of innumerable biographies, dissertations, and scholarly assessments. Much of this crowd viewed Orson as a misunderstood icon of artistic integrity and brilliance.

And within that group there was even a faction that Welles biographer Simon Callow calls "the Wellesolators":

Who will hear no criticism of their hero. . . . The Welles they have created is a fearless independent, punished by the world for being too talented, too original, too visionary. . . . If only Welles's sublime plans had not been viciously frustrated by the studio pygmies, they imply, the world would have been better off by dozens of flawless masterpieces.

Then there was the public, who knew him not only as the man behind *Citizen Kane* and *The War of the Worlds,* but also as a cartoonish talk show raconteur who would rent his rich voice and connotation
of class to anyone with an open checkbook.

Thus, to many he was a bloated, 350-pound celebrity coasting on
the fumes of his own fame and paying for good wine, rich meals, and
huge cigars by performing his act as a connoisseur and bon vivant. And
ultimately it would be his physical stature that many took as a reflection of his excess. To the world he seemed satiated, overstuffed, and
anything but hungry.

But in 1970, Orson was more than hungry; he was ravenous. Un-
derneath the image, the myths, and the big body, he was starving both
to live and to make movies. And the movie he was starving to make
was *The Other Side of the Wind,* which would restore both his depleted
bank account and his tarnished reputation.

The Hollywood to which Orson returned was different. Undone by court
rulings that took away their total control over talent, production, and
distribution, and unable to cope with either the dominant youth culture or television, the studio system was drawing its last breaths. What
remained was a bunch of middle-aged executives with little idea of what
people wanted to see.

From the ashes of the studio system, a "New Hollywood" emerged,
beginning with the 1967 release of *Bonnie and Clyde.* Mixing violence,
sex, and art, Arthur Penn's $2.5 million film did more than signal a break
with the Hollywood of Cary Grant, John Wayne, and Katharine Hepburn. It also brought in $50 million at the box office. And for the next
decade, young producers, executives, and directors who made personal
and idiosyncratic films (as opposed to big musicals and epic westerns)
came to rule Hollywood, which suddenly found itself in the hands of
the artists.

No movie made this point better than *Easy Rider,* the drug-fueled,
nonlinear hippie western in which the antiheroes die at the end.

Directed by Dennis Hopper and produced by BBS Productions, with a budget of roughly $400,000, the 1969 film sold $60 million worth of tickets.

Like Hopper's film, BBS was deeply emblematic of the New Hollywood. A partnership between Bert Schneider (a Cornell dropout whose father ran Columbia), Steve Blauner, and director Bob Rafelson, BBS also produced films such as *Five Easy Pieces* and *The Last Picture Show*, both symbols of a different film industry where there might be people who didn't care about Orson's reputation for excess in the name of film. Which was precisely why BBS and Columbia hired Orson to adapt—and possibly direct—Gavin Lyall's novel *Midnight Plus One*.

Expecting a screenplay in return, BBS rented Welles a typewriter and put him up in a bungalow at the Beverly Hills Hotel, where Orson was living on July 3, 1970—the day our story begins.

THE GREATEST HOME MOVIE
EVER MADE

ORSON WELLES'S UNSEEN MASTERPIECE SET FOR RELEASE

That was the headline for a January 22, 2011, *Guardian* article that hit the in-box of anyone with a Google alert set for *The Other Side of the Wind*. At long last, Orson's end-of-career magnum opus would be freed from cinematic purgatory, or hell, and projected onto art house screens the world over.

This, however, wasn't the first time resolution was imminent. Such developments had been rumored, reported, and alluded to by various parties on a regular basis for more than a decade. This time the source was an attorney representing the widow of Iranian producer Mehdi Boushehri.

"We are in negotiations which would lead to the finishing and public exhibition," Kenneth Sidle said. "Hopefully within the next few weeks we will know."

The story spread among newspapers, movie trades, film sites, and blogs, while Welles watchers cautiously kept an eye on the situation. Then, a week later, the story ended as it always had—with no movie. This time the bad news came from Orson's longtime companion Oja Kodar, who said that there had indeed been negotiations, but none that pushed the project closer to release. It was all, she said, untrue. And again, *The Other Side of the Wind* would remain unseen.

The reasons you've not seen this film are wide-ranging and often bizarre. They involve everything from the Iranian Revolution and runaway egos to greed, petty long-held grudges, bad accounting, corporations based in Liechtenstein, complicated ownership disagreements, self-destructive behavior, and an ever-expanding list of individuals who believed they had a legal, financial, moral, or artistic right to the film itself.

The aforementioned issues have successfully tanked a film that Welles began working on in August 1970 and which has seen a nearly continual effort by numerous parties to bring it to completion. But each time a deal is at hand, something new emerges that derails the entire process, making the road to the film's release a complicated labyrinth that's entered by party after party, but from which no one emerges, except to flee.

Like the failed attempts to complete *The Other Side of the Wind*, both the making of the movie and the movie itself are not typical stories. Instead they are multilayered, complicated journeys in which art and real life intersect time and again, creating what one crew member said was an often surreal atmosphere in which it was hard to tell what was part of the movie and what was reality.

That quality, combined with the fact that the film itself is incomplete and locked away both literally and legally, makes it important that you know the basic plot of *The Other Side of the Wind* prior to reading this book and joining the desperate adventure that was the making of what would be Orson Welles's attempt to shoot a picture that would be his end-of-career *Citizen Kane*.

The Plot

The Other Side of the Wind begins at the end, with the death of its main character, legendary movie director Jake Hannaford, which Orson describes in voice-over as we see the mangled, smoking remains of a sports car.

That's the car . . . what was left of it after the accident. If it was an accident. . . . The car was meant to be a present. Before he changed his mind, Hannaford was going to give it to the young leading actor of his last movie—John Dale.

We see a picture of Dale, a handsome, mildly androgynous young man whom Hannaford has saved from an alleged suicide attempt.

There is another picture of the car wreck and then still photos from a seventieth birthday party being thrown in Hannaford's honor, and which features a guest list that includes young members of New Hollywood and then a large faction that represents the old guard.

Orson tells us that most of Hannaford's cronies and contemporaries don't believe that he killed himself—because a great director like Jake wouldn't dream of such a *corny ending.*

But, as we see photos of guests at the party, the voice-over tells us that there are *other opinions* as to why Hannaford met his end on July 2, the day he turned seventy.

As the narration continues, it's explained that—in order to consider that mystery—the film we are about to see is made up of everything from still pictures and film shot by documentarians to footage from the sixteen- and eight-millimeter cameras brought to the party by assorted film nerds, directors, and critics.

A picture of Hannaford appears on the screen.

Hannaford's own unfinished motion picture is part of the testimony: The Other Side of the Wind—*it has been left just as it was when they screened it on the last day of his life.*

Set on the anniversary of Hemingway's suicide, the film confines its action to a single day. *The Other Side of the Wind* is the story of Jake
Hannaford, a hard-drinking, big-game-hunting, womanizing, adventure-
seeking director who loves to shoot in remote locations around the world
and revels in putting himself, his cast, and his crew in dangerous situations. Welles would joke that at least one crew member dies on the
set of every Hannaford film.

A product of the studio system, Hannaford fell out of favor and re-
treated to Europe for a few years of self-imposed exile and has finally
returned to Los Angeles, seeking end money to complete his artsy, mod-
ernist attempt at a sex-infused and violence-laden comeback movie that
reflects the style and values of New Hollywood circa 1970.

As Welles mentioned in his introduction, the film examines the last
day of Hannaford's life as viewed through the medium of film in every
manner possible. It comprises still photos and footage from 8mm
and 16mm cameras—as well as other formats—shot by a combination
of documentarians making films about Hannaford, young directors, and
video freaks who all brought their cameras to the party. In weaving together black-and-white with color images, the goal is to "sketch a film
likeness of the man himself as he looked through all those different
viewfinders," which also include lustrous 35mm footage of Hannaford's
film-within-the-film.

Thus the movie would be a mixture of Hannaford's smooth, elegantly
filmed picture and the raw, quick-cut, cinema verité footage from the
birthday party.

After Orson's introduction, the first thing we hear is Hannaford saying, "Ohh-kay . . . Cut!" as he finishes a day of shooting on a Hollywood soundstage and takes us into the loose, jumpy narrative that makes
up *The Other Side of the Wind*.

Leaving through the huge soundstage doors, Hannaford is chased by two writers: the overly serious, true believer Mr. Pister ("from the Film Institute") and Higgam, a smarmy goof who tells one of Jake's associates, "I'm doing the book on Mister Hannaford," to which the director's friend replies, "And I know someone somewhere who isn't."

Getting in the backseat of Hannaford's convertible, Higgam and Pister are joined by Brooks Otterlake, a hot young director whose first three pictures are all commercial and critical hits. A Hannaford protégé who once was working on a now unfinished biography of the director, Otterlake hops in the front and they begin driving to the party at Hannaford's ranch, with a soundman from one of the documentary crews hanging on to the trunk while he records their conversations.

Meanwhile, a school bus is at the studio loading up a second group that's heading to the party. First there is Juliette Riche, a prominent film critic who is writing Jake's authorized biography. Also on the bus are longtime friends and employees who make up the Hannaford mafia: Jake's secretary, Maggie; his hatchet man, Matt Costello; a bloated, drunken fascist named Pat; and Zimmie, a Jewish makeup man from Texas and an outsider who is fired on the ride to the party but still ordered to attend. In addition to those characters, the bus is carrying mannequins made up to look like Hannaford's lead actor—John Dale—who walked off the set angrily and has disappeared.

A third narrative strand involves Hannaford's producer, Billy Boyle, who is screening parts of Jake's film for Max David, a young studio chief they hope will provide them with end money. The rough assembly of Hannaford's movie is beautifully filmed but also clearly unfinished and essentially incomprehensible. When Max disdainfully asks about several scenes, Billy explains that Hannaford is carrying much of the picture "in his head." As things get worse, Max realizes the film has no script and that Hannaford is "just making it up as he goes along," to which Billy replies, "He's done it before."

The party itself is thrown by Zarah Valeska, a golden age movie star who has organized the event so Jake can meet young directors, critics, and film mavens, which will hopefully give him exposure and lead to funding for his unfinished film.

In Orson's script, the party attendees included Jack Nicholson, Jean-Luc Godard, Éric Rohmer, Bernardo Bertolucci, John Cassavetes, Andy Warhol, and others, though none of them actually appeared in the film. Instead, New Hollywood is represented by Dennis Hopper, Paul Mazursky, Henry Jaglom, Claude Chabrol, and horror film director Curtis Harrington.

Those directors and other film people gather at Jake's ranch, a manly paradise filled with hunting trophies, where the prime topics of conversation are filmmaking and Hannaford himself. Yet in one overheard conversation, we also learn that the director's last wife had been extremely wealthy, and after her death Hannaford had to sell their farm in Kenya and the yacht he'd been sailing in Mexico when he found the suicidal John Dale and saved him from drowning. Since then, he'd been trying to turn Dale into a movie star.

At the party, Hannaford drinks heavily while being trailed by a documentary crew and surrounded by young people thrusting cameras in his face. In public he is the epitome of a witty, genial rogue and plays the part of Jake Hannaford to perfection. But behind closed doors he has a private breakdown in the bathroom and some painfully revealing moments with Otterlake.

The pivotal scene at the party takes place while a crowd surrounds Otterlake and Riche, the latter of whom has intimated that she thinks Hannaford is gay and that he covers himself by famously bedding the lead actress or male star's lover on nearly every film he's ever made. Later Riche adds, "What he creates he has to wreck. It's a compulsion."

With Hannaford standing to the side, Otterlake spars with Riche over her review of his most recent film—and she reveals that Jake's protégé will earn $40 million when his production company goes public. Otterlake responds by saying that no matter what he does, the critics will still claim he stole everything from Hannaford, whom he calls "Skipper."

At the end of the scene comes one of the film's most revealing moments, when Riche blurts out her sudden realization that Hannaford and Otterlake are close because they have to be—they don't have any-one else.

Hearing this, Hannaford smiles, casts a benevolent but withering glance at Riche—who can't withstand his charm—and says, "Please, dear lady, don't tell us what you mean by that."

Then, as they prepare for a screening of Hannaford's unfinished film, there are several revelations. Some members of the Hannaford mafia arrive with a prissy prep school teacher who infers that Jake's been set up by Dale, whose suicide attempt was a ploy to help his career. Hannaford responds in a genial but venomous voice in which he gay-baits the teacher and invites him to take a naked swim in front of the other party guests.

After this, Billy returns and reveals that he couldn't persuade Max David to attend the party and watch the screening of *The Other Side of the Wind*. Completely undone, Hannaford has a confrontation with Otterlake and admits that he's behind schedule on the film, with no prospects for funding its completion.

Then, in an emotional scene with Otterlake, we realize that Hannaford is the one who's been stripped bare, and he shows shocking vulnerability in explaining that he is so broke, he might lose his home and knows he can neither ask for, nor actually receive, end money from Otterlake. This is the one time, it seems, that he can't pull it together and turn a mess into a movie.

When everyone gathers to sing "Happy Birthday," Hannaford humiliates his Native American lead actress by calling her Pocahontas and presenting her with a bone as a gift. He also expresses his rage during a semicomic scene where he shoots the dummies made up to look like Dale while Otterlake narrates the action in a variety of celebrity voices. Yet we realize that their relationship is broken, a point driven home further when a power failure requires that the screening be held at a drive-in theater, where we listen as the party guests analyze Hannaford's film.

"Man, that's all it is, death," one says. "It's just purely what he's all about."

During the screening Hannaford runs into Otterlake, who asks him what he's done wrong, before turning a line from Shakespeare's *Tempest* into the question: "Our revels now are ended?"

Hannaford's reply is cold and confirms the fact that their revels are indeed through.

Later, as the sun rises and the screening ends, a drunken Hannaford roars off in the car he intended to give Dale. Unsure whether or not he is in love with his lead actor, or willing to lower his guard and own up to possibly being homosexual, he is left with nothing: no money, no movie, and no capacity to save a shred of what once made him Jake Hannaford.

After he crashes the sports car and dies, the last words of the film are a voice-over by Hannaford, ending as he began: "Cut!"

Generation gap?
JIM BEAM
never heard of it.

Orson Welles is the father. And an acclaimed actor. Rebecca Welles Moode is the daughter. And an aspiring actress.

They're of different generations, these two. But they're very much alike when it comes to the love they share for their craft.

The Beams, too, have a craft. Different but no less compelling—the distilling of Kentucky Bourbon. And for 177 years now, son has followed father with a love for that craft.

It's a proud record.

It's a proud Bourbon. Smooth and light and mellow. With a rich aroma full of promise.

Jim Beam. For six generations; one family, one formula, one purpose. The world's finest Bourbon.

The world's finest Bourbon since 1795.

86 PROOF KENTUCKY STRAIGHT BOURBON WHISKEY DISTILLED AND BOTTLED BY THE JAMES B. BEAM DISTILLING CO., CLERMONT, BEAM, KENTUCKY

ACT ONE

1970–1973

He was disappointed in the world. So he built one of his own.
—Jedediah Leland on why Charles Foster
Kane built Xanadu

The greatest danger for those working in the cinema is the extraordinary possibility it offers for lying.
—Michelangelo Antonioni

July 3, 1970

Located on Sunset Boulevard, Schwab's drugstore was a legendary industry hangout with a soda fountain where, during the golden era, you might find yourself on a stool next to Mickey Rooney, Marilyn Monroe, or Groucho Marx.

Schwab's was where Charlie Chaplin played pinball and where

F. Scott Fitzgerald had his first heart attack. It's where William Holden hung out with his screenwriting pals in *Sunset Blvd.* and where Ava Gardner worked while awaiting her big break.

It has long been claimed that Schwab's was the site of a story that encompasses all we believe about Tinseltown at its peak. It goes like this: In January 1937, sixteen-year-old Judy Turner cut class at Hollywood High to grab a Coke at Schwab's, where her beauty was so stunning that director Mervyn LeRoy offered her a screen test on the spot. Later changing her name from Judy to Lana, she became Lana Turner: one of those remarkable things known as a movie star.

Like many things in Hollywood, the story is mostly true, except for the facts. Lana Turner was indeed discovered while ditching school to get a Coke, but it was at Top Hat Malt Shop where the publisher of *The Hollywood Reporter* discovered her and put her in contact with talent agent Zeppo Marx, Groucho's brother.

But to this day, many who know better will still tell you it happened at Schwab's.

The story of how cameraman Gary Graver came into Orson's life also begins at Schwab's, and like Lana Turner's discovery, it seems like something from a screenplay. It almost has to be true, because if you made it up, nobody would believe you.

In Hollywood, however, truth is often more remarkable than fiction, and it's a place where anything can seem possible—as it was on Friday, July 3, 1970, when Graver and his wife, Connie, stopped for coffee at Schwab's.

As he sat down, Graver picked up a copy of *Variety*, whose headline blared that indie films were booming and represented 39 percent of new pictures heading into production that year.

On the second page, he found Army Archerd's "Just for Variety" column, which explained that Sean Connery had set up a new production company; Laurence Harvey had fractured his knee; Patty Duke was back from her honeymoon; and actress Sharon Farrell was pregnant.

But right in between Laurence Harvey's knee and Patty Duke's honeymoon, the following item struck Graver:

Orson Welles looking very well, visiting friends here and in San
Fran., says he soon returns to film his yarn "The Other Side of
the Wind" in Italy and Yugoslavia.

Yes, Orson Welles was in town and making a new movie.

"I bet he's at the Beverly Hills Hotel," Graver told his wife before
walking to the pay phone.

"Orson Welles, please," Graver asked the hotel operator, praying
he'd picked the right place and that Welles was staying under his own
name.

Then the line began to ring and somebody picked up. And there
was *that voice*.

"Hello," rumbled a man who was unmistakably Orson Welles.

Stunned, Graver asked, "Uh . . . Orson Welles?"

"Yes," Welles responded. *"Who* is this?"

"My n-name is Gary Graver and I'm an American cameraman," the
thirty-one-year-old stuttered. "I know you have some projects and I'd
sure like to be involved with you as a cinematographer—"

Welles cut him off, explaining that he was busy and just about to fly
to New York, where he was acting in Henry Jaglom's *A Safe Place.*

"Why don't you give me your name and phone number," Welles said.

Graver did so but knew he'd blown it. Somewhere at the Beverly
Hills Hotel, Welles was sitting impatiently on the edge of a bed, waiting for the call to end and *not* writing down Gary Graver's phone number.

Returning to the table, Graver looked at his wife and said, "Let's go
home."

With Orson, one friend said, timing was everything. If you came into
his life a few minutes early, you might be gruffly dismissed. Arrive
five minutes later, however, and you could be swept into his orbit for an
evening as his dinner guest, an experience that you'd talk about for
the rest of your life and one he'd forget by the next afternoon.

But if you arrived right on time, not a minute early or five minutes late, you could be more. Meeting Welles at the right moment meant you could become his business partner or his personal assistant; his trusted friend or future enemy; Sancho to his Don Quixote; or Hal to his Falstaff. Even more, when Orson needed *you*, you became indispensable—until, of course, you weren't. You might remain in his grasp for the rest of his life or even yours. That choice was his, and resistance was futile.

The impact of falling under Orson's spell was summed up best by actress Geraldine Fitzgerald, who said he was "like a lighthouse. When you were caught in the beam, it was utterly dazzling. When the beam moved on, you were plunged into darkness."

As Graver drove back home to Laurel Canyon, he probably felt some small measure of that darkness. Soon, however, he would be caught in the beam.

As the Gravers arrived home, Gary heard the phone ringing, ran inside, and picked up the receiver. It was Orson, who said, "Get over to the Beverly Hills Hotel immediately! I've got to talk to you right away!"

Back in the car, Graver flew down North Beverly Drive to the pastel-green Beverly Hills Hotel. Moments later, he was at a bungalow door, face-to-face with Orson Welles, clad in black silk pajamas and a matching robe.

Inviting him in, Welles offered Graver coffee and they chatted for a bit. Then Orson cut to the chase.

"I'm about to make a movie called *The Other Side of the Wind* and I'd like to work with you," he said. "You are the second cameraman to ever call me up and say you wanted to work with me. First there was Gregg Toland, who shot *Citizen Kane*. Since then no technician has ever called up and said they wanted to work with me. So it seems like pretty good luck."

When he returned from New York, they would take test shots for *The Other Side of the Wind*.

Gary Graver had come to Hollywood in the early 1960s, looking to get into movies any way he could. A native of Portland, Oregon, he tried acting and took classes from Lucille Ball and Lee J. Cobb but went nowhere. So he parked cars and ushered at movie houses until he found a way to break in.

That break, strangely, came as the result of an event that wound up shaping an entire decade—the Vietnam War. Drafted into the army, Graver chose to enlist into the navy because he'd heard that Honorary Admiral John Ford sometimes trained Los Angeles–based cameramen before they headed off to Southeast Asia.

Graver didn't meet Ford, but with his naval film unit in Vietnam he got a crash course in how to be a cameraman and shot in conditions that studios would spend millions trying to re-create, while doing so from the air, ground, and water as well as under enemy fire.

Back in Hollywood, Graver found that this training made him perfect for producers such as Al Adamson and Roger Corman, whose independent studios cranked out down-and-dirty, low-budget biker, horror, and exploitation films made by eager young directors. Corman's studio in particular was a de facto film school for everyone from Francis Ford Coppola and Martin Scorsese to Ron Howard, James Cameron, and Peter Bogdanovich.

Before meeting Welles, Graver's credits included *Satan's Sadists* and *The Girls from Thunder Strip,* in which three "beautiful bootlegging sisters" fend off a violent biker gang.

At heart, however, Graver was a true cinephile who possessed an encyclopedic knowledge of film, read *Sight & Sound,* had watched the French New Wave, and loved old masters such as Alfred Hitchcock and Jean Renoir. He was also a Welles fanatic, who'd sat in an empty theater to watch *Chimes at Midnight* and had marveled at the opening shot in *Touch of Evil.* If there was a single director Gary Graver would have given his life to work with, it was Orson Welles.

That director, amazingly enough, was now talking to him in a bungalow at the Beverly Hills Hotel and mentioning him in the same breath as Gregg Toland, the legendary Oscar-winning cinematographer who'd taught a novice Welles everything he needed to know about cameras and lenses before the pair pushed every possible creative boundary to achieve the rich, deep-focus world of *Kane*. Making this all the more remarkable was the fact that Orson was now asking Graver to fill Toland's shoes on his next film.

With those thoughts undoubtedly colliding in his brain, Graver suddenly felt Welles's huge hands unexpectedly gripping his shoulders and then, just as suddenly, found himself being thrown to the ground, where moments later he was joined by Orson who used his bulk and one beefy arm to keep the cameraman pinned to the ground. Each time Graver struggled or tried to speak, Orson would simply raise a finger to his own lips, wordlessly indicating, *Silence!* Perhaps, Graver wondered, this might not have been such a great idea after all.

Then, however, Welles slowly peered over at an open windowsill, stood up, and helped Graver to his feet.

"I saw the actress Ruth Gordon out there," Welles said. "If she'd seen me, she'd have come in here and talked and talked and talked. Right now I want to talk to you."

From then on, Gary Graver belonged to Orson Welles, putting him ahead of marriage, children, money, food, and the mortgage. Of those priorities, Graver's son Sean said, "Orson would be number one."

Graver told Welles he could make a movie for almost nothing, using a young, non-union crew willing to work for less than $200 a week. He could get discounts at labs and purchase unexposed film stock left over from other pictures. He even knew ways to sneak extra days out of rental equipment.

Together they had enough equipment for a mini-studio. Graver had an Arriflex camera, while Welles owned both a 16mm and 35mm Éclair. They also had lighting, sound equipment, and an editing table.

After talking for hours, the pair agreed that they had everything necessary needed to start the movie when Orson returned from New York. At least everything besides a cast, a final script, and a financier. Until then they'd start with $750,000 provided by Orson.

Before Graver left, the fifty-five-year-old Welles said that he didn't want to spend his remaining years making movies for hire. No. He would focus on what he did best. The only movies he would make from here on out would have to be Orson Welles movies.

When Graver arrived, he'd noticed a dark-haired young woman in the background who quietly walked into another room and closed the door. With Graver gone, she returned.

The woman was Oja Kodar, a twenty-nine-year-old Croatian model, artist, and actress who'd met Orson in Zagreb during the early 1960s while he was directing *The Trial*. She was in her early twenties when they met, while the thrice married Welles was in his mid-forties, with three daughters, one of whom was three years older than Oja.

Despite the age difference, they began an intense on-and-off relationship. After an early separation, Welles took great pains to find Kodar in Paris, where he smashed in her apartment door and presented her with a love letter he'd been holding for three years. They'd been together ever since.

Though born Olga Palinkas, Kodar had picked up her stage name after Orson had described her as a "present from God" and learned that the Croatian word for "as a present" was *kodar*. Taking that as her last name and using a childhood nickname as her first, she became Oja Kodar.

A man who surrounded himself with beauty, Welles had found, in Oja, a striking woman with dark eyes, sharp features, and a lithe body, all of which emoted strength and sexuality. She was warm and tough; sweet and stern; sensual in spades; but nobody's plaything. This was not a woman with whom you'd have either a casual fling or a cozy family with a white picket fence. Orson had dated Dolores del Rio and been married to Rita Hayworth, two remarkably desirable women. But it was Kodar, somehow, who managed to maintain her grasp on him.

Things, however, were complicated. With Orson anything could be complicated, whether it was romance, setting up a shot, or financing a film. And in this case the major complication was that Orson remained married to his third wife, Italian actress Paola Mori, with whom he had a teenage daughter named Beatrice. After Orson's death, Kodar has stated that divorce was impossible because Mori was a Catholic who prized being "Mrs. Orson Welles." And while that may be true, Mori was also an intelligent, attractive woman who provided Orson with something his chaotic life greatly needed—stability.

For Kodar the situation was no problem since she didn't feel the need to marry Orson and was content to be his mistress. Welles, on the other hand, found himself maintaining two separate lives over the next twenty years: a bohemian existence with Oja in Los Angeles, Paris, and Spain; and a more formal arrangement with Paola and Beatrice in London and later Sedona, Arizona, and Las Vegas. And because he was accustomed to managing chaos, he supposedly kept Paola from even knowing about his relationship with Oja until a year before his death—though even for Orson that would have seemed to be a nearly impossible trick to pull off, particularly given that their relationship appears to have gar-nered attention in the Italian press while they visited Milan in Febru-ary 1970.

Confident, bold, and sexually expressive (something Orson was not), the fiercely protective Kodar was like "a fairy queen who could order this huge man to scurry after things." If you needed Orson to change his mind, you asked Oja.

But the most important component of their relationship may have been the unity it brought to Orson's existence, which was expressed by Christopher Welles, who wrote: "My father's life was his work. And of all the women who attempted to live with him, only Oja was capable of entering fully into his creative life."

After starring in Orson's unfinished film *The Deep*, Oja allegedly collaborated on the screenplay for *The Other Side of the Wind* and would play the female lead in Hannaford's film-within-the-film. Thus, during the next several years, while Orson shot the movie in homes where they were also living, that merger between life and art became nearly complete.

"I like this boy," Welles said to Kodar after Graver left, "and we have that story—let's see if we can make it."

When Welles headed for New York, he took the typewriter that had been provided by Columbia but left no script behind, only an unpaid $30,000 bill that was charged to BBS.

Less famous than Schwab's, the Larry Edmunds Bookshop was pure Hollywood nonetheless. Crammed floor to ceiling with scripts, lobby cards, stills, movie posters, and books about filmmaking, the store on Hollywood Boulevard was frequented by everyone from David Lean and Jean-Paul Belmondo to Carl Reiner and François Truffaut.

On August 21, 1970, twenty-three-year-old film critic Joe McBride came into the store looking for owner Milton Luboviski. A tall, earnest Wisconsin native, McBride was on his first trip to Hollywood and had already interviewed John Ford and Jean Renoir. He was about to meet Orson Welles.

Although McBride had originally intended to become a novelist, his life was forever changed in a darkened University of Wisconsin classroom when he saw *Citizen Kane* for the first time; from that moment he settled on a new career, in which he'd still be telling stories, but now he'd be telling them on film.

After leaving school, McBride took odd jobs around Madison and wrote for movie magazines. By 1970, a collection of his criticism, *Persistence of Vision*, had already been published and he was at work on another book, this one about Welles, whom he'd never met. Having read in *Variety* that critic-turned-director Peter Bogdanovich was also working on a book about Orson, McBride visited Larry Edmunds to ask Luboviski for Bogdanovich's phone number.

Later that day, when he called Bogdanovich, the director immediately said: "Can you hold? I'm on the other line with Orson."[69] When Bogdanovich returned to McBride, he gave him a phone number and said to call Welles at five thirty that afternoon, which McBride did from the phone booth outside Schwab's.

After only a few minutes of conversation, Welles invited McBride to lunch the next day at a home he was renting on Lawlen Way near the top of Beverly Hills. He also asked if McBride wanted to be in his new film, which would begin shooting in Tijuana on Sunday, August 23.

"Is this going to be a *feature-length movie*?" McBride asked, and immediately realized how awkwardly he'd posed his question.

Welles laughed and said, "We certainly hope so!"

At noon the following day, McBride arrived at a one-story modern home at the end of a half-completed block overlooking what would become Century City. He rang the bell and was greeted by Welles, who said, "Well, I finally meet my favorite critic!"

Stunned, McBride asked, "Why am I your favorite critic?"

"You're the only critic who understands what I try to do," Welles responded.

Soon McBride found himself sitting in the living room, puffing on a massive cigar (at Orson's insistence) and looking up at a copy of *Persistence of Vision* on the mantel.

During lunch and a long, informal interview that day, Welles seemed intent on explaining that the medium in which he'd worked over the last thirty years wasn't really all that important to him or to society in general.

"I've never been as excited by movies as movies, the way I've been excited by magic or bullfighting or painting," Welles said to McBride.

"After all, the world existed for a long time without people going to the movies."

Welles also used the discussion to gently mock modern cinephilia, particularly "the auteur theory," which viewed certain directors as artists who used a camera and film stock to stamp their unique signature on each of their movies. Auteur films were not to be viewed as individual pieces of art. Instead, they could be understood only within the canon of the director's work—as a part of his creative progression.

The "auteurs" included Renoir, Hitchcock, Akira Kurosawa, Ingmar Bergman, and, of course, Welles, who burst into laughter when McBride revealed that he'd seen *Citizen Kane* more than sixty times.

"You've seen *Kane* sixty times?!" Welles said, roaring. "How could you see any movie sixty times?!"

Another of Welles's objectives that afternoon was to explain the plot for *The Other Side of the Wind* and how he'd modeled Hannaford not only on Hemingway, but also on hypermanly filmmakers such as John Ford, Henry Hathaway, Howard Hawks, John Huston, and, most of all, an early studio director named Rex Ingram.

"He made terrible movies. They're awful!" Welles once said in describing Ingram as a Hannaford prototype. "[But] he was a great fascinator like John [Huston] in the high style of the great adventurer. A Super-satanic intelligence and so on. He was a great director as a figure in the way that John is."

Hannaford, Welles said, who was famous for seducing his female lead or the male star's wife or girlfriend on each of his films, would ultimately be revealed as a closeted homosexual.

"Hannaford's underlying interest had always been the leading man himself," McBride wrote. "In the desperation and abandon of his old age, the macho mask slips away and Hannaford becomes openly smitten with his somewhat androgynous-looking hippie leading man."

When the subject turned to modern directors, Welles expressed his admiration for Stanley Kubrick but confessed that he hadn't bothered to see *2001*. "I'd rather spend two hours talking to you," he told McBride.

That night, McBride had dinner at Orson's house with Welles, Kodar, and Bogdanovich, as well as Gary and Connie Graver. The festivities lasted until two or three A.M.

The following morning, Sunday, August 23, Graver woke around nine thirty when his phone rang. It was Orson.

They'd planned to shoot in Tijuana that day with a Super 8 camera and film Graver had just purchased, but Orson explained that legal restrictions prevented them from taking cameras into Mexico.

"Tijuana's out," Welles said, as was the Super 8. The new plan was to film at Orson's house, where Graver was to meet him in forty-five minutes, *with* an assistant cameraman and a soundman. Then Orson hung up.

As he was trying to figure out how he could make it all happen by ten fifteen, Graver heard the phone ring again. It was Orson, giving him more time. Now he had until eleven.

The same morning, Bogdanovich called Eric Sherman, a cameraman whose father, Vincent, was a prolific studio director. The former head of Yale's campus film society, Sherman roomed with his soundman, Felipe Herba, in an apartment that doubled as their editing room.

Bogdanovich was calling to find out if Sherman was interested in "working with Orson."

"Orson who?" Sherman asked.

"Welles, of course," Bogdanovich said.

Sherman's reply: "Is Christ Jewish?"

Bringing along Herba and their equipment, Sherman arrived at Welles's house around noon and found out that they'd be doing more than shooting film and recording sound. Orson also wanted them to appear on-screen as documentarians ("the Maysles Brothers," Welles called them), making the film *Close-up on Hannaford*. The pair would be taking actual documentary footage while they performed and also double as crew members when they weren't being filmed.

"You guys are playing a camera-sound team," Graver told them. "I'm shooting you while you're shooting [Hannaford]. Orson wants to shoot it all at once."

It was all part of Welles's creative conceit: Shoot in as many formats as possible and edit it together as a cinematic collage of moving and static images shot in both color and black-and-white, with 16mm, 35mm, Super 8, handheld, and still cameras.

As part of this, many extras were handed cameras and asked to shoot during party scenes. Welles also imagined that there would be several documentary crews, including one from German television and another from the BBC, thus creating an underlying commentary on the all-consuming modern media who try to devour Hannaford but are actually "feeding off themselves."

Knitted together during editing, that frenzied, frantic, hyper-real party footage would act as a frame, providing context and a narrative structure into which Welles could place Hannaford's beautiful but meaningless 35mm comeback movie.

A fellow cigar smoker, Sherman presented Welles with a seven-and-three-quarter-inch double corona, the largest you could buy in the United States. After examining the gift thoughtfully, Welles said, "Oh, no, thank you, Eric. I only smoke *large* cigars," and pulled out a gargantuan Cuban.

"Where on earth did you get that?" Sherman asked.

"They make them for me," Welles said proudly.

Given this and his other larger-than-life qualities, Welles, Sherman assumed, would portray Hannaford. Bogdanovich, however, thought Huston would eventually play the role, and indeed the pair had discussed the part when Welles appeared in Huston's film *The Kremlin Letter* the prior year. Huston had agreed to play Hannaford, but when he'd heard nothing from Welles afterward, he'd assumed someone else had been given the part.

Leaving the matter unresolved, Welles decided that he'd play Hannaford off-camera whenever he was needed, and they could shoot the lead actor once he'd been cast.

Work began shortly after noon, when Welles appeared on set wearing a white robe and white pajamas. On his feet were unlaced high-tops. With a $25 cigar eternally burning in his hand and one of the dozen Frescas he drank each day close by, Orson directed sitting atop a large baronial chair, because, he said, "this is *an auteur film*."

The day before, McBride had seen Welles typing at a card table with a large box of notes on the floor nearby and asked if it was the script. No, Welles said, what he'd written would be ten hours on film. But it also provided a deep understanding of his main character, on whom he told Bogdanovich he had enough material for a "three-volume novel." Orson knew Jake Hannaford and his family's entire story. "I know everything . . . everything," he said.

This knowledge of the character and his nuances was so thorough that Orson's feelings about Hannaford were both clear and complicated. "I love this man," he told Bogdanovich. "And I hate him."

Ultimately, the notes would provide a foundation for each character, allowing him to execute the idea he'd expressed in Madrid. What he had would be a springboard that provided the idea and context for each performance. Thus, when they began filming, Welles kept a typewriter nearby where he could create and rework dialogue, often in collaboration with the actor—who was usually playing some version of his or her own persona, like McBride and Bogdanovich, who were both writing books about Welles and were cast as a pair of writers working on books about Hannaford.

McBride's character, Mr. Pister, is a "high priest of cinema" writing a scholarly examination of the director. A heightened parody of his obsessive, film-centric nature and outward midwestern innocence, Mc-Bride's character had overanalytical phrases such as "mother fixation" and "Oedipal complex"[86] written in pen on his wrists. This quirk was incorporated when Welles found out that McBride had scribbled notes on his arms after running out of paper at a screening.

Bogdanovich's Higgam was a slick, smarmy composite of two film writers: Rex Reed and Charles Higham, the author of a recently published book in which he claimed that Orson suffered from a "fear of completion."

Having studied under Stella Adler, Bogdanovich was intent on questioning Welles about how to portray Higgam, who was ostensibly homosexual like Charles Higham. Should he be effeminate? No, Orson said, he should be a jumpy, high-octane nebbish. A gifted mimic who'd done Cary Grant and other celebrity impersonations since childhood, Bogdanovich jumped into his vivid Jerry Lewis impression, which Welles pulled apart and reconstructed by dialing it down and adding some measure of culture and refinement, before ultimately landing on a strange mix of Lewis and Noël Coward.

Welles had the pair play with the kinds of movie-nerd conversations their characters might have and the annoying questions they'd ask Hannaford. Responding to this, McBride described his view that John Ford's films were "an oblique reflection of the changes in American society."

Orson loved it and knocked the idea around with McBride, shaping the dialogue so that it described Hannaford, then distilling it and punching it out as "The main thrust of my argument, you understand, is that during the thirties Hannaford's predominant motif was the outsider in absurd conflict with society. In the forties he achieved salvation. In the fifties . . ."

Later, Welles convulsed with laughter when McBride made reference to Dziga Vertov, who directed Russian newsreels in the 1920s.

Never having heard of Vertov, Orson stopped laughing long enough to reject the idea, telling McBride, "C'mon now, you're supposed to be a serious character."

The first scene they shot was a very basic setup: Bogdanovich and McBride on a sofa in front of a bare white living room wall. When he entered, however, Orson saw that Graver had prelit the room in a complicated scheme, which Welles quickly had disassembled. Instead he wanted total simplicity, with the only artificial light coming from behind an open door in the background and casting a delicate pattern on the floor.

That pattern, Welles said, was "the only beautiful thing I want in this shot." Then he turned to Bogdanovich and added, "Von Sternberg," referring to the famous director of *The Blue Angel* and *Crime and Punishment.*

Despite the simple set and lighting, the scene required choreography that involved the passing of a whiskey bottle; new dialogue that overlapped with McBride's; Sherman and Herba running around chasing Hannaford; and Orson's houseboy walking into the shot while eating chicken and asking if anyone had seen a person named Andy. And in contrast with the improvisational, spontaneous dialogue, Welles wanted perfect execution.

"I give [actors] a great deal of freedom and at the same time the feeling of precision," Welles told McBride. "Physically and in the way they develop, I demand the precision of ballet. But their way of acting comes as much from their own ideas as from mine. When the camera rolls, I do not improvise visually. In this realm, everything is prepared."

McBride and Bogdanovich, however, were not capable of ballet. There were muffed lines; slow reactions; McBride's inability to seem comfortable while saddled with a tape recorder, whiskey bottle, camera, and coat; and Sherman's and Herba's failure to properly time their entrances and exits.

Despite this, Welles worked with uncommon glee. As he got caught

up in the act of creation, a light turned on inside of him that grew larger as the cameras rolled. His direction was often loud, but it was also subtle, and he elicited effective performances from non-actors such as Sherman and Herba, who'd been instructed to run as fast as they could while shooting Hannaford.

"Cut! Cut! Cut!" Welles screamed. "You're not running fast enough."

"We can't run faster," Sherman said. He explained that the equipment and the need to change film slowed them down.

Without speaking, Welles turned to Sherman and conveyed exactly what he wanted.

"He looked at us as if to say, 'Not your bodies moving, *you* need to *move*.' We ran, but we were being careful with the equipment," Sherman said. "He wasn't interested in careful. He wanted us to appear frantic."

Then, after shooting for a few hours, Welles felt he had a decent take or two and moved outside to film scenes of Hannaford driving to his birthday party, using himself as a stand-in while McBride and Bogdanovich sat in the backseat, asking questions like "Is the camera a reflection of reality, or is reality a reflection of the camera eye? Or is the camera a phallus?"

After nine hours, they'd completed nearly thirty shots and everyone was completely spent, except for Welles and Graver, whose energy never seemed to wane.

The next day, McBride returned to Madison and Welles sent Graver to scout locations in Utah. Upon his return, Graver and Welles started shooting again and kept at it for four months.

"We never had a budget," Graver said. "We just started filming. What I didn't fully understand was going to happen was that Orson worked seven days a week, every single day."

———

The University of California Press published Charles Higham's *The Films of Orson Welles* in August 1970, and because it was a semischolarly book by a first-time author, published by an academic press, it wasn't expected to receive much attention. It did, however, capture the full attention of its subject.

Claiming he'd only glanced at it in a bookstore, Welles was deeply upset by the final chapter, in which Higham described hunting "a minotaur in his labyrinth to explore the multitude of facts in the hope that they describe the real creature at the center of the maze." The conclusion he reached was that Welles simply hated to finish films.

Higham's strange last chapter included an account of the author's single encounter with his subject (whom he never interviewed) while watching a Welles magic show at a Los Angeles art museum.

> *He was grotesque . . . He was tragic . . . He was terrifying in his anger. . . . A thunderous oppressive force seemed about to break from him and destroy all concerned . . . in brief moments of pause I sensed the face of a man at once anguished by all that had been lost and afraid that behind the gargantuan meals and wine-bibbing, the anecdotes and the backslapping, the raucous laughter and the assembly of famous friends, there would be silence and loneliness and invalid rugs: the cold truth of dissolution.*

Apparently it was one hell of a magic show.

Odder still, Higham explained that he interviewed only a handful of Welles's friends and collaborators, from whom he "sensed a feeling not directly expressed by the people I spoke to, but nevertheless omnipresent, that Welles hated to see a film finished, that all his blame of others for wrecking his work is an unconscious alibi for his own genuine *fear of completion* [italics mine]."

Ultimately, Higham concluded not only that Welles feared completion (many would argue he was right, including some Welles defenders), but that it was all related to an obsession with death, as expressed

through his approach to filmmaking. "At the moment of encounter, everything is absorbed into a pattern where it becomes part of a dream and that dream is of death," he wrote. "For Welles his own films are dead, which is one reason he can't bear to look at them again."

Welles prevailed upon Bogdanovich to refute Higham's assertions, particularly those revivifying the claim he'd abandoned *Ambersons* so he could party in Rio while shooting *It's All True*.

"I don't know of any more fun than making a movie and the most fun of all comes in the cutting room when the shooting is over," Orson wrote Bogdanovich. "How can it be thought that I'd deny myself so much of that joy with *Ambersons*."

For Orson, this was more than vengeance or simply setting the record straight. It was about demolishing a legend that he considered to be the primary force that had inflicted so much damage and denied him the opportunity to have the kind of Hollywood career he so richly deserved.

"When I'd left [for Rio] the worst that can be said is that I was some kind of artist," Welles wrote to Bogdanovich. "When I came back I was some kind of lunatic. . . . The friendliest opinion was this: 'sure he's talented, but you can't trust him. He throws money around like a madman; when he gets bored he walks away. . . . Nobody cared about the facts; the fiction was vastly more amusing."

This grim reality was driven home further one day in 1970 when Orson headed happily to lunch with Joseph Cotten and returned in a dark mood. When Oja asked what happened, Orson said Cotten repeated a "Welles story" that both knew was untrue. But when this was pointed out, Cotten responded, "Come on, Orson, you know it makes a great story."

Now, just when it seemed that such stories might finally expire, they were rising from the ashes because of Higham. For Welles, destroying the myth was a matter of survival.

And despite the fact that he was in preproduction on his first studio film, Bogdanovich made time to research each of Higham's allegations and secured space to refute them in *The New York Times*.

Why Peter Bogdanovich took the time to defend Welles when he had his own career resting on the success of *The Last Picture Show* can be explained by loyalty. It was a loyalty he felt not just to Orson, but to the movies themselves.

To the Manhattan native who'd kept an extensive card file of notes on the more than six thousand films he'd seen between the ages of ten and thirty, movies were everything. They were his joy, salvation, and education. They were how he processed emotions, and sometimes the line between reality and celluloid seemed blurry enough that the world he saw on-screen was the one in which he wanted to live. There was good reason for this.

The product of a tense marriage between a Serbian father and an Austrian Jewish mother, Bogdanovich experienced a childhood shaped by events far beyond his control and comprehension.

Before his family left Europe, Bogdanovich's infant older brother was killed in a tragic household accident for which his father blamed his mother. So deep was the tension that Bogdanovich hadn't even known about his brother's existence until he was in his twenties. But the repercussions in Peter's life were clear, as he was wildly overprotected and didn't spend his days playing stickball with the other boys. Instead, according to his biographer, Andrew Yule, Peter went through his entire childhood without so much as a scratch or a bruise.

Then there was his father, Borislav, a painter unable to earn a living with his art who felt he'd been betrayed by his in-laws when they reneged on their promise of financial security if he got them out of prewar Europe. Proud and talented, Borislav suffered from depression so profound that he was hospitalized for a nervous breakdown before Peter entered his teens.

To cope, Peter became immersed in a world of fiction, imitating movie stars, writing plays, and lying about his age to take classes at the Stella Adler Theatre Studio. It was there that Brando's acting guru herself complimented him on how he'd directed some classmates, gushing, "Brilliant, my boy!"

Without graduating from high school, Bogdanovich took film classes at Columbia University. And although all the classmates fantasized about becoming great movie directors, one of his professors says that only Bogdanovich and Brian De Palma, "seemed to hold on to the dream, while the rest were too easily seduced by reality."

That refusal to succumb was one of Bogdanovich's most remarkable traits, propelling him forward through failure and success, allowing him—at age twenty—to write Clifford Odets, asking for permission to direct and produce one of his plays.

While acting and directing, Bogdanovich became a film critic and championed older directors such as Welles, about whom he wrote an early 1960s monograph for a retrospective of his work at the Museum of Modern Art.

In his early twenties, Bogdanovich married costume designer Polly Platt, who wholeheartedly joined him in his movie obsession. Bright and talented, Platt was a curious mix of someone with brassy confidence and intelligence who also harbored the old-fashioned notion that what mattered most was whether her husband was happy. Because if her spouse were happy, then she would be happy. As a result, Platt helped Peter land a position covering movies for *Esquire,* where he profiled his heroes: Howard Hawks, Jerry Lewis, Leo McCarey, John Ford, and others.

In 1963, after he'd raised $30,000 to produce a play that closed after one performance, Bogdanovich heeded the advice of director Frank Tashlin, who said that if he wanted to make movies, he should come to Hollywood. The couple packed and drove to Los Angeles, where Peter met Roger Corman at a screening. A week later, Corman called, to ask if Bogdanovich wanted to write movies.

And just like that, Bogdanovich and Platt were working on *The Wild Angels,* a twenty-two-week shoot where they rewrote the script, managed the production, scouted locations, directed the second unit, and edited the film on a Moviola. It was film school. Suddenly, they knew how to make a movie.

Bogdanovich moved on to direct *Voyage to the Planet of Prehistoric Women,* after which Corman explained that Boris Karloff owed him two days' work from the contract for another picture. What he wanted was for Peter to make a film for under $100,000 that was built around two days' use of the eighty-year-old horror legend.

In response, Bogdanovich wrote *Targets,* the story of an aging horror actor whose new film premieres during a clean-cut young man's Charles Whitman–like shooting spree. Made in twenty-three days and released in 1968, the film received mixed reviews. But it put Bogdanovich on the map and helped him get a deal to make *The Last Picture Show* for BBS and Columbia.

Though set in Texas, the plot of Larry McMurtry's novel was tailor-made for Bogdanovich, as it used the demise of a small-town movie theater to frame a bittersweet look at a dying way of life—similar to the destruction of the Ambersons and their magnificence.

One day in 1968, Bogdanovich was at home when the phone rang.

"This is Orson Welles," said a familiar voice. "I can't tell you how long I've wanted to meet you."

"Hey, you took my line," Bogdanovich replied. "But *why* have you wanted to meet *me*?"

"Because you have written the truest words ever published about me," Welles said, then paused briefly. "In English."

They agreed to meet at three the following afternoon in the Polo Lounge at the Beverly Hills Hotel.

So anxious that he'd driven to their meeting in the wrong gear, Bogdanovich came to the Polo Lounge with a copy of his John Ford book under his arm and gave it to Orson, after which he sat down and joined him at the table. Expecting to be a bundle of nerves, however, Bogdanovich found that the angst had unexpectedly vanished, giving way to a sense of total comfort and familiarity. Suddenly, Bogdanovich felt that he could tell Orson anything.

"There was, in fact, even a strangely conspiratorial quality Orson and I fell into almost at once," Bogdanovich wrote. "As though we'd known and trusted each other for a long time."

Bogdanovich was so at ease that he even told Welles that he loved all his movies, except for *The Trial*.

"I don't [like it] either!" Welles replied.°

Hours later, as they prepared to part, Welles said he regretted the fact that Bogdanovich couldn't write a book about him that was similar to the one he'd done with John Ford.

"Why can't I?" Bogdanovich said.

Within a year Peter and Orson split a $20,000 advance for a book of interviews that—for a variety of reasons—wouldn't be published until after Orson died.

But two years after that meeting, Bogdanovich had written a piece for the August 30, 1970, issue of *The New York Times*.

"Is It True What They Say About Orson?" is a ruthlessly efficient, point-by-point annihilation of Higham's book which Bogdanovich demeaned as "well-meaning" despite being filled with "half-truths . . . mythical anecdotes, factual lapses and conclusions based on false information that add up to an illustrated textbook on how to criminally impair an artist's career."

It was enough to shame any writer that wasn't named Charles Higham, who responded with unreserved glee, even sending Bogdanovich a telegram thanking him for drawing attention to his book. Higham also wrote a mock interview *with himself* that ran in the *Times* on September 13—pointing out, among other things, that Bogdanovich was more than a valiant Welles defender; he was also a competitor writing his own book about Orson. Soon Higham was getting reviews in major papers and magazines and even appeared on the *Today* show to discuss a book that should have simply disappeared into academia.

° Welles did in fact like *The Trial* and later asked Bogdanovich to stop saying he didn't like it, as it hurt his feelings. After that, Welles gleefully referred to *The Trial* as "that picture you hate" whenever he was around Bogdanovich.

At the time, it seemed like a big deal. But a far more important critic would soon become a problem—and a target—for Orson while he made *The Other Side of the Wind*.

Bob Random's audition for *The Last Picture Show* was brief. Looking like Jim Morrison's sensitive brother the handsome young Canadian clearly wasn't right for a 1950s period piece about small-town Texas. But after telling Random that he wasn't getting the part, Bogdanovich mentioned that it had been Welles who'd seen the actor on *Gunsmoke* and recommended that he let him read for the film.

"I remained cool and went, 'Oh, yeah?'" Random recalled.

But, like Graver, Random had always wanted to act for Welles more than he did anyone else. Having already found regular television work, Random said, he began "summoning" Orson into his life after talking to Bogdanovich. "I didn't want to do *The Beverly Hillbillies*," Random explained. "I just wanted to work for [Welles]."

Three days later, the phone rang at his apartment near the beach in Ocean Park. It was Orson.

"Oh, hi, Orson," Random said in a tone that indicated, *I'd hoped it might be you.*

Orson told Random he was making a movie and wanted him for one of the male leads. There would be no audition. "You have the part," Orson said.

After accepting in his casual manner, Random went to Lawlen Way the next day with his heart pounding. There he met Welles, who gave him a check for $2,000, the advance on a $10,000 salary. They talked a bit, and at some point before Random left, Welles mentioned that his character would ride a motorcycle, or perhaps a scooter, in the film.

Deciding immediately that he wouldn't appear in a Welles movie on some crappy little bike, Random headed to a Triumph dealership and quickly spent his entire $2,000 on a motorcycle. When he roared up to Lawlen the next day, he told Orson not to worry, he already had his own bike.

At Universal, Lew Wasserman decided, despite misgivings, that the way to capitalize on the magic of producers such as BBS was to create a low-budget mini-studio focused on young, independent filmmakers.

The Young Directors Program was headed by Ned Tanen, a talented but erratic executive, and Danny Selznick, the son of producer David O. Selznick and grandson of MGM's Louis B. Mayer. Wasserman told the pair to make films for under $1 million, which would simultaneously spread the risk and create more chances for success.

"For $5,000,000 they could have five pictures, five chances at a breakthrough," Selznick told Peter Biskind in *Easy Riders, Raging Bulls*.

The program would be responsible for *Diary of a Mad Housewife*, *American Graffiti*, and the John Cassavetes film *Minnie and Moskowitz*. It also, however, funded Dennis Hopper's ill-fated film *The Last Movie*, the tale of a stuntman who goes native while shooting a western on location in South America.

While filming *The Last Movie* in Peru, Hopper and crew landed knee-deep in some of the world's finest cocaine and wound up going native themselves. The result was a drug-fueled sojourn that produced forty hours of film that took Hopper a year to edit down to an incomprehensible six-hour mess. Finally cut to a reasonable length, *The Last Movie* was released in 1971 and disappeared, along with the next decade of Hopper's directorial career.

Though in his mid-fifties, Orson viewed the Young Directors Program as an opportunity to fund his film and decided to see if he could work within the new system.

Raising money, however, had always been something Orson despised. He bemoaned the fact that his post-*Kane* career was 98 percent hustling and only 2 percent filmmaking. Over the years he'd wined, dined, pleaded, seduced, cajoled, and entertained potential investors so he could get the funds to practice his art. But beneath the considerable charm he displayed was a genuine contempt for producers and midlevel executives. And now he was forced to put on a show for Tanen and Selznick, all the more galling as he'd known the latter since he was a child. The last thing he wanted to do was get on his knees for a second generation of Hollywood royalty.

Still, believing the pair had total deal-making authority, Orson considered them a good fit for the combination of funding and independence he required. He was not, however, going to make it easy—beginning with his refusal to meet them at Universal. The clear message was that if they were interested, Tanen and Selznick would have to come see him—which they did that September.

Orson set up for the meeting as if it were a scene from *Mr. Arkadin,* asking Rift Fournier, a flamboyant, wheelchair-bound commercial director, to sit in with him. Fournier, who favored white suits, lavender shirts, and Peter Max ties, was told only that "guests were coming" and that he should sit in the corner smoking Gauloises, nodding mysteriously when it seemed appropriate.

"I was just an element to head-fuck them," Fournier said.

When Selznick and Tanen arrived, Orson pointedly did not introduce or even acknowledge the mysterious man in the wheelchair, smoking the unfiltered French cigarettes.

The first order of business was to discuss rumors that Orson was shooting an erotic film. This Welles dismissed by explaining that there might be some suggestion of sensuality, but certainly nothing explicit, which would just be dull and tacky.

Satisfied they weren't funding an auteurist porno, Selznick asked if there was a script. Orson replied by pointing to a large stack of paper sitting on the corner of a nearby desk.

"Can we read it?" Selznick asked.

"Yes," Orson said. "But, it's meaningless."

"Okay," Selznick replied. "Then just tell us the story."

Orson went to work, detailing the plot and holding the pair in thrall. He explained Hannaford's tale with conviction and theatricality, stopping for the occasional dramatic pause and looking at Fournier, who'd nod cryptically and light another Gauloises. Finally, at the end of his story, Welles introduced Selznick and Tanen to "one of my colleagues—Mr. Fournier."

Taken with the story and the idea of working with Orson, Selznick asked again if he could read the script. Almost immediately Orson went ice cold.

"The word was that you and Ned could just meet with directors and, if you loved them, approve a project up to a million dollars," he said.

Selznick said that was mostly true, but they'd need a screenplay so they could go through the studio's budgeting process.

When he heard this, Orson walked to the desk and tossed the unbound script in the air, explaining that they were welcome to pick up the papers, put them in order, and read them if they were so inclined.

Mystified by Orson's behavior, Selznick tried to salvage a potential deal by telling Orson that if he could have someone pick up and organize the pages, they'd send an assistant over to get the script and the ball could start rolling at Universal.

Orson, however, was done. "Okay, Danny, that's it," he said. "Good-bye."

Pleading, Selznick said, "Orson, this is a wonderfully dramatic gesture, but I just don't understand—"

"That's it," Orson repeated. "Good-bye."

From the beginning, Orson's thematic attention was focused primarily on relationships between male characters that often resulted in some form of betrayal. Women played major roles, but their romantic entanglements with men were quite chaste, even by studio standards. Despite a long string of affairs, Welles was puritanical when it came to making films: Discussing sex or putting it on-screen, he explained in a 1970 interview with David Frost, was comparable to the depiction of religious faith.

"There's only one other thing in movies I hate as much as [an actor praying on film] and that's sex," Welles said. "You just can't get in bed or pray to God and convince me on the screen."

Yet despite those words and his assurances to Tanen and Selznick, Welles sat on a chair in an empty lot across the street from the home on Lawlen, drinking a Scotch, smoking a cigar, and preparing to shoot the first graphic sex scenes of his career.

The desire to do this sprang from two sources. The first was Kodar, who'd inspired the erotic elements in the script and came from a culture and a generation that were more open about sexuality.

But while Kodar opened the door, it was the film's structure that freed Orson to journey into sensuality, because he could do it in the guise of Hannaford attempting to make a sexually charged comeback movie for the youth market. He would be filming sex, but not doing it as Orson Welles. Instead, he'd be imitating Hannaford imitating the style of someone such as Michelangelo Antonioni. In directing, Orson could wear a mask over a mask while he filmed Kodar making love to Bob Random in the front seat of a car late that evening in early September.

Orson preferred not to crap on other directors in public. But with Antonioni he'd made an exception.

Ironically, the two directors had much in common, as both were child prodigies from well-to-do families who'd grown up with a passion for creating their own worlds and carried it into adulthood.

But the world Antonioni created on screen bothered Orson to no end. Because while Welles tangled with love and hate, life and death, and the unknowability of man, Antonioni's films were about existential ennui with characters who lived empty lives covered by another layer of ennui. It defined all that Welles despised about the auteur theory.

"According to a young American critic, one of the great discoveries of our age is the value of boredom as an artistic subject," Welles told *Playboy* in 1967. "If that is so, Antonioni deserves to be counted as a pioneer and founding father."

With a visual style featuring long, lingering shots of inactivity (for example, a woman staring at an electrical post), Antonioni's work galled Welles.

"One of the reasons I'm so bored with Antonioni [is] the belief that because a shot is good, it's going to get better if you keep looking at it. He gives you a full shot of somebody walking down a road and you think, 'Well, he's not going to carry that woman all the way up that road.' But he does. And then she leaves and you go on looking at the road after she's gone."

It was empty art, Orson felt, consisting of beautiful images that created no value or meaning. Antonioni was "an architect of empty boxes" whose plots had no beginning, end, or context. It gave real art a bad name and made people mistake nonsense for complexity.

Worse yet, Antonioni, actually three years older than Orson, had thrived during the 1960s and had a three-picture deal with producer-director Carlo Ponti and MGM that included substantial artistic control over his films.

Blowup, the first of those films, was a success partially because of its use of boundary-pushing sexuality circa 1966. The second film, however, was *Zabriskie Point,* a 1970 commercial and critical disaster exploring the emptiness of consumer culture.

And it was that film that would be Orson's inspiration for Hannaford's attempt at a youth movie.

Welles would not only mock Antonioni, but also outdo him at his own game, capturing stunning shot after stunning shot in vivid 35mm and doing it so well that one crew member marveled at an astonishing image and said, "Antonioni never got a shot like that!"

"You bet your sweet ass he hasn't!" Orson yelled back.

In this manner, the man who only wanted to make "Orson Welles films" was working on a major artistic statement that contrasted Hannaford's flawless Antonioni knock-off with the jumpy, raw, documentary footage of the party. Welles was making a film in two distinct styles—neither of which was his own.

After midnight on September 6, Orson, wearing pajamas and an over-coat, directed a small crew as they prepared for the first night shoot of the sex scene on the empty lot across Lawlen.

The crew included Graver and his wife, Fournier, Sherman, Herba, television producer Ed Sherrick, and Curtis Harrington, who went on to direct the Shelley Winters horror films *Whoever Slew Auntie Roo?* and *What's the Matter with Helen?* Tipped off that Orson was shoot-ing that night, Harrington was caught watching from a nearby hill, after which Orson asked him to help on lights.

There were also two other crew members who'd remain with Or-son for years: Michael Stringer and Glenn Jacobson. Both were friends of Graver's, Stringer from the B-movie world and Jacobson from their childhood in Portland. Over the years, Stringer worked for Orson as a grip, camera operator, or anything else he needed to be. Jacobson had an open-top Willys Jeepster, so he frequently drove Welles around and did whatever he asked both on and off set.

That night, there would be three performers working in the front seat of Graver's 1967 Mustang. Robert Aiken would play the driver, with Oja, naked except for a raincoat and beads, sitting next to him—and Random, in jeans and an open shirt, on the other side.

As the crew prepped, Orson had Oja open her raincoat so the cam-era captured more of her body as she seduced Random, who was to sit in stunned obedience as Kodar undressed him and sat writhing in his lap.

Welles explained to Aiken that he should be driving fast through a rainstorm, trying to pretend that there wasn't a couple having sex right next to him. Then, toward the end of the seven-minute scene, Aiken would explode in aggravation and toss Oja out the passenger door into the rain.

Because Orson didn't have the resources to close streets, the action was filmed using the "poor man's process," in which the car never actu-ally moves, but the illusion of motion is created around it with sun guns and handheld lights that simulate passing cars and traffic lights via the use of colored filters. Meanwhile, several crew members would rock the car gently back and forth. Jacobson's job was to create the storm by spraying the window with a garden hose that hooked up to Orson's house across the street.

With Graver contorted in the backseat to shoot from one of Orson's low angles, Welles screamed, *"Rain!"* One hundred and fifty feet away, someone turned on the hose and Jacobson began nervously hitting the windshield and hood with water while Fournier, Connie Graver, and Stringer moved around the car with sun guns. Meanwhile, inside, Oja mounted Random and began grinding up and down.

Sitting in back, as his naked girlfriend straddled a handsome young actor, Orson helped rock the car by shifting his weight, screaming directions to the lighting crew.

Knowing he wanted to create a quick cut blur of images and lights that would flash as beads flapped against Oja's chest, Welles orchestrated a scene of intense rhythm with footage that is as disorienting as it is erotic. Take after take and angle after angle, Welles was in total command and enjoying every minute of creation.

"He just loved the filmmaking process more than anyone I've ever met," Stringer said of Welles. "His vision was what everyone else was focusing on—and that's an intoxicating process."

Orson sent everyone home before sunrise and said to come back for an early call the next day. Drained from an eighteen- to twenty-hour workday, the crew left and did their best to get a nap and a shower before returning. But Welles, a hopeless insomniac, remained energized, and it wasn't uncommon for cast and crew to leave him at the end of the night sitting in his pajamas pounding out revisions and then find him in the same position—still typing—when they returned in the morning.

Although a number of people came and went over the years, Graver, Stringer, and Jacobson began forming a group that was there for the long haul. Several years later, line producer Frank Marshall would coin the term *VISTOW*, but this was the beginning. They were "volunteers in service to Orson Welles."

VISTOW membership required several personal and professional qualities but first and foremost you had to come in with the right intentions. You had to be there because you loved film and wanted to make a great movie. If you came simply to meet the great Orson Welles, you were doomed. Welles would eat you alive.

"[Orson] simply wouldn't suffer a fool," Stringer said. "And we had our share of fools show up."

Stringer learned this on day one. Never having met a movie legend, Stringer sat down at lunch and said, "I can't believe I'm eating fried chicken with Orson Welles."

For the next week Orson ignored Stringer, unless it was to be verbally abusive. Not understanding the situation, Stringer approached Graver, who said, "You can't treat him like he's your pal. You need to show professionalism and respect."

Putting his head down, Stringer did his work and was repaid when Orson gave him the ultimate recognition: assigning him a specific task and referring to him by name. "Mike Stringer would be good at that," Welles would say. "Have him do it."

Others, who didn't pick up signals or lacked a thick skin, disappeared quickly, while anyone who resisted or fought back against Orson vanished as well. During the first months of work, this meant that 50 percent of the crew turned over on a daily basis.

Some couldn't deal with the hours. Work began around six A.M. and ran until early the next morning. There was, however, a long, two-hour lunch break each day, at which cast and crew devoured buckets of chili brought in by Chasen's or a spread laid out by the Beverly Hills Hotel.

The conditions were probably illegal and sometimes dangerous, but those who loved Welles never thought about it. Instead, they were driven by the simple belief that *The Other Side of the Wind* was important. Thus they would submit to the biggest demand of all—remaining on their game at all times and giving themselves almost completely to Orson.

This meant holding the same awkward camera position for ten minutes, without moving. It meant ignoring the bombast and doing precisely as they were told. But most of all, it meant accepting that they were there to make Orson's vision a reality. No matter how impossible the request, they never thought, "That won't work." Instead, it was, "How do I make that happen exactly as he wants?"

Graver was the ultimate example of this.

"Orson would demand a shot that was beyond human ability, and I never heard Gary say, 'C'mon, Orson,'" Sherman said. "[Gary's] duty was to deliver Orson whatever he wanted."

Those such as Graver also accepted the surreal aspects of the job and the sometimes surreal and childish needs of their boss.

Among those who couldn't hack it were a still photographer who likened Welles to "a mean Santa Claus" and one man who was overwhelmed by the weirdness of spending more than an hour trying to lower Orson's gigantic body into the trunk of a Lincoln Continental so he could direct a scene through a hole in the backseat. With a look that said, *Am I seriously lifting the great genius of American cinema into the trunk of a car?* he finished the job and never came back.

But then there were those such as Jacobson, who once received an early Sunday morning call from a moaning Welles, who sounded as if he might be near death because he'd run out of some important medication that needed to be filled immediately. Driving across Los Angeles intent on saving Orson's life, Jacobson arrived to find a seemingly healthy Orson who handed him a slip of paper that was not a prescription. Instead, it was a list of pastries he wanted Jacobson to pick up at the bakery.

Their payoff didn't come in money. Orson paid the going non-union rate, though he grumbled mightily every time it went up. Nor did it come in appreciation, since having Orson call you by name was often as good as it got.

What you did receive was the opportunity to be in the presence of genius; to witness that genius; to help that genius; and to work in the glow of that genius. Because working with Welles was like performing behind Thelonious Monk or Charlie Parker, artists who so totally took over what they were doing that it was rehabilitating to be part of their creation. Or perhaps it was like being a spot-up shooter next to Michael Jordan, who is present to complement his brilliance and, in doing so, finds his game raised to its highest level.

During his few weeks on the film, Sherman said, he did the best camera work of his life simply by following Orson's directions and witnessing his process. Welles would stalk around the set, look through a circle he made with his fingers, and explain precisely which lens and focal length were required. Without looking through the camera, he always knew exactly what image would be captured if its operator followed his instructions. While such precise instruction from a director might feel constrictive in the abstract, it had the opposite effect on Sherman and others—who found that Orson's intense control of the process relieved pressure and doubt. It required enormous work, but the outcome was artistically fulfilling and of colossal depth.

Then there was his conceptual ability, as he seemed to be creating each frame as if it were its own work of art and then—in his head—weaving them together into a creative whole that exceeded the sum of its parts.

"Each shot had something to do with the larger creation, but the shot itself would be stunning and staggering in its magnitude," Sherman said. "The concepts Orson had for shots were utterly astounding and his ability to conceptualize them was total."

But there were still moments when the execution of a shot was so difficult that it seemed as if he needed another medium, beyond film, with which to communicate. And although he pulled it off more often than not, there were rare instances when he tried over and over to get a shot, killing himself, Graver, and everyone else in the process. On one such occasion, when Graver provided a stewing Welles with a solution, Orson waved him off.

"No, Gary," he said. "God doesn't want me to make this shot."

Though seemingly in control of his art, Welles clearly lacked discipline concerning his health. When he was between cigars, Orson smoked cigarettes. And though he suffered from gout, he would seem to go long periods of not eating at all punctuated by gigantic binges in which he ate huge amounts of food (allegedly including an entire turkey) in one sitting. That food was chased by gallons of coffee and a dozen daily Frescas, not to mention gulps of cough medicine and painkillers. Yet despite trouble with his knees and weight-related problems, he appeared to be unbreakable and chugged along like a tank, seemingly unaffected by what he was putting in his body.

Though he drank early in the shoot, Orson's alcohol consumption went down dramatically after he excitedly stopped work early on September 17 so everyone could watch him appear with Joey Bishop and Petula Clark on Dean Martin's variety show.

But when Orson saw himself on-screen, the joy turned to self-recrimination.

"God, I'm fat," he said.

Graver claimed that Welles immediately cut back on his wine consumption and quit hard liquor entirely, though he continued doing ads for Jim Beam and Japanese whiskey. Clearly self-conscious about his weight, he spent most of the next fifteen years on diets that either didn't work or to which he couldn't stick—including one that consisted of stewed tomatoes and another in which he was allowed to eat only shrimp.

Three days later, Christopher Welles was remarried, and—again—her father didn't attend. In fact, he hadn't even responded to the invitation.

From early on, Christopher had been warned not to expect Orson to act like a normal dad. Welles proved this to be true, popping in and out of her life for thirty-two years, with dramatic, exciting visits during which he filled his daughter with the sense that he loved her very much. Then he would disappear once more.

"Orson may not be the father you've always been looking for," Skipper Hill told Christopher. "But, in his own way he cares about you. As much as he can, that is."

Some of this wasn't Orson's fault, as his first wife (Virginia Nicholson) conspired with her second husband and her mother to estrange him from Christopher. It wasn't until adulthood that Christopher began to accept what Skipper told her. But accepting that didn't make it easier when he missed her first wedding trying to save *Touch of Evil* and didn't even acknowledge that she was marrying again, this time to a man named Irwin Feder.

Then, six weeks later, acknowledgment, of a sort, arrived in a letter postmarked Beverly Hills.

> Darling Girl,
>
> Very nearly my first frustration upon landing on these shores was to find that the Feders had moved. I should have remembered that New Yorkers always do that, but what good has it done me? The migration of birds can be charted New Yorkers are something else again. Forgot the name of your place of business—if indeed I ever knew it—so what to do?

Over several pages, Orson implored Christopher to write a Christmas card to her half-sister Beatrice and mentioned a Jim Beam print ad he'd done with his other daughter Rebecca. The letter included no mention of her wedding or Irwin Feder, whom Orson didn't meet for another decade.

Though he loved his daughters, it had always been difficult for Orson to fully engage with them; as he told Bogdanovich, he "never knew what to do with girls." Which was possibly the reason Welles enmeshed himself in father-son relationships with men such as Bogdanovich and Graver.

With Gary, it was simple. There was a deep bond born of many things, including the fact that both lost their fathers at a young age. Orson loved Gary like a son, spending more time with him than almost anyone during the last fifteen years of his life. Essential, however, was Gary's subordinate position, in which he served Orson even to his own detriment. Making ends meet shooting low-budget films and directing borderline pornography such as *Sandra: The Making of a Woman* and *Erika's Hot Summer,* Graver occasionally received money from Orson as payment for his services, or Welles gave him work if he was filming a commercial. But while he was making *The Other Side of the Wind,* his marriage to Connie disintegrated and he remarried a woman named April, with whom he had a son. That marriage also ended in divorce before principal photography on the film was completed.

Still, Graver was loyal to Orson and knew what an opportunity he would have to be launched into a much more lucrative and higher class of film work once they finished *The Other Side of the Wind*.

With Bogdanovich, the bond was far more complicated and would evolve (over the next decade) into an increasingly difficult, sometimes torturous, relationship that bordered on Shakespearean. But in 1970, the roles remained clear. Bogdanovich was a young director in the thrall of a charming, brilliant Hollywood immortal whom he both admired and emulated.

Thus, as he began to work on his first major studio film, *The Last Picture Show,* Bogdanovich bounced his creative challenges off Welles. Most notably, they discussed how he could shoot a 1950s period film that captured a bittersweet nostalgic beauty against the grim, desolate backdrop of his location in Archer City, Texas—which had been selected because it emitted a visceral sense of loss and desperation.

The answer was to attain the depth of field in which Welles had filmed *Kane* and *Ambersons*. The problem was how to achieve it, something they discussed at length before Orson finally said the only way to make it work was to shoot in black-and-white.

"You'll never get it in color," Welles explained.

When Bogdanovich said he didn't think BBS and Columbia would let him make a black-and-white picture, Orson recommended that he at least ask. This turned out to be good advice, because after discussions with Schneider and Columbia (which polled their theater owners on the subject), it was decided that the film didn't need to be in color after all. And in the end, the black-and-white cinematography would be one of the most stunning and important creative elements of *The Last Picture Show*.

In addition to offering counsel, Welles wanted to be cast as Sam the Lion, a venerable Texas-style father figure who owns the local pool hall and movie theater. Though he'd been offended by the screenplay's sexual content, Welles told Bogdanovich that whoever played Sam would win an Oscar. Wanting a movie without any stars, however, Bogdanovich stuck to his guns and cast Ben Johnson, an Oklahoma-born rodeo champion who played grizzled cowboys in John Ford movies. And just as Orson predicted, Johnson won the Oscar for Best Supporting Actor in 1971.

With Bogdanovich heading off to make *The Last Picture Show*, Orson continued working in Los Angeles, now shooting scenes at Century City, which had once been a 20th Century–Fox back lot that covered nearly two hundred acres before the studio capped off a run of early 1960s box office disasters with Taylor and Burton's *Cleopatra* and decided to sell the land. The developers who bought that land envisioned turning it into a city-within-a-city, consisting of skyscrapers and modern architecture that would stand in contrast with the sprawling hodgepodge of styles that made up Los Angeles.

In 1970, the development was still in its infancy and Century City was little more than a few mirrored buildings and lots of construction dirt, which Welles decided to transform into a neo-futuristic landscape he could use as a backdrop for scenes from Hannaford's film-within-the-film. He literally achieved this effect with mirrors, as he'd done in

The Lady from Shanghai, having his crew put large, smoked and clear glass mirrors on rolling platforms that he positioned at different angles so they'd capture reflections off the existing buildings and create the image of a strange, seemingly uninhabited city that didn't exist anywhere but in his mind and on the camera.

Because it was large and nearly empty in the fall and winter of 1970, Century City also offered Welles the chance to shoot without interference from others and on the cheap. Welles had Gary secure permits for Gary Graver Productions and skirted additional fees by having him erase dates and enter new ones each time they expired. This was done so frequently that by the time they finished shooting, the permits had holes where the dates were supposed to go.

Though intricately composed and set up, the Century City scenes were shot without sound and under highly improvised circumstances. Having conceived an idea for a great visual, Welles ran with it and directed on the fly. Random described the shoot as "like a silent movie, except that you never knew what you were going to do. . . . [Orson would say,] 'Now you see the girl, she's over there, you're interested, so your eyes are following her. . . .'"

But somehow every direction made sense, as Random chased Kodar across the barren wasteland.

Another day, it was almost too windy to shoot, but when they viewed Graver's footage, it was so dynamic that Welles decided to start creating wind on his own. "Anything that made the shot more interesting stimulated Orson," Stringer said. "He then took that stimulation and magnified it."

To make the wind, the crew mounted an airplane propeller on a giant motor. Orson fell in love with the device, having it dragged to dusty areas under unfinished overpasses and near big portable tunnels, where he had Random drive the motorcycle into a blistering dust storm. On another occasion, he shot Random riding up Bunker Hill into the wind, and later, at MGM, Random spent half a day walking toward the fan with a jacket pulled over his head while crew members tossed garbage into the fan, which shot it back in the actor's face.

Though seemingly arbitrary, the fan was in keeping with Welles's theory that directors "preside over accidents." The wind was an accident whose limits he was now exploring with by playing god and creating gales of his own.

For the crew, what sometimes came off as madness was tempered by the knowledge that Welles was carrying the entire film in his head. "He knew exactly what he needed and wanted," said cameraman Leslie Otis. "He could accommodate bad luck, timing, and circumstances and come away with something better. We didn't know how, or how it would turn out, but we had complete trust in his ability to turn it into a magnificent film."

Welles also shot scenes from Hannaford's movie on MGM's back lot, which he was able to rent at a rate of $200 a day, as long as Graver and the crew pretended to be UCLA film students—meaning Orson had to duck every time they passed a security gate.

Once its own little city and Hollywood's most glamorous movie factory (boasting "More Stars Than There Are in the Heavens"), MGM sat on 185 acres that housed offices, soundstages, film labs, and massive departments for makeup, lighting, costumes, and publicity. It also had its own one-hundred-officer police force, a florist, a zoo, its own railroad, and a sixty-three-million-gallon lake.

Although in disrepair and being sold off to developers, MGM maintained a number of crumbling western sets that were also among the divine accidents over which Welles chose to preside. Reduced nearly to rubble, with tumbleweeds blowing across the streets, the sets offered some old catwalks, rafters, a few façades, and half-demolished structures with staircases to nowhere that were crisscrossed by beams.

This provided more fuel for Orson's imagination, and he began to think about how to use the old lot as part of Hannaford's surrealist world. Letting the set dictate what would work, rather than forcing his own preconception onto it, Welles would see beams or staircases and say,

"That's what's important here," after which the crew worked the shadows Welles found most interesting.

Much time at MGM, however, was consumed by Orson searching for inspiration and without a clear vision of how he wanted things to appear on-screen. Many scenes were rehearsed and filmed numerous times, after which Orson would change things around and do it again, and again, until the right image or interpretation emerged. Then he'd move the camera again and reenvision the action from a different perspective.

On another film, the producer might have pushed Orson to be more efficient. But since it was his own money and he had an accommodating crew, Welles had total control over the set, how long they worked, and what they shot. As a result, when the lot was available for only one final weekend, Welles had the crew work seventy-two hours straight until they got all the footage they needed.

Because of the free-form nature of the MGM shoot, Welles often became exasperated over technical glitches or shots taken from the wrong angle. Many times he would lament that they were "losing the light" and explode in a way that terrified some but was part of the job to most.

One outburst took place when Welles sent someone out for dinner during the late afternoon. Upon his return, the crew member handed out wrapped plates of food and plastic silverware. Orson went ballistic, launching into a twenty-minute tantrum about how they'd lost the light.

"I wanted sandwiches!" he screamed as the precious light dissipated behind him. "So that they could eat with one hand!"

Everyone, including those stifling laughter, put on an appropriate face out of respect for Orson and to avoid the line of fire.

Random recalled that Welles blew up on another occasion and told everyone to get off the set and never return. Knowing it was just another explosion, they left and then came back as if nothing had happened when Graver called later that week.

"Everybody excused him for everything and we didn't care why he was having a tantrum or what was wrong. We just did whatever he said. 'Get out,' we got out. 'Come back,' we came back," Random said. "He just made things up. I knew about his madness. I liked it."

"Where's the lighting?" Dennis Hopper asked when he arrived at Orson's house one evening to find that they were filming in the backyard with kerosene lamps as the only illumination.

"This is it," Orson replied. "These kerosene lamps."

"That's cool, man," Hopper said.

Hopper was there for a portion of Hannaford's party during which the power goes out and the documentary crews conduct interviews with young filmmakers. Hopper played a director named Lucas Renard, clearly based on himself, the idea being to film Hopper discussing movies in general and Hannaford in particular.

With a big untrimmed beard, long hair, and a black cowboy hat, a clearly stoned Hopper appears on camera sitting by a fire, rambling about how he'd like to get John Wayne's audience to watch his films and mumbling about the FBI visiting his house.

Probably still editing *The Last Movie* when he shot his scenes in November 1970, the disoriented Hopper is strangely compelling and captures the essence of all that he embodied, talking about how the idea of "a god-director" (later he says, "I'm still confused about the area of the magician as director") is "a very dangerous area"; then he unknowingly points to a theme at the heart of *The Other Side of the Wind* when he says, "The whole thing becomes a movie in front of that camera."

Hopper's *Easy Rider* producer Bert Schneider called Paul Mazursky at his office and said, "Orson Welles wants you to be in his new movie."

The first-time director of the 1969 blockbuster *Bob & Carol & Ted & Alice*, Mazursky was in postproduction on *Alex in Wonderland*, a semiautobiographical film about a director with one hit, trying to figure out his second movie.

Having never met Welles, Mazursky was suspicious, as he'd been in a legal battle with Schneider a few years before. And though they'd patched things up since then, the pair weren't friends. Mazursky assumed it was a prank.

"Why would Orson Welles want me?" Mazursky asked.

"I don't know why, he just asked for you," Schneider said. "He's doing a picture called *The Other Side of the Wind* and wants Paul Mazursky for a party scene."

Mazursky said he was insanely busy but asked when Welles wanted him. Schneider gave him Orson's address and said to be there at eight that evening.

Arriving around seven forty-five, Mazursky circled the neighborhood a few times. Either he was the butt of someone's joke or he was about to meet one of his heroes.

Finally he parked, went to the door, rang the bell, and was greeted by a very heavy Orson Welles, dressed in a black smock and laughing.

"Ho, ho, ho, Paul Mazursky!" Welles said. "Come in! *Bob and Carol and Ted and Alice*—wonderful! Wonderful! I can't tell you how happy I am that you came to my party."

Together they walked through the dark house to a room where Mazursky saw Henry Jaglom sitting at a table near two 16mm cameras. Now Mazursky had some idea why he was there.

A fiercely independent writer, actor, and director, who seemed to need friction in order to do his best work, Jaglom had met Welles in the late 1960s and settled into a less complicated mentor-student relationship than the one Orson had with Bogdanovich.

Smart and handsome in the scruffy, offbeat style of the era, Jaglom had come from New York to be a contract player at Columbia, appearing on *Gidget* and *The Flying Nun*. He was waiting for his big break when he auditioned for the lead in *Alex in Wonderland*, where he'd have portrayed a fictionalized Mazursky.

According to Mazursky, Jaglom was never promised the part but was in the running before it went to Donald Sutherland. Jaglom, however, said that he'd been cast and claimed to have spent months fielding late night phone calls from an anxious Mazursky, who sought his total commitment to the project.

"He needed to know it was the most important thing in my life," Jaglom said. "He wanted me to be as enthusiastic and overwhelmed as him."

Months later, however, after turning down roles in films by his friends Jack Nicholson and Dennis Hopper, Jaglom said he received a call from Mazursky, who told him he knew Jaglom was working on *A Safe Place* and feared that his attention would be divided, so Sutherland would get the part.

Knowing they hadn't spoken since, Orson hoped putting Jaglom and Mazursky together would give him real tension he could use as the catalyst for an improvised debate about the merits and philosophical underpinnings of Hannaford's films.

As Mazursky greeted Jaglom, the strain between the pair was everything Orson wished for.

"Hello, Henry," Mazursky said.

"Hello, Paul," Jaglom responded.

"Paul, I want you to sit here, right across from Henry. You know each other, but you have opposite opinions of Jake Hannaford," Welles said, laughing again. "Johnny Huston is going to play Jake Hannaford, but since John isn't available tonight, I'll be off camera so you can have someone to refer to."

After pouring Mazursky the first of several huge glasses of brandy, Welles handed him a Churchill cigar and the conversation began.

"What sort of man are you, Mr. Welles?" Mazursky asked. "I mean, Jake Hannaford."

"Hannaford has been living in Europe for some time. A director, filmmaker, someone who's been blackballed by Hollywood," Welles said, and emitted a thunderous, earthshaking laugh. *"A great man!!"*

When Welles decided to cast Mazursky, he told Jaglom: "I'm going to bring him to my house. He won't know why. Go at him. Tell him that he's a lousy filmmaker. Berate his films. Take my character and beat the shit out of him. Mazursky will defend the character because he thinks it's me. I want you to question my masculinity."

Filled with indignation, Jaglom did just that, railing at the forty-old Mazursky, whose owl-like face and cigar are visible against a backdrop of almost complete darkness.

Jaglom infers that *Bob & Carol* was a sellout. Exasperated, Mazursky calls Jaglom a spoiled rich kid and refuses to apologize for making a successful movie.

"But what about people who can't first make a movie that makes money?" Jaglom asks, cutting off Mazursky's response. "Maybe they're not interested in making pictures that make money. That's my point."

With Welles refilling their brandy glasses and someone passing a joint, the pair went on like this for a long time until they began screaming at each other like a pair of stoned philosophy majors having a three A.M. argument.

Jaglom: "Don't condescend to me! Don't patronize me!"

Mazursky: "Let me finish—"

Jaglom: "Don't patronize me!"

Mazursky: "Let me finish now—"

Monstrously frustrated, Mazursky even throws up his hand at one point and says, "Let's not talk about pictures, then."

Seeing that they were sufficiently whipped up, Welles approached.

"Cut!" he said. "Don't say a word. It's brilliant!"

Now it was time to start talking about Hannaford.

When the cameras roll again, Mazursky defends Hannaford and

explains how the director's work is thrilling. He invents names for various Hannaford movies on the spot and praises them. In response, Jaglom calls Hannaford a fascist and says he helped put Franco in power. When Orson interjects, as Hannaford, Jaglom confronts him about the role of women in Hannaford's films, asking why he always turns men into stars, then has a falling-out with them. Why hasn't he ever launched or shaped the career of an actress? Why, he asks pointedly, is it always men?

"Are you asking him if he's a homosexual!" Mazursky yells. "What are you asking him?! What is it that you're asking him?!"

"We did this for two or three hours and I was getting drunker and drunker," Mazursky said. "I had no idea what was going on, except that I was having fun."

With no clue how he'd gotten home, Mazursky was at the office the next morning when Welles called.

"Now I have a film," Welles said. "You're the greatest improviser I've ever seen. Unlike Dennis Hopper. He can't improvise."

Flattered, Mazursky said, "Mr. Welles, it was such a thrill and an honor. I hope we can get together sometime."

Welles said that sounded great, but not to call him. Instead, he would get in touch once *The Other Side of the Wind* was completed.

Taking a break in December, Welles told Bob Random to go to Hawaii and lie in the sun for a while. When he returned, Orson said, they'd finish the film.

After getting back, Random waited a few weeks but didn't hear anything, so he waited a few more weeks and then called Orson.

The phone was disconnected.

Random phoned Gary, who said Welles was in Europe and would be in touch when he returned to Los Angeles.

Not satisfied, Random began searching for Welles's number in

Europe. He asked everyone and tried everything, until finally, through a backdoor channel, he was given a number in France. He dialed and was soon on the phone with one of Orson's secretaries. After explaining that he was looking for Orson, he heard her tell Welles that there was a call.

When Welles grumbled loudly in the background, the secretary asked who was on the line. Random just told her it was important and that Orson was needed on the phone.

The director's voice grew louder and louder as he approached the receiver. "Hello?!" he barked.

"Hi, Orson," Random said. "This is Bob."

"Oh," Welles said. "Good to hear from you. Busy, Bob." The line went dead.

Random would neither see nor hear from Welles again until 1975.

1971

Orson has no friends, only stooges.
> —SCREENWRITER BEN HECHT

Carefree, Arizona, wasn't easy to reach in 1971. More than thirty miles from Phoenix, it required driving through raw desert on roads that went up and down like a washboard and flooded quickly, leaving drivers stranded after any decent rain.

Populated by aging cowboys and wealthy folks so conservative that Orson said they thought Reagan was a Communist, Carefree seemed an unlikely place to shoot a movie about Hollywood. But early in the year, Welles had a crew member rent a home there on the premise that Orson would use it to sit quietly by the pool and write his memoirs.

Like Orson, the home was dramatic. Owned by a New Jersey family named Slingman, the rental was a recently completed, architecturally significant structure designed to blend with the desert landscape. It had been built into the side of Black Mountain, with only one boulder moved to make way for a home that looked as though it had been lifted up and placed there by a giant.

Constructed from native, desert-toned red granite, the home featured huge picture windows, and each room opened to a patio or balcony from which there was a remarkable view. The pool, meanwhile, was nine and a half feet deep, with no shallow end or diving board, since the Slingman kids just dived off surrounding rocks.

The house was perfect for Orson, with the right look and feel to double as Hannaford's ranch, a desert backdrop they could use in Hannaford's film, and the irony of being located down the road from the home Antonioni blew up (on-screen) at the end of *Zabriskie Point*.

Finally, Carefree was so remote that Orson could shoot in private, without journalists or Hollywood folks poking around asking about his film.

Meanwhile, the Slingmans were back home in New Jersey, probably thrilled that they were renting their vacation home to a highly cultured living legend, while that very same legend was turning it into a movie set.

In Arizona, it became clear that Gary needed more help. Up to this point, he'd been much more than a cinematographer: He hired, fired, and managed the crew; procured meals; purchased and altered work permits; located props; and made sure Orson had everything he needed. But even Welles could see it was too much and decided they needed to hire a production manager and beef up the staff.

Among those Welles contacted was Polly Platt, who was back in Hollywood with her two children, living in the home she shared with Bogdanovich on Outpost Drive. Bogdanovich, however, wasn't there, as events that took place during the making of *The Last Picture Show* had dramatically altered not only his career, but also his personal life.

The Archer City, Texas, set of *The Last Picture Show* had been a mix of creative brilliance and virtuoso filmmaking, enhanced greatly by the creative rapport between Bogdanovich and Platt, the former bringing his innate sense of story composition and the latter her impeccable visual instincts. It was a partnership that remained intact even while their marriage crumbled because of Peter's affair with Cybill Shepherd, the twenty-year-old model he'd cast as the spoiled, small-town ice queen Jacy Farrow.

A tomboy turned Memphis beauty queen, Shepherd was discovered by Bogdanovich and Platt while they waited in a checkout line at Ralph's Supermarket in the summer of 1970 and saw her picture on the cover of *Glamour*.

"Doesn't that look like Jacy?" Platt said of Shepherd's mixture of all-American blonde and cool, seductive carnality that jumped off the magazine cover.

After his casting director tracked her down, Bogdanovich went to New York so he could interview Shepherd for the part. What he found was more than a typical model or southern belle. Cybill was smart, tough, funny, and rebellious—not to mention so unimpressed with movie people that she showed up to meet Bogdanovich in his room at the Essex House hotel wearing jeans, sandals, and no makeup.

Accustomed to stopping men dead in their tracks, Shepherd ironically found herself on the other end of the equation when Bogdanovich opened the door and she felt an intense and immediate attraction and spent the interview sitting nervously on the floor and casually pulling petals off the flower from a room service tray while she answered questions.

For Bogdanovich, what Shepherd said wound up being much less important than what she was doing with the flower.

"I thought, 'That's kind of the way [Jacy] plays with guys. Just kind of offhandedly,'" Bogdanovich said. "And that little gesture made me feel that she could do this part."

In Archer City, however, the sexual tension between the pair was clear to everyone on the set, including Platt, who—for the most part—sat by as her husband fell in love with his lead actress. In fact, Platt later said that she even mildly encouraged it on some level, making Cybill up each day to embody Peter's Hollywood-based fantasy girl. Although she believed that Bogdanovich almost had to fall in love with his lead actress for the good of the film, Platt figured that any relationship wouldn't last after they wrapped. Ultimately, she even understood why Peter couldn't avoid the inevitable.

"Cybill was irresistible," Platt said. "If I was a man and a beautiful girl like that made a pass at me, I don't know what I would do. I could see why Peter was head over heels in love with her."

In November, after nearly two months on set, a flirtatious conversation between Bogdanovich and Shepherd crossed the blurry line between film and reality when Peter said, "I can't decide who I'd rather sleep with. You or Jacy." Ultimately, however, the answer to that question didn't matter, as Peter wound up in bed with his lead actress.

Upon returning to his hotel room later, Bogdanovich had a huge fight with Platt, who kicked him out. From that day forward, they could barely speak to each other as husband and wife. But the movie came first, and the pair drove to work together each day and talked through setups, then sat side by side on set, working through each shot.

No matter how well they worked together, the tension between Platt and Bogdanovich bled onto the set, where the crew was already bristling at Peter's perfectionist ways and tendency to make them take shots over and over until they were just as he wanted. Equally annoying was his determination to maintain control over the set, which included a rule that cast and crew couldn't eat together. And along with all this, there was the perception (among those who didn't care for him) that Peter was arrogant. It was a feeling that only got worse as he seemed to walk around gloating over his affair with Cybill.

Then in late November Peter's father died unexpectedly of a stroke. Heartbroken and deeply shaken, he remained focused on his film. "That's what movies are like," he said of all that happened. "You just kind of keep going . . . the present definitely intruded personally on our lives and the making of the film, but it was an obsessive . . . movies are an obsessive thing."

Knowing the entire story, Welles called and spoke to Platt for the first time since Peter and Cybill's affair, which he said was a laughably hackneyed Hollywood story straight out of a crappy screenplay.

Orson told Platt that the best thing for her would be to join the crew in Carefree.

"Come to work for me," Platt recalled Welles telling her. "I need you."[172]

Meanwhile, with Peter living at the Sunset Tower, *The Last Picture Show* production manager Frank Marshall was between jobs and occupying a spare room at the house on Outpost, where he was helping out with Bogdanovich and Platt's kids.

After she spoke to Welles, Platt told Marshall, "I'm going down to do this movie with Orson. Do you want to go?" And soon after that, Platt flew to Arizona while Marshall drove his VW bus to Carefree, arriving in time to find Orson's secretary—an Englishwoman named Margaret Hodgson—in the garage, typing the script while smoking a cigarette through a long holder.

When he met Orson, Marshall received a grunted, "Hello," after which he ran around for three days doing whatever he was told. Finally Welles yelled, "*Frank!* Go move that thing over there."

"My God! I've been accepted," Marshall thought, blown away to hear Welles refer to him by name.

Now part of the team, Marshall was asked to construct a small table that seemed like one of Orson's bizarre tangents but became a key element in the creation of something remarkable.

The table, Welles said, was being used in a "forced perspective" shot: an effect created in the camera that alters the viewer's perception by placing small objects of varying size and scale between the audience's vantage point and the on-screen image.

Often used in low-budget movies, forced perspective allowed Japanese directors to make a toy Godzilla tower over scale model Tokyo skyscrapers. More artistically, the effect was used at the end of

Casablanca when Humphrey Bogart says good-bye to Ingrid Berg-man in the rain as her plane waits behind them. The scene was shot in the studio, with an airplane painted on the wall and the actors stand-ing in the foreground, while dwarves (in order to achieve proper scale) prepared the aircraft for takeoff and the rain created enough distrac-tion between the view and the backdrop to make it work.

Orson's forced perspective shot was from Hannaford's film, where the foreground remained in sharp focus while Oja's character walked across a distant volcanic wasteland. It was something a moviegoer wouldn't notice, but for Marshall, making the idea work was fasci-nating, as it required the table (covered in rocks that had been painted black) to act as the foreground miniature while Kodar stood atop a bread truck parked half a mile away.

Maintaining sharp focus on the rocks, the resulting image ap-peared to be a tiny Kodar atop a huge black tundra, which had been created with a table and rocks.

"It was the most amazing thing I'd ever seen," Marshall said.

What Welles had done was use the struggle to stimulate his imagi-nation. The more impossible the shot, the more creative he became. Often it seemed he created problems just to get the results that came from overcoming them. "Visually and in a cinematic sense, [Orson] was creating shots in his head with these crazy ideas," Marshall said.

It was just another part of his genius.

On the set of the 1970 biker pic *Bury Me an Angel,* Graver and Stringer met Mike Ferris, a big guy and a movie fanatic with no practical training whose on-set function was to carry heavy things. Working as an unpaid grip, he did whatever was asked and began working on non-union films.

Soon the three were close, with Stringer becoming Ferris's best friend. Graver, meanwhile, would kill downtime on the set with Ferris as they challenged each other's movie knowledge. According to Ferris, he would often name a little-known actor from a rarely seen film, only to have Graver describe its plot and recite the names of the cast and crew.

When it became apparent they needed more people in Carefree, Stringer called Ferris, who was in his car thirty minutes later, headed for Arizona.

Arriving the next afternoon in the waning desert light, Ferris saw standard filmmaking equipment as well as numerous items Orson had asked crew members to make out of papier-mâché. He found Graver and Stringer, and soon after that he met Orson, who extended a big hand and asked him to kneel down to help him get a shot.

Three or four feet from the camera, but on a ninety-degree angle from the lens, Ferris and Orson sat on opposite sides of the camera. When they were ready, Welles said, "Let's roll!" and began throwing dirt at Ferris, exhorting, "Mike, throw dirt at me!" So Ferris threw dirt, with no idea what purpose it might serve. But Orson Welles was throwing dirt and telling him to do the same with such clarity of purpose that Ferris's dumbfounded amazement turned to compliance.

To Ferris, what they'd been doing looked insane. It was two men just throwing dirt. But with Orson, he said, "the amount of dirt; the way he tossed it; the angle; the exposure; the setting: All made it look like some kind of strange storm that could only take place in this particular desert at this particular time."

Like Marshall, Ferris adapted to Orson's work methods, realizing that part of the process was for Orson to invent problems and situations for which he would need to *create* a solution. Each day included the constant surprise that arose from Orson's fertile mind, which spewed forth new ideas that were always outside anyone's experience.

"Once we got used to it, we expected it," Ferris said. "But we never stopped being amazed."

Equally amazing was Bogdanovich's new life, which included Cybill; friendships with Orson, Jerry Lewis, Howard Hawks, John Ford, and Cary Grant; and a new film that was already the talk of Hollywood, despite the fact that it wouldn't hit theaters for nearly a year.

Representing the hottest young director in town, Bogdanovich's agent, Sue Mengers, spent her days fending off requests to see the film and granting access only to the biggest stars, including Barbra

Streisand and Steve McQueen, the latter wanting to see if Peter would be right to direct *The Getaway*. Though he'd blown off Bogdanovich before the screening, McQueen came to him afterward and said, "You're a picture maker, man. I'm just an actor, but you're a picture maker."

Streisand was more dramatic. Unable to stop bawling, she loved the film and spent over an hour discussing possible projects with Bogdanovich, who suggested that they make a screwball comedy with the actress playing off her own persona. Streisand, however, wanted to do something serious, like *The Last Picture Show*.

When McQueen took on another project before *The Getaway*, Bogdanovich pitched his idea to Universal. The studio green-lighted his concept of a Hawksian film like *Bringing Up Baby*, starring Streisand as the wacky Hepburn type who disrupts the life of a stuffy academic, and offered him $125,000 to direct, plus 8 percent of the profits. Bogdanovich cast Streisand's boyfriend Ryan O'Neal in the Cary Grant role, and by October they were shooting *What's Up, Doc?* in San Francisco, where Polly Platt was again at his side, talking through the setups.

Though they were still not divorced, their marriage was clearly over. Peter was with Cybill, and Platt, still hurting, had become deeply wary of his almost dreamlike, cinematic view of life and the limitations it created.

"You can only feel for people on celluloid," she screamed at him during one fight. "You have no concept of what it's like in real life to feel any grief . . . Picture it in a movie . . . and maybe you'll get it."

That quality allowed her to understand—and empathize with—where he was coming from. "It's almost impossible to hate Peter," Platt told writer Rachel Abramowitz. "You realized he never knew what to do. Because he only learned things from the movies."

Meanwhile, with her psyche and self-worth in a shambles from the way the relationship had ended, Platt was also sitting by as Bogdanovich was launched into the stratosphere by a film to which she'd made a substantial contribution. Though the picture had rested on Peter's shoulders, Platt felt she wasn't getting any credit—it was as if she didn't even exist. Home alone with two children, she was nobody. Which was why Orson's job offer had been so important and why she was able to compartmentalize her personal relationship with Peter and go to work on *What's Up, Doc?*

But if Platt had been at a low point when Orson called, her savior was about to cast her, briefly, in a role based on someone who seemed intent on driving him to similar depths by taking away the one thing he'd always had, no matter what: *Citizen Kane.*

Before the *Kane* crisis, however, Charles Higham reappeared to write a short, highly inaccurate, piece in the January 31, 1971, *New York Times.* In it, he revealed the plot of the self-financed film Orson was "secretly" making without a lead actor, but with a cast that included Mazursky and Marlene Dietrich (playing a character based on herself), who interrupted filming to attend Coco Chanel's funeral in Paris.

Higham was indeed correct that Dietrich was the model for Zarah Valeska, the legendary actress throwing Hannaford's birthday party. But, though Welles may have considered her for the part, he hadn't shot a millimeter of film with his old friend, whose cameo as a fortune-teller in *Touch of Evil* included a line that became symbolic for the way many perceived Orson.

When Welles's corrupt cop, Quinlan, asks Dietrich's Tana (who once loved him) to read his future, she says he doesn't have one and explains, "Your future is all used up."

Dietrich was either unavailable for the part or feared that she wouldn't be lit properly in the documentary-style scenes and therefore wouldn't do the film. Instead, Welles cast German actress Lilli Palmer (costar of Fritz Lang's *Cloak and Dagger*).

Shooting at Palmer's home in Malaga, Spain, on several occasions, Welles matched up her scenes to existing footage using photos to duplicate the lighting, inserting tight shots of other actors and having someone dressed as Hannaford cross before the camera at the beginning of shots in which Palmer appeared. Thus, her scenes involved pairing performances on different continents, filmed years apart by actors who had never been in the same room.

"That was my father to a T," his daughter Beatrice said. "I don't think he even knew what the word continuity meant. He'd have done that even if he'd had the money."

Five years after she'd referred to him as "the one great creative force in American film in our time," Pauline Kael wrote the following about *Citizen Kane* in *The New Yorker*.

"It is difficult to explain what makes any great work great, and particularly difficult with movies and maybe more so with *Citizen Kane* than with other great movies," she wrote in the essay "Raising Kane," "because it isn't a work of special depth or a work of subtle beauty. It is a shallow work, a shallow masterpiece."

In the five years between her endorsement of Orson's genius in *The New Republic* and the publication of "Raising Kane" on February 20 and 27, 1971, things had changed for Pauline Kael. Upon moving to *The New Yorker*, she'd effectively become the most influential movie critic in America. A gifted writer with a wry sense of humor and contrarian taste, she liked to stir things up and now could do it from atop a gigantic soapbox.

Which is exactly what Kael did in 1970 when she decided that it was time to take on the auteur theory championed by her rival, Andrew Sarris of *The Village Voice*. There was no better (or more ironic, given Orson's feelings) way to do that than by taking down the greatest act of auteurism in Hollywood history, the making of *Kane* by actor, writer, and director Orson Welles.

Keenly sensitive to the plight of the screenwriter, who received short shrift when it came to handing out money and fame, Kael had developed a theory, based on a hunch, that the true author of *Kane* had been

Orson's co-writer, Herman J. Mankiewicz, with whom he'd shared the writing credit and the Oscar that followed.

Extremely career-savvy, Kael knew a piece that questioned Orson's role in *Kane* would generate controversy and allow her to take a big dig at Sarris and auteurists everywhere. So, armed with the belief that Welles's co-writer was the real genius, she went about finding support for her theory that "Mankiewicz died [in 1953] and his share faded from knowledge, but Welles carried on in the Baronial style that always reminds us of *Kane*."

Beyond the irony that Orson also hated the auteur theory was the fact that Kael's essay would be the introduction to *The Citizen Kane Book*, which contained the film's script, whose publishing rights Orson had sold to Little, Brown and Bantam in return for a share of the royalties. But Welles wasn't the only one getting screwed by Kael.

The other victim was Howard Suber, an assistant film professor at UCLA, where Kael often lectured and was friendly with the department chair. During a 1969 visit, Kael met Suber and found out he was working on a scholarly book about *Citizen Kane* for which he'd interviewed Mankiewicz's widow, who'd, not surprisingly, rhapsodized about her husband's influence on the script.

Upon her return to New York, Kael called Suber and invited him to write one of two essays that would appear in her *Kane* book. With Kael offering half her advance ($375) and promising to extract him from his current publishing contract, Suber would have seemed a fool not to accept.

Soon Kael sent Suber a check and asked for his research, which included interviews with Dorothy Comingore (who played Charles Foster Kane's second wife) and Orson's friend and associate Richard Wilson. Each contained evidence, Kael thought, supporting her beliefs.

Only Suber's wife found the situation suspicious and was worried about her husband working without any written agreement. Unconcerned, Suber asked her, "Why would the biggest film critic in America need to screw with some little assistant professor from UCLA?"

Kael spoke to only a few people, the most notable being John House-man, Orson's longtime partner whom he'd taken to calling "an old enemy of mine."

Houseman, whose existence once revolved around doing everything else so that Orson had the freedom to just create, was hardly unbiased. Though he'd taken the alcoholic Mankiewicz to remote Victorville, California, in order to keep him dry and focused on putting together early drafts of the script, Houseman wasn't going to explain what Welles did to transform that work into *Kane*.

Estranged for nearly thirty years, Welles and Houseman had gone from an edgy symbiosis to—at best—bitter dislike. Orson believed that Houseman may have been in love with him (despite the fact that Houseman was twice married), an idea that was further solidified by his former partner's 1972 memoir, *Run Through*, nearly a third of which concerns his relationship with Welles and is written in the tones of a spurned lover.

In Houseman's defense, however, Orson was either unaware or unable to acknowledge just how valuable his partner had been, and that since they'd parted, the organization of his work life, the financing of his films, and his ability to concentrate fully on manifesting his genius had been badly compromised. Thirty years later, he still didn't have anyone who made sure that his projects had reliable funding; sets and costumes that arrived on time; and budgets managed by someone who understood his creative patterns and needs. Perhaps Houseman was intolerable, but he'd also been invaluable. All of which made Orson's former partner happy to tell his unfavorable side of the story to Kael.

Meanwhile, Suber heard from Kael less frequently, until the calls stopped. On February 20, he received the issue of *The New Yorker* containing her essay, but there was no mention of his name. Without a contract, Suber had no recourse against the famous critic who was friends with his boss.

Though Suber was not mentioned, Kael had (without naming names) mocked McBride in her essay. Either feeling guilty or trying to cover herself, she called McBride, saying she hoped he wasn't upset. McBride said he wasn't hurt, but he wanted to know why "Raising Kane" took such an unfavorable view of Orson's contributions and why she'd spoken only to unsympathetic sources. And why hadn't she spoken to Welles?

Kael said she'd avoided Welles and his confidants because she already knew what they'd say, summarily dismissing a gigantic flaw in her fifty-thousand-word piece that had eluded *The New Yorker*'s famed fact-checking process. Kael was a critic, not a journalist, and her research files for the piece contained little more than a few phone numbers, including Suber's.

According to her biographer, Brian Kellow, Kael's behavior regarding the essay was both entirely in and out of character for a woman he'd found to be kind, brilliant, and generous for the most part. But, because of her ego, Kael had concluded that she'd discharged her obligations to Suber by giving him $375 and believed that having his work appear, even uncredited, in *The New Yorker* as support for *her theory* would make a larger impact than any academic book. Thus, she'd done him a service.

Regarding Welles, one of Kael's flaws was that she was frequently unaware of how her writing impacted its subjects. Though capable of such hubris, Kellow said he was still baffled that she'd taken such an enormous risk, particularly since it was unlike anything she'd ever done before.

One thing was clear, however. Kael thought she'd have no trouble getting away with it.

For two days after "Raising Kane" was published, Welles refused to come out of his bedroom or speak. When he emerged, he called his attorney, Arnold Weissberger, to discuss a libel suit against Kael and legal action against her publishers.

Weissberger said the lawsuit was a bad idea that would generate greater publicity for Kael and draw more attention to "Raising Kane." Breaking down in tears of anguish and frustration at the great indignity of the accusation that he'd stolen credit on the film for which he was revered, Welles took another blow when Weissberger pointed out the cruel twist of fate in which Orson was essentially partners with Kael and her publishers, with a financial stake in the success of a book featuring her snarky essay.

Then the defense began. Comingore angrily disputed her testimony. McBride, Sarris, and Wilson wrote anti-Kael articles for respected film magazines. And Orson turned to Bogdanovich again, this time asking him to respond to Kael.

Once more Bogdanovich came through, because "Orson was shattered by it and I thought, 'This is bullshit.'" Doing the legwork needed to decimate Kael's article and expose her as a fraud, he allowed Orson a very heavy editorial hand in "The *Kane* Mutiny," which appeared in *Esquire* shortly after *The Last Picture Show* opened in fall 1971.

In the article, Bogdanovich explains that Kael seems to have no idea how films are made and eviscerates her in a way that makes his Higham response look like a well-considered reflection upon a flawed but valuable work. Questioning every bit of evidence and providing information to the contrary, Bogdanovich even exposes Kael's violations of journalistic ethics, including the story of how she'd taken credit for Suber's work without mentioning his name.

Publishing the story under his own name was an act of colossal bravery, ego, and borderline foolishness for Bogdanovich, who was pissing in the face of America's most powerful critic at the moment his career was taking off. But his respect for Welles knew no boundaries.

And now it was Kael who felt blindsided, as Kellow's book recounts, describing how she had been with Woody Allen while she read the *Esquire* story. "How am I going to answer this?" Kael asked Allen.

Allen gave her perfect advice.

"Don't answer," he said.

Welles, however, sought retribution in his own way, by either revising an existing character or adding a new one—the bitchy, pretentious critic Juliette Riche. Originally, Welles had cast Polly Platt in the role; then, briefly, he'd replaced her with Janice Pennington, a *Playboy* centerfold and future *Price Is Right* model who was married to Glenn Jacobson. Ultimately, however, he chose Susan Strasberg, daughter of legendary acting teacher Lee Strasberg, recognizing that her fragility and intelligence would add balance and humanity to the Kael-inspired role.

Meanwhile, Platt was doing set design and various odd jobs. At one point, for instance, she was called upon to walk into a Phoenix radio station and tell the receptionist that she needed a private meeting with station manager Pat McMahon. The receptionist buzzed McMahon and said there was a strange but seemingly not dangerous woman looking for him. McMahon walked to the front desk and met Platt, who said she was working on a major motion picture whose director (wishing to remain anonymous) needed use of a radio studio.

McMahon told Platt the studio was booked and offered to call other stations. Wearing sunglasses and a trench coat, Platt looked at McMahon "like Pussy Galore in *Goldfinger*" and said, "May we go to your office for a talk?"

Once they were alone, Platt confessed that she'd been lying about the studio. "The director is interested in you," she said.

"This unnamed director of an unnamed movie is aware of me?" McMahon asked.

"Yes," Platt said. "He saw you on some kids' show."

A regular cast member on the popular local children's show *The Wallace and Ladmo Show*, McMahon was also a frequent victim of the elaborate pranks of his costar, Wallace.

"But, I'm not a film actor," he said to Platt. "At least tell me who the director is, so I can decide if I want to do this."

"I'm sworn to secrecy," Platt responded.

McMahon said that he couldn't agree unless he knew that he wasn't going to be wasting his time. Platt relented.

"You must promise not to tell anyone," she said. "It's Orson Welles."

Now McMahon was convinced it was a prank, given that everyone knew he idolized Welles. Telling Platt he'd do it, McMahon hoped to catch Wallace in the act. But he also asked for a script.

"Only Orson has a script," Platt said. "But here are some pages he'd like you to memorize. Are you free Saturday?"

McMahon said he could work after doing an amusement park appearance with Wallace and Ladmo. Platt told him to meet her beneath a bridge that ran between Phoenix and Tempe.

On Saturday, after wrapping up his appearance, McMahon thought, "Wallace isn't as good as he used to be," and drove to an access road under the bridge. There he found a small crew and Orson, who came directly to the car and introduced himself.

"God, I've admired you," Welles said, then gave a detailed description of how much he enjoyed McMahon's work on *The Wallace and Ladmo Show.*

Orson then began to explain McMahon's character, a fawning Hannaford fanatic who runs up to introduce himself as Hannaford arrives at the party.

"Mr. Hannaford," he says, beaming, "I'm Marvin P. Fassbender."

Looking him up and down, Hannaford takes his hand and says, "Of course you are."

Despite his suspicions, McMahon had memorized his lines, and Welles began talking to him about how to play a scene in Hannaford's car. But when Welles looked at the sides Platt had given McMahon, he exploded:

"We've invited my friend Pat McMahon and interrupted his extraordinarily busy day to come and be part of this company of players and yet somebody gave him the wrong sides!" Welles shouted. "How do you expect him to have any respect for what we are doing here?"

Quickly someone gave new pages to Welles, who handed them to McMahon and said, "Can you memorize these lines rapidly?"

With no context except that they were going to Hannaford's birth-day party, Welles got in the front seat of a Jeep with his camera, while McMahon sat in the back, where he was going to speak to a nonexistent Hannaford, reading his lines from a page taped to the fly of Orson's pants.

For the next few days, they spent hours working on the scene, until they wrapped one evening and Welles said that McMahon, being a long-time Phoenix resident, would recommend a restaurant where they'd have some privacy.

Stunned, McMahon suggested a dimly lit place nearby, where he wound up sharing a booth with Orson and Oja. Drinks were ordered and everyone was looking at the menu when a waitress interrupted.

"I'm sorry to bother you, but could I get you to sign this?" she said, handing a piece of paper past Orson and to McMahon, whom she asked to sign as one of his *Wallace and Ladmo Show* characters, tell-ing him that her kids would treasure the autograph.

When she left, Welles began to laugh hysterically and told Mc-Mahon, "I've always enjoyed dining with the stars!!"

After everyone left, McMahon was on his way out when he saw the waitress again.

"I really didn't want to bother him," she said. "The gentleman who just left . . . that was Burl Ives, wasn't it?"

The next day, when McMahon told the story to Welles, the director smiled broadly and said, "Had I known that, I would have gone back and done the first eight bars of 'Big Rock Candy Mountain' for her."

Among the presenters at the Forty-third Annual Academy Awards that April was a young, giggly Goldie Hawn, who would give a Best Actor Oscar to either George C. Scott (*Patton*); James Earl Jones (*The Great White Hope*); Ryan O'Neal (*Love Story*); Melvyn Douglas (*I Never Sang for My Father*); or Jack Nicholson (*Five Easy Pieces*).

Opening the envelope, Hawn gasped, "Oh, my God, George C. Scott in *Patton*!" The audience exploded, and producer Frank McCarthy took the stage and graciously thanked the Academy for recognizing a remarkable performance.

Hawn hadn't gasped over Scott's win because he was an underdog. She'd known, as had everyone else, that he'd refused to attend the ceremony (which he described as a demeaning "two-hour meat parade") or accept the award if he won. Though Scott had also withdrawn his name when he was nominated for *The Hustler,* nobody had turned down the award before, and Hollywood was split on whether he was a genuine artist or a raging asshole. Gregory Peck and other establishment stars felt Scott was inappropriate and wildly disrespectful, while Ryan O'Neal and his contemporaries applauded his bravery.

But Scott wasn't the only person who didn't accept his own award that night.

In December, the Academy of Motion Picture Arts and Sciences told Orson that he'd be receiving a "Special Oscar" for career achievement. What may have been intended as a heartwarming welcome home wasn't interpreted as such by Welles.

Only fifty-five, he was receiving the same award as seventy-eight-year-old Lillian Gish, who'd made her film debut in 1912. For Orson, this was the industry sending him into retirement with a gold watch.

"'They're not going to get me like that,'" Bogdanovich said Welles told him. "As if it were humiliating for him to get the Oscar."

There was no way, Orson said, that he'd summon fake tears and false sentiment or play the jolly dancing bear to assuage the guilt of everyone who'd turned away his projects. He was a working filmmaker, not a dried-up museum piece.

"He didn't want to give them the pleasure of having him show up," Bogdanovich said.

But, unlike Scott, Orson didn't decline the award. He just didn't attend the ceremony, having John Huston accept in his stead.

Clean-shaved and distinguished, Huston strode to the podium and unleashed his seductive, hypnotic, whiskey- and cigar-ripened voice that was capable of convincing anyone of anything.

"Genius is a word that must be used very sparingly, especially in the world of films," he began. "Those who claim it don't have it, and those who do have it, keep the fact concealed for fear of being called difficult. Which usually translates to unemployable."

He paused.

"So at one time or another, Orson Welles has been considered both difficult and unemployable. I know only too damn well. But from the time of his very first picture, the unforgettable *Citizen Kane*, Welles's mastery of the medium was evident. Unfortunately, only once, in *Kane*, was he free to exercise his talents without restraint. Subsequent productions were cut by other hands or, like his *Macbeth*, made on impossibly low budgets. Yet in every picture he ever made, his brilliance shone through.

"Thirty-three years ago, Orson Welles received what he liked to call 'half an Oscar,' for the script for *Citizen Kane*, which he coauthored with Herman J. Manckiewicz. Tonight the Academy is honored to give him an Oscar all his own. . . . Because he is truly that most difficult, unforgivable, and invaluable of God's creations, a man of genius."

After explaining that Orson was filming abroad, Huston introduced a video Welles had prepared for the occasion.

Made up and lit to look younger and trimmer, a tuxedo-clad Welles spoke in one of the many voices he'd perfected over the years. Dialing down his commanding baritone, he was "humble Orson."

"Ladies and gentlemen, with this great honor, let me say that it's a lot more fun to look forward. Looking backwards over some thirty years in the movies is something that I like to do as seldom as possible, but I can't forget that I didn't spend those years alone. Every filmmaker knows how much was done for him and by how many. If I could call just half of all those who deserve it to stand beside this camera, just to get them in one shot we'd need Cinerama."

Glancing down shyly, Welles asked forgiveness because this award meant more than others, because it came not from the critics, but "from movie people themselves, the ones who love movies the most. . . . And if we didn't love movies as much as we do, if we weren't a little crazy on the subject, there wouldn't be any movies at all. I treasure this award as an expression of the happy lunacy, and may I accept it, please, not so much for what I may have done, but for what I hope to do. . . . Meanwhile, this encouragement is very welcome. With all my heart, I thank you for it."

Amid the applause, the camera cut to Huston, who said, "Happy lunacy, that's really telling it like it is. . . . On my way back to Ireland, I'll stop in Spain and give this to him." And he left the stage with a mischievous grin on his face.

The whole thing had been perfect. Huston's speech was a tightly written defense of Welles and a charming "I know you and don't care what you think" repudiation of an industry that kept his friend from expressing his genius, simply because *he was a genius*. Orson followed with a performance of such bashful modesty that it was hard to imagine why anyone would stop him from doing anything, much less making a picture. Was this thankful, innocent man someone who'd steal credit from poor dead Herman J. Mankiewicz?

Then there was the real joke. Orson wasn't in Spain, but was actually sitting in a bungalow at the Beverly Hills Hotel, watching the awards with Bogdanovich and Graver.

Thus, while Huston smiled, Orson busted out laughing. "Thanks, John!" he said to the TV. "Bring it over!"

Making the situation even more ironic was the fact that, according to one document, Huston also seemed not to know that Orson was in Beverly Hills and genuinely intended to bring the statue with him to Europe.

French actress Jeanne Moreau, who played opposite Welles in *Chimes at Midnight,* once said about Orson: "If he calls and says, 'I need you,' then you say, 'Orson needs me and it's something important.' His career is so strange because he's capable of such beautiful things and it's so hard for him to make a film, you wouldn't be the little stone that would stop the machine from going once he has the chance to make a film. I think that's why we all do react that way."

Nobody knew this drill better than Mercedes McCambridge, who'd received "the call" before. Often it came from a secretary. But the last time, it had been Welles himself.

McCambridge was home in Los Angeles during the late 1950s when Orson (who'd called her "the world's greatest living radio actress") phoned to see if she'd like to have lunch with him that afternoon at Universal. During the conversation, he also asked if she could wear black pants and a sweater (of course she could) and whether she had a black leather jacket as well (of course she didn't).

An Oscar winner (for Best Supporting Actress in *All the King's Men* [1949]) then in her early forties, McCambridge was a tough Irish wit from Joliet, Illinois. With a husky voice to match her personality, she was the perfect foil for Orson and his drama.

So when McCambridge arrived on the *Touch of Evil* set and saw Welles working from a distance, she didn't care that she'd been barely acknowledged by her host. Rather than go to him, she simply watched the chaos that swirled around Orson and waited to find out what her friend really wanted.

Soon a panicked assistant director came to her and said, "He's going to cut your hair. He's going to do it himself." McCambridge acted as if this unthinkable actress's nightmare were nothing unusual.

Then Orson came over. Cigar in hand, he embraced "Mercy" in a manner that suggested her presence was little more than a delightful surprise.

"I understand you're going to cut my hair," she said.

"No, no, no, no, no, my dear, sweet girl, not cut your hair," Orson cooed. "I'm going to trim it ever so slightly to give the perfect effect of the character you are going to play."

There was no mention of lunch.

Unflappable, McCambridge let Welles go at her with a scissors, snipping here and there, then a little more here and some more there, before standing back to admire his work and deciding what else was required. The answer: black shoe polish, which he used to curl her hair, outline a mole, and turn her eyebrows thick and bushy. Finally, to complete the transformation, Welles gave her a black leather jacket—and McCambridge became the toughest lesbian member of a Mexican gang ever seen.

After telling her to walk around like a "masculine hood-type broad" with a "heavy, coarse Mexican accent," Orson turned on the cameras and his lunch date became the strange thug he'd imagined overseeing the gang rape of Janet Leigh.

She was back home by four P.M.

"That's what it's like to work for Orson Welles," McCambridge wrote.

For a man who one biographer said was always searching for his Judas, in McCambridge he'd found Mary Magdalene. "If [Orson] asked me to jump off the Empire State Building," McCambridge told McBride, "I would do it and not ask why."

Having appeared in a string of forgettable films and TV westerns during the 1960s, Mercedes McCambridge was now in her mid-fifties, twice divorced, and a newly recovered alcoholic whom Orson cast as Maggie, Hannaford's loyal secretary. Joining the cast that May, while they shot in Los Angeles, she and other old Welles associates were playing "the Hannaford mafia," or "Jake's stooges."

In addition to McCambridge there was Paul Stewart as Matt Costello, Hannaford's snarling hatchet man who's involved with a Hollywood anti-Communist organization. With a gravelly voice and large, unsympathetic eyes, Stewart was one of Orson's Mercury Radio friends and looked every bit the villainous mobsters he'd been playing since his film debut as Kane's butler.

An Oscar winner (for Best Supporting Actor in *The Barefoot Contessa* [1954]), Edmond O'Brien also knew Orson from his New York days. Now a character actor, O'Brien had appeared in everything from James Cagney's *White Heat* to Sam Peckinpah's *The Wild Bunch*. Cast as Hannaford's friend Pat, O'Brien played a red-faced, whiskey-swilling former actor who openly harbors fascist political leanings.

Finally, there was Zimmie, the Texas Jewish makeup man who'd helped Hannaford mold actors into stars. Kept out of Jake's inner circle because of his religion, Zimmie was played by veteran actor Cameron Mitchell, who'd been Happy in the original Broadway production of *Death of a Salesman* and now played Uncle Buck on TV's *The High Chaparral.*

In late May, McBride joined the cast while Welles was shooting on a bus filled with dummies made up in wigs and trench coats to look like Random's character. It's Jake's weird joke now that his lead has run away from the set after the director humiliates him during a sex scene. Tooling around Encino and other parts of the San Fernando Valley in the sweltering heat, Orson, Graver, Stringer, Ferris, and other bearded hippie crew members filmed the older actors as they established the film's political undertone.

Tossed from the car after asking about the suicide of Hannaford's father, McBride's character rides with the dummies and the director's cronies to the party and screening at Jake's ranch. During the ride, Costello fires Zimmie but still orders him to attend Hannaford's party.

The more often he showed up, the larger McBride's part grew simply by virtue of his presence on the set. Typically, Welles treated the writer with great kindness punctuated by torrents of anger, such as the day he canceled the shoot because McBride brought the wrong trench coat for his character. After screaming until his biographer began to cry, Welles sent everyone home because of McBride's "carelessness."

By contrast, Welles was compassionate when McBride was unable to read back a transcript of Hannaford ranting against hippies and beatniks. Taking the writer aside, he explained privately that Mr. Pister should hand the transcript to O'Brien, whose character was really the one that should be reading it. Removing the blame from McBride, Orson said it would be better because "Eddie is such a magnificent ruin."

Welles could also be lighthearted when dealing with problems, such as when he tried executing a difficult shot in which the light changed from blazing sun to the darkness of a tunnel and back. With his powers focused on making it work and the crew trying to turn his vision into reality, Welles yelled, "Cut!" and asked, "How was it, Gary?"

Unsure of what to say, Graver began, "Well, Orson . . ."

"Magnificent!" Welles said.

"Y-yes," Graver stammered, "but the problem with the shadows and the lighting . . ."

"Don't say that," Orson replied. "I only want to hear one word: Magnificent!"

"Okay," Graver said. "Magnificent!"

Satisfied, Welles took a few steps, paused, and asked Graver, "Can we use it?"

Orson was less playful that month when he gathered the cast in a Howard Johnson's parking lot, only to have Peter Bogdanovich suddenly appear with a soundman. In addition to awaiting release of *The Last Picture Show* and plotting *What's Up, Doc?*, Bogdanovich was making the documentary *Directed by John Ford,* with Orson narrating.

In front of everyone, Bogdanovich told Welles they had to record. Now.

"Peter, I'm trying to make a movie here," Welles said.

Bogdanovich insisted, saying they'd waited too long and had to tape some of the narration then and there.

Embarrassed and furious, Welles said, "You know, Peter, sometimes you can be a real shit." He stormed into the motel with the soundman and returned thirty minutes later to angrily hand the tape to Bogdanovich, who roared away in his new convertible.

That moment seemed but a blip in the affection and devotion the two directors felt for each other, but it was also symbolic of the inevitable change in the relationships people have with their heroes. Soon they would have to either treat each other as equals or confront the unspoken gap in their friendship.

That spring, Welles continued shooting as inexpensively as possible. Despite a reputation for extravagance, he was thrifty and resourceful while spending his own money on *The Other Side of the Wind*. Having once shot Roderigo's murder in *Othello* using towel-clad actors in a Turkish bath when financial problems held up the arrival of costumes, Welles now reused gaffer's tape and had someone stand behind Graver to shut off his camera immediately after Orson cried, "Cut!" Even a few seconds of film wasted was too much.

Welles also continued shooting on locations where he didn't need permits or could avoid paying fees. Thus, after cast and crew had successfully posed as film students at MGM, Orson had Frank Marshall use the same excuse when they tried to shoot Hannaford's screening, without permission, at a Reseda drive-in one morning.

Soon, however, the police arrived. Marshall began the UCLA film school explanation, while just behind the cops sat a big convertible where a cigar-smoking Orson was slouched down in an attempt to remain out of view.

There was no doubt: This was guerrilla filmmaking.

When he returned home from Los Angeles, McBride received two boxes of cigars from Welles with a note:

> Dear Joe: We didn't get a chance to say a proper goodbye and I certainly didn't begin to say a proper thank you.
>
> Yours was a very real and valued contribution. We hope to make you proud to have been part of our picture. All my most affectionate regards—Orson.

On July 25, McBride sent a letter of his own, to *Focus on Citizen Kane* author Ronald Gottesman. Giving some sense of his role, the story line, and Welles's unconventional filmmaking method, he wrote:

About my part in the Welles picture: it's called *The Other Side of the Wind*, and as you know from the Higham piece in the Times, it's about an aging film director (*not* Welles either in person or proxy) who returns to Hollywood for a last fling. I play a fatuous intellectual critic, and so I have plenty of lines, mostly inane babbling while incredibly complex things are happening all around me. It's a cliché, but you don't appreciate the talent of a man like Welles until you actually witness it in process. To stand in the middle of a Welles shot is a fantasy experience. . . . I'm not supposed to say anything about the plot, which is good because I don't really have all of it quite clear, but from hanging around Welles, keeping my ears open, talking to the crew, I've managed to pick most of it up. I think.

On August 2, a page one *Variety* story reported:

Orson Welles has one of those "guess who" ventures coming up in "The Other Side of the Wind" to be filmed here. . . . The new film, which Welles will direct, is about an old filmmaker who finds the world changed when he tries to make a picture after a long hiatus. Welles says it's not autobiographical.

Orson reiterated that point when speaking at USC later that month. "It's not a cute thing, not Felliniesque, where you have to guess who it is," he told a group of film students. "It really is about a fictional movie director."

The event at USC had been Orson's idea but didn't go off as intended. Having contacted the film school's Arthur Knight, whose students had included George Lucas, John Milius, and John Carpenter, and explained that he wanted to film students on a soundstage posing questions to Hannaford (with Orson acting as stand-in), Welles arrived to find that Knight had reserved a huge auditorium for what was essentially "Arthur Knight Presents: Orson Welles."

Making the best of things, Graver shot as planned, with Orson directing while he spoke, stopping whenever there was a particularly inane question and telling Gary, "Get the camera over there," while the student asked the question on film for a second time.

Thoroughly annoyed with Knight, Welles had his revenge when a first-semester student asked what his goal should be while studying at USC.

"To get out of film school as quickly as possible," Welles said. "Everything you learn here you can learn in three weeks out there."

Though the ire was intended, Welles believed what he said. It was the school of life, not film school, that created great filmmakers.

Another student held up a magazine with one of Orson's Jim Beam ads and asked a question worthy of Mr. Pister.

"Mr. Welles, I appreciate your obligations as an artist," the student said. "But, I wonder how you would correlate this ad with your comments on artistic integrity."

Taking a deep breath and then puffing his cigar, Orson paused a bit more before he lamented, "Please, oh, please, allow me this bit of petty harlotry."

Then, just before the lecture concluded, someone brought out what was allegedly the actual Rosebud sled. Though several had been used in the film, Welles didn't let on. Instead, he sighed and said that it was smaller than he'd remembered it being.

Years later, hearing that Steven Spielberg had purchased Rosebud for $60,000, Welles told Graver, "I think you and I should go down to the basement and start making sleds."

When *The Last Picture Show* was released in October 1971, Bogdanovich sat in stunned silence as Bert Schneider read the opening sentence of a review in *Newsweek* that declared it "a masterpiece" and the most extraordinary film by "a young American director since *Citizen Kane.*"

Bogdanovich had only one thing to say: "Jesus Christ." It was an understatement, given that his first movie was being compared with *Kane*.

Other raves continued to roll in. Kael liked the film, and *The New York Times* loved it, running two features about Bogdanovich within weeks of each other. The second, a full-fledged profile, bore the title "Peter Still Looks Forward to His *Citizen Kane.*"

In that article, Peter confessed that his life was so remarkable that he hated for each day to end and had to take sedatives at night simply because things were so good that he didn't ever want to sleep.

After explaining that he didn't compare his films with those of his contemporaries, but instead measured himself against "Hawks, Lubitsch, Buster Keaton, Welles, Ford, Renoir, Hitchcock," Bogdanovich was humble enough to add that he was good, but not *as good* as those legendary directors. Yet he also explained that he'd begun to worry about how sad and disengaged he'd feel someday when "all the Bogdanovich pictures have been made. . . .

"What will I do then?" he wondered.

1972–1973

> *Orson was horrified by money.*
> —DOMINIQUE ANTOINE

Luck and money. They were always inextricably linked for Orson. Together, along with talent, they were the key elements of his story after *Citizen Kane.*

Welles said he began with "the best luck in cinema history," total artistic control over *Kane.* That this was afforded to such a young man enraged more than a few Hollywood veterans, including Ward Bond, an ultra-right-wing member of John Ford's stock company who approached Orson one night at Chasen's and cut off his tie. Who the hell did Welles think he was?

After *Kane,* Orson had "the worst bad luck"—a karmic repayment for his good fortune. That bad luck always seemed to begin with making a movie but ended up having to do with money. Were it not for money, Orson surely thought, there would have been so much more unparalleled art; so many more Welles movies; so much more of everything.

But, much as he despised it, Orson knew money was essential and the lack of it was an albatross around his neck that became the explanation for greatness that might have been.

If he'd been born centuries earlier, Orson would have been a perfect Renaissance artist, as what he required was a patron with infinite money, impeccable taste, and unending patience. Someone who gave him the time and funds to create masterpieces. If he were a novelist or painter, Welles said, nobody would care how long it took him to create. But he was in the movies, which had a clear commercial purpose—even if Orson was simply an artist.

Given that he was hamstrung by the requirements of the industry, what Orson managed to create over thirty years has been unimaginably superlative.

In the winter 1971–1972 issue of *Sight & Sound*, *Citizen Kane* topped the magazine's list of greatest films ever made. *Ambersons* came in at number eight. Today, *Touch of Evil*, is twenty-sixth on the British Film Institute's rankings of the top one hundred movies. Decades after its release, *The Lady from Shanghai* came to be regarded as a masterpiece and "the weirdest great movie ever made" (according to critic Dave Kehr). At Cannes, *Chimes at Midnight* won two awards and earned Orson a lengthy standing ovation, while *Othello* received the festival's Palme d'Or. Even *The Trial* was named best picture by the French Syndicate of Cinema Critics.

Thus, though he never achieved the staggering productivity of Ford or Huston, Orson's batting average was unprecedented, with nearly half of his dozen movies eventually considered to be great films.

Artistry, however, rarely resulted in profits for Orson or his partners. After *Kane* broke even, the only Welles film to turn a genuine profit was *The Stranger*, a 1946 noir thriller that Orson directed, starred in, and co-wrote with, among others, John Huston. Portraying an escaped Nazi living as a small-town Connecticut prep school teacher, Welles costarred with Loretta Young as his fiancée (later wife) and Edward G. Robinson played the UN investigator sent to track him down. Welles made the film to show studios that he "didn't glow in the dark" and could say "Action!" and "Cut!" the same as any other director. Hopefully, he thought, it would kill off at least a few myths and demons.

The Lady from Shanghai came to be after Welles found himself in Boston in 1947, ready to premiere his musical version of *Around the World in 80 Days,* only to find out that his producer, Mike Todd, was bankrupt and needed $50,000 for costumes—immediately. Welles took action.

According to the oft-told tale, Welles called Columbia's Harry Cohn from a pay phone in his hotel lobby and said that he'd direct a movie for $55,000. Cohn asked what movie he had in mind and Welles said *The Lady from Shanghai*, selecting the title from books for sale on a nearby rack in the hotel lobby. When the studio chief said he'd agree, on the condition that it starred Orson's soon-to-be-ex-wife Rita Hayworth, Welles made the deal—as long as he could have the money within an hour. The money arrived, the show went on (and closed quickly), and Orson made *The Lady from Shanghai*, a production which was hamstrung by Hayworth's frequent illnesses and the delays they caused.

Thus began a decade in the wilderness, starting with *Macbeth,* shot in twenty-three days for a Poverty Row B-movie factory. After that he became almost totally independent, a setup he enjoyed for its freedom but whose frustrations and almost Homeric financing adventures swallowed huge amounts of time and energy.

In addition to possessing no aptitude for business or the management of personal and professional finances, Welles had an uncanny ability to choose lousy partners. The result was several films beset by money problems.

First was *Othello,* financed by an Italian who went bankrupt immediately after shooting began. Then there was *Mr. Arkadin,* funded by Spanish, Swiss, German, and French investors, and ultimately taken away from Orson when he missed some editing deadlines. In 1962, after making *Touch of Evil,* he went to Europe and directed *The Trial,* but the French father and son producing it didn't have the money they'd promised, causing the Yugoslavian government to withdraw its funding and support for the film. Finally, in the mid-1960s there was *Chimes at Midnight,* which Welles financed by promising producer Emiliano Piedra that he'd simultaneously direct *Treasure Island,* while seemingly not making any plans to actually do so.

Ironically, *Treasure Island* returned to Orson's life in 1972 and introduced him to the first source of outside money he needed for *The Other Side of the Wind,* the production of which had begun to follow a familiar pattern.

"He'd have a new [house] for three or four months, and that . . . would be our studio," Stringer said. "Then Orson would go away for three to six months and we'd shoot again when he returned. When funds ran out, he'd close up and just go find more money."

In the early 1970 Welles would chase money by appearing in *Necromancy, Get to Know Your Rabbit* (both released in 1972), and a television production of *The Man Who Came to Dinner*—playing Sheridan Whiteside, of course.

Welles also funded his life and art by lending his magnificent voice and sophisticated reputation to Jim Beam, Eastern Airlines, and—by the late 1970s— Japan's G&G Nikka Whiskey and, more famously, Paul Masson wine. With a daily fee that some say was nearly $15,000, Orson had no problem practicing what he called "the most innocent form of whoring I know" while remaining "virginal" when it came to directing film.

But earning the modern equivalent of $75,000 a day was often insufficient, because no matter how many commercials he made, Orson seemed to teeter back and forth between a simple need for more money and the brink of financial collapse.

According to his daughter Beatrice, the state of her father's finances was typified by their accomodations while shooting the Paris-based portions of *The Trial.*

"[At the beginning] We were living at the George V, then two months later we stayed someplace a little [less luxurious] and we wound up in a small B-and-B on the left bank because all the money was going into the movie," Beatrice Welles recalled. "It was perfectly normal. One minute we were just rolling in it and the next we were wondering how we were going to live."

Rarely discussed during this period of Orson's career—or in terms of *The Other Side of the Wind*—Paola was possibly the most dependable woman in his life since his mother, and played an integral role by creating stability within the disorder brought by Orson's lifestyle and frequently changing financial situation. Beautiful, intelligent, and deeply grounded, Paola had the capacity to make any hotel room, succession of hotel rooms, or other living circumstance feel as if it were home.

"It may have been chaos," Beatrice Welles said. "But I never knew it."

And that quality was one of the things that had attracted Orson to her in the first place and made their marriage enormously valuable to him, despite his simultaneous relationship with Oja.

It did not, however, settle Orson's longtime and endlessly recurring inability to deal prudently with finances on almost any level.

One of the problems with Welles's approach to money went back to his Broadway days, when he poured his own funds into his plays, including those underwritten by the government's Federal Theatre Project. The product had always been the only thing that counted, and having been raised with money, Welles believed it would always be there—not an unreasonable assumption given his initial inheritance and huge salary as a radio actor. Leaving details to people such as Bernstein, Houseman, and Weissberger, he lived well, was dedicated to his work, and had no idea what things cost or how much was in the bank.

Some of this stemmed from his upbringing and the attitudes it produced. Though his knowledge of the arts was superb, he'd never had an education in everyday life. To an extent, this was a great source of strength. His imagination was allowed to run wild, and others were magnetically drawn to ensuring the execution of his ideas. It was wonderful, but it shielded him from the skills required for the real world.

His aristocratic nature was also a factor, in that it fostered the belief that talking about money was beneath his breeding. This, combined with his education and experience, makes it easier to understand why he was able to live with the pressures of unpaid hotel bills and huge tabs at expensive restaurants.

All these influences together kept Orson detached from the realities of his financial situation and the nature of his obligations. He knew he needed money or when things were desperate. But the details were hazy, and like many famous or wealthy people, he had no concept of everyday expenses. It was a quality he displayed shortly after arriving in Hollywood to make *Kane* while still commuting back to New York each week for his radio show. Since air travel was expensive, Orson ran the numbers, incorrectly, and told Weissberger it would be thriftier to buy a plane and hire a pilot.

Having been protected from reality until his blowup with Houseman, Welles spent the next thirty years seeking cash for movies and personal expenses, which had become the same thing by 1972, with funds frequently disbursed among a multitude of film projects that generally included the cost of custom-made cigars, rental homes, and good food.

Then there were the fund-raising meals, which Orson found demeaning but necessary. Time and again, he'd dined with potential investors, turning on the charm and giving an Oscar-worthy performance over expensive wine and rich food. Puffing a cigar as waiters cleared the table, he'd be left with a check he couldn't afford while the financiers went home with the money and the ability to spend the rest of their lives telling people that they'd had dinner with Orson Welles. It had happened so often that he no longer had the expectation of landing fresh money.

A frequent companion at these meals, Bogdanovich found the charade depressing. Finally, after yet another evening of wooing investors, he expressed his rage and despair to Orson as they walked through New York.

"It's funny," Welles said. "I've been doing that for so long I guess I'm used to it."

A young European movie distributor and his partners had originally wanted Yul Brynner to play Long John Silver in their adaptation of *Treasure Island*. Then, however, the man remembered that Orson had long wanted to be the lead in a film version of the Robert Louis Stevenson classic, and, in the winter of 1972, they sent a copy of their script to Welles's office in London.

A week or so later, the pair shared a long lunch at Maxim's in Paris, where they ate, drank wine, and talked about movies. Like Bogdanovich, the man immediately felt completely at ease in Orson's presence.

When lunch was over, Welles handed the young producer a "revised" screenplay, written under the nom de plume O. W. Jeeves. That script was superior to the one they already had—and Orson was offered the part for $150,000. Orson accepted, with the following conditions: They would use his script; give him control over wardrobe; and allow him to provide his own parrot.

That summer, Orson came to Almería, a harbor town on Spain's Mediterranean coast where portions of *Lawrence of Arabia* and several "spaghetti westerns" had been filmed. Shooting had begun the week before, and when Welles visited the beach house his producer was renting, he decided to rent one next door. As filming went on, the pair became close and discussed collaborating on the completion of Orson's unfinished films, including *The Deep;* his never-ending *Don Quixote;* and their first priority, *The Other Side of the Wind.*

When the film wrapped, Welles stayed in Europe, spending most of the fall and winter in Spain and France, while the young producer courted investors such as Klaus Hellwig, who operated the German production company Janus Films with his brother Juergen. Eager to work with Orson, the Hellwigs became partners in *The Other Side of the Wind* and started raising $200,000. Meanwhile, Welles claimed that the distributor-turned-producer had agreed to invest $150,000 as well.

With his $150,000 *Treasure Island* salary, $200,000 from the Hellwigs, and $150,000 allegedly promised by his young production partner, Orson had new lifeblood and began editing at a Parisian film lab in 1973.

Meanwhile, back in Hollywood, Peter Bogdanovich was finding money much easier to come by after the March release of *What's Up Doc?*, which premiered while *The Last Picture Show* was still in theaters and had been nominated for eight Oscars.

Despite not winning in any of the three categories in which he was nominated, Peter watched Cloris Leachman pick up Best Supporting Actress while—as Orson predicted—Ben Johnson took home Best Supporting Actor. Meanwhile, *What's Up, Doc?* was the third-highest-grossing film of 1972, hauling in $66 million.

The success of *What's Up, Doc?* along with *The Godfather* and *The French Connection* sparked an idea for Gulf+Western's Charles Bludhorn, who'd purchased Paramount and hired former actor Robert Evans to turn it around, which he did with *Love Story* and *The Godfather*. A tough, perceptive businessman, Bludhorn wasn't a creature of Hollywood—but he could smell money and thought there was a potential gold mine in creating a unit that would combine elements of First Artists (a production company whose partners included Sidney Poitier and Paul Newman) and Universal's Young Directors Program.

To do this, Bludhorn planned to lock up three of Hollywood's hottest young directors (Bogdanovich, Coppola, and William Friedkin) and give them $30 million to $40 million in capital, artistic control, 50 percent of the profits, and a green light for any movie budgeted under $3 million. If each director committed to at least three films, Bludhorn said they'd all get rich.

On August 20, the formation of the Directors Company was announced by Paramount chief Frank Yablans during a press conference at New York's 21 Club. Though he'd told Bludhorn he thought the idea was idiotic, the thirty-six-year-old Yablans put on a happy face and spoke to the press.

"What made the deal possible was the degree of simpatico between the directors and the studio; we're all in our early thirties and we don't have a great hierarchy," he explained. "They've all gone through their growth period, indulging their esoteric tastes. Coppola isn't interested in filming a pomegranate growing in the desert. They're all very commercial now."

Behind the scenes, however, Yablans was playing a remarkable game of poker in which he didn't even have to show his hand. Because Yablans ultimately realized that mixing big money with big egos in an artistic context would bring out the worst in everyone and could have only one result: a nightmarish auteurist mini-studio more than capable of killing itself without any effort on his part.

The creation of the Directors Company, according to Peter Biskind's *Easy Riders, Raging Bulls,* "marked the zenith of director's power in the 1970s and its fate prefigured their fall from grace."

In addition to his difficulties financing pictures, Welles frequently suffered problems on the back end as well. According to some, his prolonged absence from Hollywood in the 1940s and 1950s was about more than breaking with the studio system; it also involved disputes over fines from the IRS and other tax authorities.

Those issues appeared to be in the past until the early 1970s, when the IRS questioned his business practices after CBS paid Orson's salary for a television special to a Swiss production company he'd established for his European film projects.

Although he claimed it wasn't a dodge, Orson was still hounded by the revenue department, which took the money from his Swiss company and placed him in a precarious financial state, after which, he formed Avenel, a Liechtenstein-based partnership with Oja that would help prevent similar problems in the future.

Then, in early 1973, the state of California levied a $30,000 fine for income dating back to 1958. So just as he was returning to sound financial footing, Orson was forced to dig out from beneath new troubles once again.

Some of the pain of this situation, however, might have been alleviated by the fact that he was doing what he loved most: editing a film. Setting up camp at their home in the Paris suburb of Orvilliers, Welles was busy at the postproduction facility Antegor, where he was assembling the initial footage from *The Other Side of the Wind* while he finished a BBC show and put together *F for Fake,* his remarkable essay film about art forger Elmyr de Hory.

At Antegor, Welles worked with and was impressed by Yves Deschamps, a twenty-eight-year-old journalist turned editor who helped solve a seemingly intractable problem with the BBC show. In addition, Orson loved the fact that Deschamps wasn't in awe of him.

"I wasn't impressed by his legend, which was such a burden," said Deschamps, who literally didn't know Orson was still alive when they met. "I was really just a stupid guy, and he liked that."

Early on, Deschamps realized that Welles was the greatest editor he'd ever meet. And by the time Welles asked him to work on *The Other Side of the Wind,* Deschamps knew he wasn't being hired to cut the film. Orson didn't need editors. What he needed were assistants, and Deschamps accepted that his role would be to supervise and make sure that Orson's orders were carried out.

After hiring him, Welles told Deschamps to meet him in Los Angeles, where they'd begin work. Following orders, the young editor went there and waited for three weeks—yet Orson never appeared.

When he returned to Paris, Deschamps heard editing would take place in Madrid, but this time he decided to stay in France until he heard from Orson. Sure enough, Welles called soon after Deschamps's return and set up a meeting at a film lab in Montparnasse. The meeting went well, but the lab's editing rooms were accessible only via long staircases, and Orson's weight and knee problems made working there impossible. So they decided to edit at a facility named LTC.

Knowing almost nothing about *The Other Side of the Wind*, Deschamps asked Welles if he could see a script, but Orson would share only the one or two pages that pertained to the scenes he wanted marked.

"Orson, it would be easier if I knew what the story was about," Deschamps said.

"You don't need to know," Welles replied. "I know the story. That's enough."

Despite this, Deschamps was fascinated by watching Orson's editing process, where the first step was to view all footage of a scene (often twenty to thirty takes) and eliminate only shots that were useless or beneath his standards. In keeping everything else, he wasn't simply finding a properly executed scene and printing it, as many filmmakers would. He was working the opposite way, avoiding choices and judgments after seeing a scene only once or twice. Then everything, even the same line repeated more than a dozen times, was organized by the assistants so Orson could watch the scenes again and again, paring down as he went along. Working intuitively, Welles began reorganizing material in new ways that arose organically from the footage. Taking a few lines or interpretations, he watched until he had exactly what he wanted because it fit perfectly with the next line.

"That was the way he rebuilt the interpretations of the actors," Deschamps said. "It was wonderful, because instead of choosing it by himself, he let the movie speak to him, progressively. It was like the movie gave itself the answer to what he was searching for."

As they worked, Welles was like a dancing symphony conductor. With his imagination fired up, he underwent a physical transformation. Gone was the heavy breathing and constant pain. Once he was rolling, Orson would float around the room with fluidity and grace, moving from one editing machine to the next and telling each editor to cut here or mark there.

Watching this brilliant man edit beautiful footage with such enthusiasm, Deschamps wondered how Welles could be having financial problems and was mystified that nobody would give him money to finish his comeback film.

"It's impossible that you can't find money," Deschamps told Orson. "I know at least ten people who'd be happy to give you the money."

"Introduce me to at least one," Welles replied.

Before making his first call to a wealthy young French producer named Carole Weisweiller, Deschamps told his friend Dominique Antoine about Orson's problems financing *The Other Side of the Wind*.

"You're working with Orson Welles and want to introduce him to Carole?" said Antoine, who'd once worked for Weisweiller. "You have to introduce him to me!"

"But you're broke and Carole is rich," Deschamps said.

"Yes, but I have more money than Carole Weisweiller and more than Orson Welles," Antoine replied. "I'm working with one of the richest men in the world."

And indeed she was, because Antoine had joined the recently formed Les Films de L'Astrophore, a production company under the direction of Mehdi Boushehri, third husband of Princess Ashraf, the shah of Iran's iron-willed twin sister. As part of the shah's modernization plan, Boushehri founded Astrophore to boost Iran's profile as a location for non-Arab directors while also setting up co-productions with well-known filmmakers.

Orson Welles seemed like the perfect place to start.

Antoine met Welles at LTC in January 1973, while Orson was working. Barely looking up, he reached a limp hand over the editing table and hardly acknowledged her existence. Then Deschamps explained that this was the producer he'd mentioned, and Welles hopped to his feet, turned on the charm, and enunciated every syllable of a suddenly warm, "How do you do?"

Believing she had only one opportunity with Welles, and that it required giving as good as she got, Antoine said, "So, for producers we stand up and say hello?"

There was silence, and Welles blushed before all but bellowing, "*You bet!*" and belting out a huge laugh. Sitting back down, he told Antoine about *The Other Side of the Wind* and said he had enough footage for one completed hour of film. Then he veered off, saying there were also other projects.

"No. No. No. Orson," Antoine said, "we should finish *The Other Side of the Wind* first, then we can see what to do next."

From then on, whenever she saw Welles, Antoine decided that she must be completely on her game all the time, because Orson would be hard to persuade and was too smart for her to bullshit. "That was part of his genius," Antoine said. "The relationship put you at your best—always."

Antoine also knew it was important to understand the kind of relationship their collaboration required. For things to work, she would have to devote herself to Orson in every way, while also maintaining discipline over his creative personality and ability to complete the film. She had no idea how complicated the latter would be, but the former was much more easily accomplished.

"I don't wait for you to love me," she said at lunch one day. "I am loving you and that's enough."

Because she'd offered her respect and affection while asking for nothing in return, Orson's wariness melted. Now, with the dynamics of the relationship cemented, Antoine had to persuade Orson to participate in the financing process that he so despised, as his dearest wish was for others to respect what he'd already created and give him money without meetings and contracts. And just as he'd bristled at Danny Selznick's inability to provide instant funding, Welles made Antoine plead with him to meet Boushehri in his office at the Maison d'Iran on the Champs-Élysées.

"That was when I understood the big baby that was in Orson," Antoine said of begging him to meet Boushehri.

That big baby, however, wasn't necessarily born of ego. Instead, Antoine realized, it was the behavior of the sensitive, easily hurt little boy who'd been abandoned by his parents. Though larger than life, Orson was filled with an easily shaken pride.

When Welles finally relented and went to see Boushehri, he found the shah's brother-in-law to be profoundly cultured, well educated, and seductive, with a deep well of patience and enormous respect for artists in general and Orson in particular.

Politically savvy, Boushehri was long separated from Ashraf, but they remained married and on good terms, allowing him to retain great influence in the shah's regime. He was smart enough to see the brutality and injustice perpetrated in the name of his brother-in-law but was motivated by an altruistic desire to further the Iranian arts.

A year younger than Orson, Boushehri was excited about having an artistic adventure with the great director—and Welles didn't disappoint at their first meeting.

"He was acting," Antoine said. "He was Shakespearean when he tried to impress people, and he was trying to impress Mehdi."

It worked. On December 26, *Variety* reported that Welles was getting $150,000 to finish *The Other Side of the Wind,* noting, "Welles has shot most of the pic except the director himself. He does not want to play it and has yet to find somebody to his taste."

Though Welles had flirted with the idea of character actor Dean Jagger as Hannaford, he realized there was only one person who could portray the swashbuckling director. Now needing to hire his lead and having already offered him the part at least twice, Welles contacted Huston, who agreed to a fee of $75,000 for several weeks of work that would commence in Carefree early the following year.

Desert Forest Motel and Apartments

CAVE CREEK and SCHOOLHOUSE ROADS

CAVE CREEK, ARIZONA

May 2, 1974

Frank Marshall
652 Veteran #21
Los Angeles, California

Dear Frank:

The Maricopa County, Arizona prosecutor's office has filed
Criminal charges against ████. They have completed their initial
investigation and will issue a warrant for his incarceration
should he return to the United States. Grand Larceny is an
extraditable offense and, as of May 5th (I believe) he will be
considered a fugitive by both the State of Arizona and the
United States. His Federal Offense will be interstate flight
to avoid prosecution.

All this crap, however, does not get me any closer to the
$1,788.40. When he gave me the check I gave him a receipt (properly
noted that the account was paid by check with Bank, location
and check number) along with the phone receipts (of which I have
copies). The actual total was $1,433.83 in phone charges and
$1,154.57 in room charges and tax - a total of $2,588.40. Eight
hundred of this was paid in cash by Rick - leaving the balance
of $1,788.40. I suppose I can afford to be screwed for the room
charges.....BUT the phone thing is something else. I am going to
have to come up with all the phone charges - OR - lay them off on
someone responsible for their collection.

I realize that you are having financial problems. I also realize
that you are gambling on the success of the motion picture for
your personal recovery. But, when I got the motel built (and it
was no small gamble, either) I thought my gambling days were
pretty much over. However, things do change. I am willing to
gamble on the room rent (receiving it or not receiving it as the
case may be), but the phone charges are out of pocket - direct
expense items and I am not willing to go that route.

Please let me know what the financial situation is and when any
possible payment can be expected.

Sincerely,

(over)

JIM and MAT HINES

Mailing address: P.O. Box 312, Cave Creek, Arizona 85331 • Phone: (602) 448-3668

ACT TWO

The great danger for any artist is to find himself comfortable. It's his duty to find the point of maximum discomfort, to search it out.

—ORSON WELLES

1974

It was really hard to tell what was the movie and what wasn't because what was happening was such a mirror of what was going on.

—SCRIPT SUPERVISOR MARY ANN NEWFIELD

―――――――――――――――――――――――

REPORTER: *Describe a typical day on the set of "The Other Side of the Wind"?*

JOE MCBRIDE: *Every day was different.*

PETER BOGDANOVICH: *Every day was different.*

Larry Jackson was sent to pick up John Huston at the Phoenix airport, where he would be arriving after a long international flight.

It was January, and Jackson, who headed the Orson Welles Cinema in Harvard Square, had been a recent addition to the crew.

Waiting for Huston, Jackson was nervous, as his interest in film had been kindled by the 1956 premiere of *Moby Dick* in his hometown of New Bedford, Massachusetts, where he watched Huston and Gregory Peck parade through town in an open convertible.

Just twenty-five, Jackson had only recently met Welles, and here he was watching Huston stride off the plane dressed in a safari outfit and Irish tweed cap. Tall, with white hair, a gray beard, and a craggy ex-boxer's face, he was everything one imagined when thinking of John Huston.

Courtly and down-to-earth, Huston quickly eased Jackson's nerves while the latter carried the director's luggage to the parking lot, which he'd forgotten was surrounded by a low chain-link fence. Realizing it would require a long walk to the car, Jackson said he'd take the luggage and drive back to pick him up. Although he suffered from emphysema so severe that his breathing could be heard through the walls of his motel room, the sixty-seven-year-old Huston wouldn't hear of it.

"Oh, no, no, no," he said, vaulting the fence and landing gracefully on the other side. Jackson stood there in disbelief, thinking that even he couldn't jump the fence. But he wasn't John Huston. Nobody was.

The only child of actor Walter Huston and journalist Rhea Gore, Huston spent his childhood shuttling between his divorced parents. Walter's influence included a love of theater and the gifts of charm and generosity. Rhea made John tough, instilling a desire for adventure and an ability to live close to the edge, such as when she'd put her last ten dollars on a hundred-to-one shot that came in. Huston's mother celebrated by immediately purchasing a fur and returning to the track the following day, where she blew all her winnings and had to hock the coat just to get back home.

"She taught me that money is for spending," Huston said. "And to hell with the rest."

At age ten, John was diagnosed with an enlarged heart, which doctors said had made him so fragile that whistling might kill him. Put on two years' bed rest, John decided one night that if he was going to die, he at least wanted to swim in a nearby canal. So he snuck out a window, jumped in the water, and lay there floating. A few nights later, he returned and swam toward large floodgates, which suddenly opened, sucking a huge amount of water—and John—beneath them. Stuck under the water and convinced he'd drown, Huston was surprised to come exploding out the other side. Exhilarated, he returned night after night to nearly drown and have the excitement of riding the waterfall back to life.

After that, nothing could kill him, as author Ray Bradbury learned while joining the director at his Irish home to adapt *Moby Dick*. Overwhelmed by Huston's personality, Bradbury found himself spellbound, intimidated, occasionally horrified, and frequently uncomfortable. Despite his charm and charisma, Huston scared the crap out of Bradbury, and he did so in particularly dramatic fashion one afternoon as they walked across a field near the director's home and suddenly came upon an angry black bull that was staring right at them. Crippled by fear, Bradbury watched in terror as Huston removed his jacket and waved it at the bull, beckoning the snorting beast to engage with them, only to seem terribly disappointed when the animal didn't charge.

But the story that seems to best sum up Huston took place in the 1940s, after he'd just become an independent director and formed a company with Sam Spiegel when he could have made more money paired up with any number of well-respected, more reliable, and better-known producers. When Peter Viertel asked why he'd made such a choice, Huston said, "Because it was the wrong thing to do, kid."

When he arrived at the Slingmans' house in Carefree, Huston's reunion with Welles was almost too cinematic, as the legendary pair gave each other a gigantic bear hug while framed against a gigantic picture window through which there was a backdrop of red rocks and desert.

Among those present as they embraced was Mercedes McCambridge, who'd received a call from Frank Marshall asking her whether she still had her costume.

"I have it, darling," she said. "I packed my bag and put the suitcase in my closet. It's always ready."

At a table by the pool, Welles and Huston caught up and fleshed out how Hannaford should be played. Discussing the characteristics of the fictional filmmaker, they began talking beards, with Huston wondering if his current facial hair would be appropriate. Welles, with his own beard, thought about it and declared Huston's beard perfect. Then they talked some more and decided it somehow wasn't right for a great director to have a full beard.

Sitting with them, the hard-boiled McCambridge could barely contain her amusement at the two immortal filmmakers with big beards debating whether a big beard was right for an immortal filmmaker.

"My God, he's matured!" Welles said when Joe McBride arrived, twenty-five pounds heavier than when he'd last appeared on film—a time period in which Huston had completed four films and was about to work on a fifth, *The Man Who Would Be King*.

Thus, when McBride met Huston shortly thereafter, he introduced himself and said that he was excited to finally meet the film's lead actor after three years of waiting.

Unflappable in the face of an angry bull, an incredulous Huston asked McBride, "You've been in this picture for three years?"

Huston had completed nearly thirty features since he and Welles each directed their first films (*The Maltese Falcon* and *Citizen Kane*) in 1941. Much of this difference in output was the result of the fact that Huston understood how to work within the system and knew he might have to make one or two films for hire in order to direct one that satisfied him as an artist. He made some mediocre films and some very good ones, however, while also turning out classics such as *The Treasure of the Sierra Madre, The Asphalt Jungle,* and *The African Queen.*

For Huston, the ultimate non-auteur, there was no trademark style. Instead, he let each film take its own shape, using his painter's eye to dab color and texture on celluloid and then preserving his work by cutting movies in the camera, which left almost nothing for the studios to monkey around with after he submitted a film.

Huston could also walk away and move on to new projects. He realized when a film was "done" rather than "perfect." Restless, he was always ready for the next adventure and indulged this by shooting in the Belgian Congo, rugged parts of Mexico, and other far-flung locations. And once there, he would display a superhuman ability to thrive while others wilted under often horrific conditions, such as the wave of intestinal illness that swept *The African Queen* set, where only he and Bogart were spared because they drank whiskey instead of the local water.

The unifying theme of Huston's work was that of men, often failures and outcasts, on a quest that ends with them losing their object of desire or realizing that it was illusory. The excitement, camaraderie, and futility of the journey were what captured Huston's interest, a story line neatly summarized by Viertel as "an adventure shared by desperate men that finally came to nothing." He was about to find that type of adventure in Carefree.

John Huston and Orson Welles had much in common. Each could write, direct, and act. They were gifted painters with a deep knowledge of art and culture. Both had strong mothers and charming fathers, nontraditional educations, great intelligence, and broad curiosity.

Among their other similarities, Welles and Huston were uncommonly horrible with money. Orson would blow his on making films, fine wine, and custom cigars, while Huston preferred horses, an Irish castle, and pre-Columbian artwork.

Both expatriates at various points, the two mavericks had worked together at least five times, including their collaboration on *The Stranger* and Orson's appearances in four Huston films, most notably as Father Mapple in *Moby Dick*.

By the time both were seventy, at least four novels had been written about collaborating with either Welles or Huston, between whom there were innumerable romantic conquests and shattered marriages, including Huston's fifth, which was crumbling when he arrived in Arizona.

Brooks Otterlake is a Hannaford protégé who starts writing a book about his mentor but never finishes after he directs three consecutive hits and becomes the hottest young filmmaker in Hollywood. Unctuous and slick, he still comes off as being devoted to Hannaford, whom he calls "Skipper."

Since Otterlake's primary character tic was a predilection for celebrity impressions, Orson's choice for the role was comedian Rich Little, whom he'd met on the set of a TV show called *The Kopykats*. Little, who could do anyone from Nixon to Jimmy Stewart, seemed like he'd be perfect for the role.

When the pair met in Las Vegas, Orson gave Little a basic plot outline but went into more detail regarding the Otterlake character. Offered a salary of $50,000 and the chance to work with Orson, Little happily accepted the part, with one caveat: He would have only slightly more than a month to work on the film because he'd already booked several sold-out stand-up gigs for late winter and early spring.

"Don't worry," Orson said. "We'll shoot your stuff in about two and a half or three weeks."

Anticipating no problems with the schedule, Little headed to Carefree that January, where Welles introduced him to Huston as follows:

"John, I want you to meet Rich Little," Orson said. "He's probably the world's greatest impressionist."

"Oh well, then we're going to get along just fine," Huston replied.

"I have a lot of paintings, and that's one of my hobbies. We'll have a great many discussions. I'm thrilled."

"No! No! No!" Welles shouted. "Not that kind of impressionist!"

Living in the Slingmans' house with Oja, Orson would arrive on set early, wearing a purple terry-cloth robe and carrying new dialogue he'd written the night before. Despite claims that there was "no script," there was usually a massive screenplay at Welles's side from which he'd give each actor pages to memorize.

Huston, however, was told to use cue cards after Orson watched him struggle with committing dialogue to memory.

"John, you're just causing yourself unnecessary agony," Welles said. "Just read the lines or forget them. The idea is all that matters."

And that's what he wanted—for Huston to carry the idea of Hannaford inside him so that Orson could extract a deep, genuine performance. Huston's job was to behave like Hannaford, and the dialogue would take care of itself.

This worked well except when Huston got lost or forgot the purpose of a scene. Then, instead of telling Welles he'd gone up or asking the script supervisor to feed him a line, Huston would just say something—anything—with enormous authority and confidently exit the scene.

Where the script might say, "I'm going to talk to Billy about that," Huston would look at a scene partner and say, "We'll set it up for Tuesday. I'm going to the kitchen," and walk off, leaving another actor alone in the frame. Moments later, Huston would innocently reenter and ask, "Was that the line, Orson?"

"Well, not exactly," Welles would say, laughing. "I don't know what the hell you just said!"

Where he might become frustrated with others, Orson put Huston at ease, knowing the film turned on his performance. Welles wanted two things: Huston's manly rogue persona was the first. That was easy. The other was to find something raw at Huston's core. Orson realized that Huston's greatest creation was John Huston, and it would be essential for his fellow director to remove that mask, even if for just a few moments.

Knowing he couldn't just ask Huston to be emotionally naked, Orson handled him with calculated humor, as he demonstrated one evening when they sat on set with a beam of light shining on them.

"What the fuck is this movie all about?" Huston asked.

"It's about a bastard director," Orson said. "It's about us, John. It's about us."

His answer, however, was different one evening when Little found Welles propped up in bed, making script revisions.

"Orson," Little asked, "what does *The Other Side of the Wind* mean?"

Welles looked over his glasses and said, "I haven't the foggiest."

With Little, Welles was more traditional, flattering him and doing everything to caress a performance from a non-actor. The early results pleased Welles, particularly an intense scene they'd filmed with Huston in a small bathroom, during which Little appeared to have tears in his eyes.

After hours in a confined space, Welles gleefully told Little he'd shown a remarkable range of emotion. "You were crying! Legit! You can turn it on!" he said. "You were just great!"

The crying, however, wasn't a performance. Little was wedged into the washroom with two compulsive cigar smokers, and his tears had been genuine.

Huston, meanwhile, was astonished as he watched Orson's filmmaking process. Everything appeared to be happening on the edge of an artistic cliff, without any formal structure or rules. And making things even more to his liking, the shoot was a series of strange adventures, including an afternoon when they filmed in a residential area of Phoenix and a policeman arrived and asked to see their permits.

"We're not making a movie," Orson told the officer, and proceeded to explain that they were filming real estate for his sister in Chicago who was moving to the area. Seeing all the equipment, the cop wasn't buying that story, so Huston stepped in.

"Let me tell you the true story. What we're doing is making an amateur movie with amateur actors and crew," he said. "It's not really a film, it's just a private thing for our own amusement. So we don't need a permit."

Seeing that the officer found that explanation less plausible than Orson's, Huston started over.

"No, that's not the story," he said. "We're making a film about how beautiful Phoenix is."

At this point, the policeman suggested that they follow him to the station, where they could either buy a permit or post bail (Orson, according to Little, chose the former).

Another strange moment arose when Huston, Little, and Welles were eating at a Denny's where the waitress recognized Little and asked, "Who's your fat friend?"

Without missing a beat, Huston said, "You know, we don't actually know this man. We picked him up on the highway and he seemed undernourished. Seems he hadn't had food in over a week, so we brought him here. We're going to feed him and then send him on his way."

On set, however, Orson was in command, frequently gathering actors around him to take instruction and rehearse scenes until he was satisfied. As this often caused performers to add enormous nuance to their roles, these practice runs could be so exacting that it was sometimes a letdown when the scenes were filmed.

When there were problems, it brought out the best in Welles, who'd go after sequences that didn't work, reshaping them from take to take until he'd manipulated them into something better. At one point, he took a major scene from an actress and gave it to another line by line in a way that enhanced everything without embarrassing her.

Watching his actors with a perfectionist's eye, Welles saw things that nobody else could. Often running a scene over and over until he saw the problem, Welles kept McCambridge and Huston into the wee hours performing a simple sequence in which her character turns toward Hannaford and says, "What other girl?" while he slowly stands up.

Take after take, Orson looked for the flaw while McCambridge became exasperated and Huston wilted. It was there, he just needed to find it. Then, after hours, he asked McCambridge if she'd taken dance lessons. Yes, she said, as a child. That was it. She was turning like a dancer.

"I thought he'd lost his mind, [but] he was right," McCambridge wrote. "I was pivoting. It was mechanical, like a clay figure on a turntable. There was no body movement, no shifting from one foot to the other, and it flawed the picture. It was a phony turn."

When they nailed it, Orson was ecstatic. "Very good, John," he said to an exhausted Huston.

Huston mustered whatever was left and replied, "Thank you, Orson," before someone took him back to the motel, where he collapsed.

Despite the late night, Orson continued to treat Huston with delicacy. And on the day they filmed a drunken, self-loathing monologue Hannaford unleashes upon himself in a bathroom mirror, Welles created the kind of intimacy usually reserved for young actresses' nude scenes, barring everyone but essential personnel from the set.

Welles encouraged Huston to drink throughout the day (which he did), wanting fragility and power during a moment of dark self-realization. He filmed it from the top, the middle, and the end, shooting the scene fourteen times until Huston did it perfectly.

"That's the one, John," Welles said.

"Yes, Orson," Huston responded. "That's the *only one.*"

Welles nodded in agreement, then turned to a crew member after Huston left and said, "We'll print them all," knowing there were great moments in fumbled takes that he could edit together to make the scene even better than the one Huston hit out of the park. When finally cut together, what McBride called "the King Lear scene" was one of the film's most powerful moments.

———

Described by Orson as "a rat of a woman," the character Juliette Riche is a smart, pain-in-the-ass film critic with a decidedly bitchy side and a desire to poke at Hannaford's image. Heavily influenced by his feelings about Kael after she wrote "Raising Kane," Welles made a compelling choice in hiring Susan Strasberg for the part.

Now thirty-five, Lee Strasberg's daughter had peaked at seventeen, playing Anne Frank on Broadway while also starring in the film *Picnic*. Since then, she'd worked regularly but had done nothing to match her early success. What made her interesting as Riche was that Strasberg's sweet, vulnerable personality stood in sharp contrast with Orson's feelings about Kael and the malevolence of the character based on her.

Unlike Huston, who was bulletproof, Strasberg exuded a tenderness and sensitivity just beneath her skin that turned Riche into more than a bitchy critic. Perceptive and bold, Strasberg's characterization also makes it seem as if Riche could be destroyed with a glance.

Having been sent the script by Orson's secretary and given a day to respond, Strasberg called her agent and said she'd been asked to do a Welles movie. The agent told her that another client had done a film with Orson years ago and loved it.

"What film was that?" Strasberg asked.

"The Other Side of the Wind," the agent said.

Thrilled about working with Orson, she accepted. Less thrilling for Strasberg, however, was the Orson and John show that played at most meals, with a rapt audience watching the pair telling stories about their famous friends, exotic location shoots, and never-ending adventures. Topics included a mutual dislike of James Mason's acting; Orson's intense disdain for Laurence Olivier; and (as recounted by Orson) the night Huston beat the crap out of Errol Flynn at a Hollywood party. Humbly, Huston claimed it was a draw.

When they worked together, Strasberg found Huston charming and egoless. When she said he'd been wonderful in a scene, Huston responded, "I'm no actor, dear. I don't know what I'm doing."

Yet, Strasberg was unsettled by Huston. In his eyes she saw brilliance and charm, but also, the actress thought, a heartless, scornful quality that felt contempt for everyone, especially himself. And while nobody but his soon-to-be ex-wife found him openly disdainful, many shared Strasberg's belief that there was an unseen sadness behind the noble hell-raiser he presented to the world. In small moments, when he was smoking a cigar or studying his lines, Huston seemed incredibly re-mote. It may have been old age, encroaching mortality, or the demise of his marriage. Maybe it was the price of being a great director. But whatever the root, John Huston often seemed like the loneliest man in the world. This was a quality he shared with Hannaford and so many other central characters in Welles's films, which, according to François Truffaut, are about one thing: "the angel within the beast, the heart in the monster, the secret of the tyrant . . . the weakness of the strong."

Unlike his undercover coddling of Huston, Orson's treatment of Stras-berg frequently was geared to switch on her insecurity and vulnerabil-ity. He did this on several occasions, including a scene where she had to recite the names of fictional movie stars who'd been created by Han-naford: Courtney Saxon, Branch Sutter, Glenn Garvey, and others. When she proved unable to do it without stumbling, Orson implored her to use cue cards. He used them, Brando used them, and Huston assured her that it would be fine. Finally, after explaining that he didn't want to see the terror in her eyes as she searched for the names, Orson yelled, "What's wrong with you? Use the damn cards."

Nevertheless, Strasberg resisted—until she remembered that Spen-cer Tracy once said that his poignant and thoughtful pauses weren't part of any performance, but were simply the result of looking down to find his mark. So she taped the cards on the floor in order to read them as she walked through the scene.

With the cameras rolling, they tried her method. Afterward there was a painful silence.

"Where's Susan?" Orson asked.

"I'm right here," Strasberg said.

"Where's Susan?" Welles repeated.

"Orson, I'm standing right here," she said again.

"Oh no," Welles replied. "That couldn't possibly be Susan. She would never do a scene that badly."

Though embarrassed, Strasberg knew he was right. She hadn't been present during the scene, and her performance was inadequate.

Orson also wasn't above bullying the actress, a tactic he employed by asking Strasberg to remove her boots after she'd been unable to properly execute a scene over the course of several takes. When Strasberg refused to take off the boots, Orson said it was fine, but added that he wouldn't turn off the cameras until she did.

When submissive Strasberg ultimately lost the standoff and removed her boots, everyone saw that she was wearing mismatched stockings that were covered in runs. She was humiliated, but even that humiliation had served a purpose by revealing Strasberg's fragility. Through intuition, Orson knew there was something embarrassing under the boots, or that they gave her a sense of confidence. Taking them off reduced her, giving Orson control and allowing him to extract the performance he wanted.

To the crew, Orson was like the Wizard of Oz, both a gigantic, omnipotent force who infused the set with electricity from the moment he arrived and also a mere mortal, prone to outbursts and childish emotions when things didn't go his way.

"He was real and fake at the same time—this big, amazing person and also a blowhard," said Constance Pharr, who was on the crew with her husband, cameraman Bill Weaver. "One minute you'd feel this whirlwind of power, and then there were moments where he pouted like a two-year-old, emitting all of this enormous disappointment he was feeling."

Frequently self-aware, Welles often seemed to realize that he was being difficult and provided metacommentary on his behavior while bossing everyone around: "You need to do this . . . We need to change the lighting . . . And for God's sake we need to get Orson to shut up . . . Now move this sofa."

Orson also felt entitled to his dark humors, particularly when he was feeling a sense of creative impotence and knew everyone was waiting until he found inspiration. Once, as a stymied Welles fumed silently, someone asked where to place the camera or a piece of scenery.

"Idiot!" Welles shouted. "Can't you see I haven't the foggiest notion of what I want? I wouldn't be sitting here if I did!"

Yet one thing was certain: Orson wanted everything and wanted it now. He frequently screamed, "Bring me that . . . ! *Run! Do not walk!*" This kept the set in such a state of frenzy that production assistant Rick Waltzer once ran through a sliding glass door while trying to get an apple box Orson wanted.

Many on set found that chaos intoxicating, a feeling shared by Orson, who loved having a group of people anticipating his needs to such an extent that many knew something was in the wrong place and moved it before he could even tell them to do so. When things were done correctly, he doled out praise and recognition, which bought loyalty and allowed him to get people to go the extra mile under duress. And some needed no recognition at all, particularly Graver and Marshall, who would endure anything.

Welles fired Marshall on a regular basis. Each time, the line producer would go to the Desert Forest Motel, get on the phone, and talk someone through his job until Orson summoned him back. Once, having replaced Marshall with actor Peter Jason, Welles demanded, "Nineteen hippies! I want beards on them! And I need them today!" Jason called Marshall, who sent him to Arizona State University, where he could round up students with a promise of Rich Little, hot dogs, and free beer.

Then they needed a generator, and Jason told Orson he had no idea how to get one.

"Well! Who does!?" Welles asked.

"Frank," Jason replied.

"He's in Hollywood!" Welles said.

Jason explained that Marshall could be there in five minutes, and Welles roared, "Well! Get him back here!"

When Marshall returned, Orson didn't apologize. Instead, he said, "Frank, what we need is a generator and we need it in . . ." Marshall, however, understood. He knew Orson needed him, always, which was why he never left.

Among the other things Orson needed during the shoot were: a real human bone; fake but authentic posters for old Hannaford films that existed only in Orson's imagination; dummies to fill a crowd scene; a cigar store Indian for Jake's den; and hunting trophies, including a swordfish for the mantel.

Anywhere other than the desert, it might have been easy to find a swordfish, but in Arizona they were hard to come by, so Orson sent Jacobson to a Hollywood prop house. After driving from Carefree to Los Angeles and back, Jacobson proudly placed an enormous grouper over the mantel.

Welles took one look and said, "No! I want a swordfish! Like in Hemingway!"

So the grouper sat in a corner and the search continued until Jason asked a bartender where he could find a big stuffed swordfish and was given the name of a local taxidermist with one on his own mantel.

Jason called the man, explained his predicament, and was lent a beautiful, much treasured swordfish *only* because it was for Orson Welles. Jason placed it in the back of a station wagon and drove back to Carefree, holding the fish's delicate bill the entire way.

Knowing how happy he'd make Welles, Jason was beaming as he and Marshall brought the swordfish inside and placed it carefully on the living room floor during dinner.

"Oh, my God!" Welles said. "It's fantastic!"

While Welles continued to express his pleasure, Jason warned everyone that he was responsible for the swordfish and that no one was to touch or move it. But minutes later there was a crunch, and Jason turned to see that Larry Jackson had accidentally stepped on the bill and broken it into three pieces.

With everyone shrieking and moaning "like they were at an Italian funeral," Jason tore Jackson to pieces and then spent the next several days finding the proper shades of black, blue, and silver spray paint to glue the bill back together so they could use it over the mantel. It then remained there for weeks and weeks, while the taxidermist called to see when he'd get his swordfish back.

Nobody, not even Marshall, showed as much loyalty, suffered as much abuse, or provided as much energy as Graver.

While others groaned as they waited all day for Orson to figure out a lighting scheme, Graver set it up, took it down, and set it up again. When Orson didn't know what he wanted until he saw it, Graver would try anything and was willing to scrap an entire day's work and then happily start all over the following morning.

During their four years together, Orson and Graver had come to an informal agreement where Gary would check if Welles needed him before taking a job. If it was okay, Orson gave him clearance. If not, Graver said no and accepted that no money might be coming in for a while.

Yet, even for Graver, there had to be limitations. Needing to feed his family and keep a roof over their heads, Graver often directed erotic films under the name Robert McCallum, including *3AM*, a picture that starred Georgina Spelvin (of *The Devil in Miss Jones*) and had a crew that included Stringer, Ferris, Jacobson, and *Wind* soundman Paul Hunt.

A perfect demonstration of the affection, manipulation, and codependence that defined their relationship, *3AM* was in postproduction during 1975 at a point when Orson suddenly needed Gary and he needed him *now*! Graver, however, put his foot down. This time he couldn't do it. He had to finish *3AM* and get paid before he could go back to Welles. This time Orson wouldn't come first.

Realizing he couldn't win and wanting Graver back as quickly as possible, a frustrated Welles offered to help him and allegedly wound up editing a hard-core lesbian shower scene that he couldn't resist cutting in Wellesian fashion with low camera angles and other trademark flair.

But that was the exception. Otherwise, Graver was completely self-less when it came to Orson and was accustomed to withstanding the tantrums that Welles directed at him in moments of failure and despondence. "The person Orson yelled at most was Gary," said crew member Lou Race. "But, it wasn't really yelling. It was more like oration."

But Welles also saved the greatest possible tribute for Graver, delivering it one day in Carefree after shooting a scene in Hannaford's den, where his *Kane* Oscar was used as a prop. Becoming quite emotional, Orson presented the statue to Gary, telling him that it was payment for all the work he'd done without compensation.

"Keep this, Gary," Welles said. "I want you to have it."

Overwhelmed, Graver said he couldn't take it.

"No," Orson insisted. "I want you to have it once we're done shooting."

With that, Welles rewarded Graver's devotion by giving away his greatest symbol of recognition for the film that defined his life.

By March, there was serious progress toward shooting everything they needed. But there was also confusion, as almost nobody seemed to know much of the plot beyond his or her own role. Huston knew more than others, but every shot seemed to exist primarily in Orson's head, creating an undercurrent of disarray.

"The script I had was over two hundred pages," said script supervisor Mary Ann Newfield. "It was really disjointed and we were doing the other half of conversations he'd filmed before and shooting so out of order that we never knew what we were matching to. Only Orson knew what was going on."

And there were days when even Welles appeared confused by what he was filming and why he was filming it, something that was further compounded by the constant creation of new dialogue via both Orson's typewriter and the actors' improvisation. As a result, no one who worked as script supervisor could keep up, and ultimately there were several versions of the screenplay, rather than just one.

Adding further complexity was the addition of new characters, many based on Hollywood people or taken straight from Orson's life. Some were shots at perceived enemies, while others represented particular themes. Those new characters included the following:

Dr. Bradley Pease Burroughs, a prim, effeminate teacher whose prep school John Dale once attended. Portrayed by Dan Tobin, the character bears some physical (and professional) resemblance to Skipper Hill and is the source by which Hannaford realizes that he's been set up by Dale, whom he rescued from what he now understands was a fake suicide.

German actor Tonio Selwart played "the Baron," a strange, vaguely European Hannaford associate loosely based on John Houseman; while actor Gregory Sierra portrayed Jack Simon, a parody of manly screenwriter John Milius, who'd requested a gun as part of his payment for *Dirty Harry*. In the film, Simon challenges Hannaford's manhood in front of Otterlake, insinuating that he is possibly homosexual.

Orson cast his sweet-natured old friend Norman Foster (who directed *Journey into Fear* as well as several Charlie Chan and Mr. Moto films) as Billy Boyle, a recovering alcoholic who is the most fully realized character in the Hannaford mafia, and who has been assigned to show Jake's film to a young actor turned studio executive named Max David (played by Graver's B-movie friend Geoffrey Land), who is clearly modeled on Robert Evans. And it is Foster's Billy who sits uncomfortably with David during the revelation that Hannaford's film may be visually remarkable, but is also completely incoherent.

Frequently reminded that Little's time was running out, Welles shot as quickly as he could, believing they could film all his scenes before the comedian had to leave.

Among those scenes was one that took place on a rooftop where Little, McCambridge, Strasberg, O'Brien, and Foster are dancing and sipping cocktails at Hannaford's party.

After they'd shot it several times, Welles finally said they had the scene, but added that he wanted to keep the camera rolling and then directed the cast to begin looking down at their feet—in disgust.

Mystified, Little asked Strasberg, "What the hell is this about?"

"Don't ask," she said, continuing to do as she'd been told.

"Keep it up! This is excellent!" Orson said as the shrieking and hysteria continued. Finally, he cried, "Cut! Beautiful! Let's move on to the library!"

Approaching Foster, Little asked him what just happened.

"Don't ask," Foster said. "There's always a reason."

But on the way to the next scene, Little stopped and talked to Welles. "Why were we looking down at our feet in total disgust?" he asked.

"Midgets," Orson said. "Midgets running between your legs."

"But Orson, what midgets?" Little replied. "There weren't any midgets running between our legs."

With a look suggesting that he couldn't understand why anyone would ask such an insane question after he'd provided a perfectly reasonable answer, Orson sighed, rolled his eyes, and said that he'd "shoot them next month in Spain" and cut them in later.

Days later, while filming another scene, Orson screamed, "Midgets on the roof!" and the horrified reactions resumed immediately. Little remained mystified.

"I never found out what that was all about," he said.

Their meaning, however, wasn't important to the crew, particularly Rick Waltzer, who suffered from a recurring fear that one day Orson would wake up and say, "I'm going to need those midgets tomorrow!"

The circumstances of Little's departure depend on the source. Many believe he was fired because he couldn't act. Others say Orson liked Little, so he fired him in a way that allowed the comedian to walk away feeling he'd quit. In Little's version, he simply hit the deadline and didn't have a choice, claiming that Orson drove with him to the airport, filming the entire way.

"What should I do?" Little asked.

"Just make up dialogue," Orson told him.

And then there is the version in which Orson hired a bunch of extras and planned to shoot through the weekend before Little's departure at Southwestern Studio, a nearby production facility he rented to shoot interiors.

"I just need you until Sunday," Welles told Little.

But according to Marshall and Peter Jason, Little simply disappeared into the night on Thursday evening, without telling a soul that he was leaving for the airport.

When he found out, Orson went ballistic. Having blown $50,000 on an actor whose role was central to the film, he was left with a bunch of nearly completed, now useless footage. It was, Marshall said, "one of the rare instances where Orson didn't cause the drama."

At first, everything shut down and Welles went into a tailspin brought on by feeling defeat just as he was about to cross the finish line. Then, however, he gathered his energies, refocused, and decided to proceed.

"Orson used it as a way to start over," said Marshall.

They'd scrap Little's footage and find a new Otterlake.

Edmond O'Brien's departure was less impactful but decidedly more spectacular than Little's. The frequent outlet for Orson's frustrations, O'Brien was nearly deaf, suffering from emphysema, and wearing thick glasses after cataract surgery. Acting strangely since he'd arrived in Carefree, the actor would mutter incomprehensible and odd things to anyone he encountered and often didn't seem sure of who he was, where he was, or why he was there. Under the assumption that O'Brien's problems were related to heavy drinking, almost everyone on the set pitched in and tried to help him function.

When he needed O'Brien, Welles would scream, "Go and get Eddie!" and send someone to find the Oscar winner, who was usually in the bathroom, coughing. Knocking on the door, the messenger would say, "Mr. O'Brien, Mr. Welles is ready for you." In response, there was just more coughing.

After being told that O'Brien wasn't leaving the bathroom, Orson would yell, "Get him out here!" and send the poor soul back, where he'd try again to get O'Brien's attention. Finally, the actor would emerge from the bathroom, leaving a trail of used Kleenex tissues behind him.

When O'Brien walked onto the set, said Jason, "Orson would whip him and yell at him and O'Brien just took it and did his job."

In fact, O'Brien did more than his job. Suffering from dementia or Alzheimer's, he would transform before the camera as if by magic and suddenly be 100 percent there, never missing a beat and giving a spot-on performance without complaint.

Finally, when O'Brien had completed his last shot, the cast and crew gave him a gigantic round of applause, after which he thanked them and turned to Welles.

"Orson, it's been a pleasure working on this movie," he said. "Anytime you ever need me again you can always call my agent care of— *Peking, China!!*"

Nobody laughed harder at O'Brien's surreal rage than Orson, who roared from the bowels of the earth.

It wasn't until Marshall and Jackson went to help O'Brien move out of the Desert Forest Motel that they realized how far gone he was. Finding drawers of rotting bananas and raw hamburger, the pair were still in shock when O'Brien insisted they pack a large number of lightbulbs that he'd taped together in bundles to take to the airport. Later, they had to explain the bundles to security as they rushed the actor through the concourse in a wheelchair so he wouldn't miss his flight.

Though now an important director, the brash, confident Peter Bogdanovich still worshipped Welles, and the two spoke every day for at least thirty minutes around lunchtime. With their conversations often turning contentious, Orson had no problem letting everyone hear how cruelly dismissive he could be toward his protégé. This included one incident when Bogdanovich sought Welles's advice on how to solve problems on an upcoming film.

"Shoot it in black-and-white," Welles said, echoing his advice on *The Last Picture Show* and Peter's success with *Paper Moon*. Then, putting his hand over the receiver, Welles looked at the large crowd eating lunch and roared, "Black-and-white!"

On another occasion, after a lengthy call, Welles got off the phone to find lunch already over. Asking Marshall why he hadn't been informed, he was told, "You were on the phone talking to Peter."

Annoyed, Welles said, "Don't you know that the one thing I want out of life is a meal after I've been on the phone with Peter Bogdanovich?"

But on March 13, the call was different.

"I just finished shooting with Rich Little," Welles said. "He did great impressions, but he can't act. I don't know what to do. I've got John waiting. I'm in terrible shape."

Bogdanovich suggested that he could play the role.

"That never occurred to me," Orson said after a thoughtful pause.

"The guy's a young director who had three hits and he does impressions all the time and it never occurred to you?" Bogdanovich asked.

"But you're playing [Higgam]," Welles responded.

"That's just a few scenes, anybody could do that," Bogdanovich said.

"My God," Orson replied. "Of course you could do it. You'd be great for it. My God, will you? You just saved my life."

Bogdanovich arrived the next day and was greeted warmly by Welles, who proceeded to chat with him about a range of topics unrelated to the film. After some time, Bogdanovich said that maybe they should be working on the movie. Orson, however, was in no rush. He wanted Bogdanovich to relax and settle in a bit before the shooting started again.

Not long afterward, Welles asked to see the clothes he'd had Bogdanovich bring from Bel Air so that he could put together his costume. Sifting through the pricey wardrobe, Welles arranged the clothing until there were several combinations that satisfied him.

Then, when Peter said he'd never worn any of the outfits Orson had created, Welles smiled and said, "Now you know how a successful young film director dresses."

Strasberg, however, recalled the event differently. She sensed that Bogdanovich was deeply intimidated by Orson, who rifled through the clothing and dismissively said, "My God, that's not what a successful director would wear!"

"But these are my own clothes," Bogdanovich replied.

"That's just what I mean," Welles shot back.

Intimidated or not, Bogdanovich's arrival added a strange new element to the set, with everyone knowing that Welles had cast another person from his own life as a character based on himself. "When Peter came in to play Peter, it was bizarre," Marshall said. "I always wondered whether Peter *knew*."

On set with her new husband (*Paper Moon* prop master Tony Wade), Polly Platt was concerned that Otterlake was a slap at Peter, who seemed to be the only person who disagreed with her. To others, it was obvious that Bogdanovich's story was so close to Otterlake that there was no other interpretation. And Orson did nothing to soften the blow, once asking the crew for a line that an annoying cineaste could ask Hannaford. "Could you talk about the aesthetic difference between a dolly shot and a zoom?" someone said, suggesting an almost exact re-creation of a question Peter once asked Welles. Then, with Bogdanovich watching, Welles explained to the actor, "That's exactly the kind of bullshit question I'm looking for."

"It was so surreal that you couldn't make it up," Rick Waltzer said of Bogdanovich playing Otterlake.

Bogdanovich, however, approached Otterlake as if he were a character based on someone *like* him, and he treated anything derogatory as having been added to serve the story.

Meanwhile, Huston, also playing a role close to his own personality, seemed as unaware of Bogdanovich's career as he'd been of Little's, asking him, "So Peter, how many movies have you actually acted in now?"

"This is my second, Mr. Huston," Bogdanovich replied.

"Two . . ." Huston said, stopping to consider Bogdanovich's body of work. "Must make it very easy to count them."

While Huston teased him, the relationship between Bogdanovich and Welles intensified, with Orson orchestrating a game of cat and mouse, reeling in Peter when necessary and pushing him away when he got too close. "Mercedes knew just how to deal with Orson," said producer Juergen Hellwig. "But, with Peter, Orson kept him in his place."

Beyond his desire to maintain control over their friendship, Welles wanted Bogdanovich in the same mind-set as Huston. Beneath Peter's cocky swagger was a genuine, innocent sweetness that was palpable and needed to emerge in certain scenes. Thus, Orson's passive-aggressive behavior was tempered by his acknowledgment of Peter's talents, which was expressed in ways that made Bogdanovich incredibly malleable.

Directing Bogdanovich in one scene, Welles ran him through the dialogue again and again, pushing him in one direction and then the next, simply telling him, "Okay, try it another way." And giving himself over to Welles's direction, Bogdanovich did exactly as told. When they finished Orson said, "Now I know how you get those brilliant performances in your films."

"What do you mean?" Bogdanovich asked.

"You show them how to do it, don't you," Welles said.

"Well, sometimes," replied a flattered Bogdanovich.

"Because you're a brilliant actor," Orson purred.

Whether manipulation, a momentary feeling, or God's honest truth, the impact of that exchange released enormous tension and provided Bogdanovich with the freedom to find the guilelessness within Otterlake.

Bogdanovich also pushed Welles, challenging him to get certain shots simply so he could witness the process of their creation.

"Why don't we do a shot where there's no cut?" Bogdanovich asked one day. "[Like] one of those shots from *Ambersons* or *Kane*?"

"I haven't got the actors," Welles said. "I can't do that kind of thing." But the next day he declared, "We're going to do one without a cut," and orchestrated a complicated, cutless multicamera scene with Bogdanovich and Huston.

That scene is particularly poignant, as it depicts the end of a conversation between Hannaford and Otterlake, where the latter is caught sitting in his mentor's kingly chair. At the time, Bogdanovich believed he was acting, but later he realized that the scene was a reenactment of how Prince Hal betrays Falstaff.

"I think Orson thought that dynamic was at work with me and him, and I didn't feel that way at all, but he did. I think he kind of wanted it to be that way," Bogdanovich said. "It was all sorts of stuff I didn't think existed in my relationship with Orson at all, but I guess it did as far as Orson was concerned. He basically fictionalized our relationship."

The meaning was unmistakable, Bogdanovich said. "I was thinking about being him."

Art also imitated real life during another scene in which Hannaford, Otterlake, and Juliette Riche engage in a revealing confrontation. Using a spinning whirl of shots taken from multiple perspectives, with characters coming and going in precise rhythms designed to enhance the moment, it is one of the film's most complicated scenes.

Surrounded by a crowd of partygoers and media, Riche asks Otterlake a question about himself, which he declines to answer, saying, "This is Mr. Hannaford's night, let's save the questions for him."

When Riche persists and begins prying into the Hannaford-Otterlake relationship, Bogdanovich's character dismisses the critic by mocking her review of his latest film.

"She wasn't that kind to me," Otterlake says. "Not that you can do much harm . . . [switching to Cagney's voice] I mean, how much harm can you do to the third biggest grosser in movie history?"

Watching warily from the side, Huston's Hannaford chimes in with cheery sarcasm, "Did you really make that much? How marvelous!"

Parrying back, Riche looks to Hannaford and says, "Did you know that when his production company goes public that your friend stands to walk away with forty million dollars?"

Then, before Hannaford can respond, Otterlake says, "Yes, and she's going to keep writing that I stole everything from you, Skipper. I'm never going to walk away from that."

Putting the topic to rest, a gimlet-eyed Hannaford tells the crowd, "It's all right to borrow from each other, but what we must never do is borrow from ourselves."

But despite whatever invective Welles was directing at Bogdanovich through the clear reference to the Directors Company and the idea that the student might be stealing from the master, Orson invited Peter to lunch one day when everyone else had gone out, during which he said, "If anything happens to me, I want you to promise me that you'll finish the picture."

"Oh Jesus, Orson," Bogdanovich replied. "Why would you say a thing like that? Nothing's going to happen to you."

"I know . . ." Welles said. "But if it does, I want you to promise me that you'll finish making the picture."

"Of course I would, but—," Bogdanovich began.

"That's okay," Welles stopped him. "We don't have to discuss it any further."

"Don't worry," Welles assured Larry Jackson, who was lying on the trunk of a convertible, holding a boom mike. "We won't even be going that fast."

Welles and Jackson were about to shoot a scene in which Hannaford drives to his party, with Bogdanovich (formerly in the backseat as Higgam in August 1970) now sitting in the passenger seat with a crew member crammed into his footwell. Orson and Graver, meanwhile, strapped a camera to the side of the car and squished into the back with handhelds.

Having already consumed a considerable amount of vodka that day, Huston pulled the car onto a street, where he drove only briefly before running up a curb onto somebody's front lawn, clipping a tree, and destroying the side-mounted camera, which swung violently toward—and nearly decapitated—Bogdanovich.

When the car stopped, Welles looked at the camera and said, "I'll have to do another commercial to pay for that." Then he turned his attention to Huston, wanting to know what just happened. Though Hannaford was supposed to be driving recklessly, this was more than Orson had in mind.

Huston, however, was neither acting nor drunk. Instead, he explained that long ago he'd concluded that drinking and driving didn't mix and that he'd have to make a choice of one or the other. Drinking won, and for decades he'd hardly been behind the wheel.

Undeterred, Orson yelled, "Action!" and Huston steered back onto the road and drove for a bit before he was told to merge onto a highway. Following the directions, Huston turned the car and entered by going the wrong way down an exit ramp and into high-speed traffic on an expressway, with Jackson clinging to the trunk, thinking, "The obituary won't even mention that I was here."

With everyone screaming and the cameras rolling, Huston swerved away from oncoming cars until he was able to jump the meridian with a hard left and then calmly join the flow of traffic on the other side.°

When they exited the highway and Huston pulled over, everyone

---

° The Huston driving incident is one of the more frequently told stories to have come from the set of *The Other Side of the Wind*. In addition to the account that appears here, there is also Rich Little's version, which is cited in a 1977 letter from the comedian to Welles and was apparently told on at least one television talk show. In that version, Little is still playing Otterlake and gets into the car with Huston and Welles, who was working the camera. After Welles instructs Huston to drive both fast and recklessly along a canal, Huston makes the same confession as the one he made after driving the wrong way on the highway—namely that he'd barely driven in thirty years. Hearing this Little asked to be let out of the car. Attempting to calm him, Huston explained that if god forbid they did drive into the canal, having Welles in the backseat would take them down so rapidly that they would be quickly put out of their misery. Not surprisingly, this did not calm Little, who demanded to be let out of the car. Orson then took over and said that on the outside chance they were to die Little's name would look great with his and Huston's in the headline for the *Variety* cover story about their demise. Then, after Orson forced Little to remain in the car, Huston very nearly drove it into the canal and eventually rammed it into an embankment. Though most witnesses claim it was Bogdanovich in the car, Little and Welles did exchange letters that seem to acknowledge the incident.

was deadly silent, until Welles sighed deeply and said, "Thanks, John. That'll do."

When someone Orson relied upon was in a relationship that seemed to be getting in his way, Welles tended to do one of two things. One option was to hire wives and girlfriends so that they were invested in the project and were working the same sixteen-to-twenty-hour days as their boyfriend or husband. Option two was to send them packing. Sometimes he did both, as was the case with Graver's wives Connie and April, who had jobs on the set, but were ultimately driven away by the clear message that Orson almost always came first for their husband.

"Orson didn't want any women around," Jason recalled. "He didn't like for anyone else to love Gary."

He had the same feelings about Cybill Shepherd, whom he'd first met when he and Oja had dined with Cybill and Peter at a Paris restaurant. Orson's conversation with Peter had been so intensely exclusive that the two women had lit their menus on fire in order to get their attention.

Welles could be warm and paternal toward Shepherd, such as the time he gave her a copy of *Daisy Miller* and insisted she'd be perfect for the title role in an adaptation directed by him or Bogdanovich. That was the Orson who offered her advice and encouraged her to pursue her interest in singing opera (but cautioned that she couldn't be an actress at the same time).

But there was also the disdainful, rage-filled Welles, who, while living at Bogdanovich's home, once exploded during breakfast after Shepherd mentioned something she'd learned in school. Turning red, he screamed, "Everything you've learned in school is balls! Balls, do you hear!"

Similarly, when Shepherd visited Carefree and was asked to be an extra, Welles jumped down her throat when the camera got too close.

"Orson yelled at me in that incredible voice," Shepherd recalled. *"Turn away from the camera, Cybill! We can see your face!!"*

Perhaps this was the side of Orson that decided to create the character of Mavis Henscher, a pretty, dim young blonde who arrives on Otterlake's arm but is stolen away by Hannaford. Describing the actress he wanted for the role, Welles told Marshall and Jason that in addition to youth and looks, he sought someone naïve and unspoiled. And as he continued, the pair realized Orson was describing the waitress who served them breakfast at a local restaurant each morning.

That waitress was Cathy Lucas, a shy, Bambi-like, blond teenager whom they approached the next day, asking if she wanted to be in an Orson Welles film. Apprehensively, Lucas agreed to come to the set with her mother, with whom she shared a trailer in the middle of nearby cowboy country.

When Cathy and her mom arrived, they sat nervously in the living room with Huston and Welles. Clearly terrified, they listened as the directors explained how they wanted Cathy to take time off school and promised she would be in good hands on the set, which they characterized as a wholesome enterprise not unlike a 4-H club. Despite her misgivings, Lucas's mother agreed to let her take the role.

Since she'd never acted, casting Lucas was a challenge for Orson, who spent hours trying to help her understand what she'd need to do in each scene. On several occasions, everyone sat watching as two of Hollywood's greatest directors huddled with the teenager, doing everything they could to coach her into a believable performance. At one point, Huston was on his knees, trying desperately to get a line reading from Lucas, to whom he suggested gently, "My dear, why don't you try it like this. . . ."

"Gee, I don't know," she responded.

Willing to accept her limitations, Orson expanded Lucas's role, believing that it was his job to get the right performance from his cast. He would generally take responsibility for bad acting or a sequence gone wrong, but only to a certain point, as he adhered to the following philosophy:

"For any given scene, the actor and director each have responsibility to get it correct," he told the cast one day. "Takes one through three are on me. Takes five and after are on the actor."

When someone asked, "But what about take four?" Orson replied, "Exactly."

No matter how many takes she required, Lucas's naïveté was a refreshing counterpoint to the collected cinephiles standing in awe of Welles and Huston. Having no idea whom she was working with, Lucas was unaffected by their fame. When a cast mate told her she was lucky to be playing Huston's love interest, her only response was that he seemed kind of old.

It was that sincerity, innocence, and lack of training that ultimately made her perfect. Thus, while everyone watched Lucas struggle with dialogue, Orson was untroubled, working her painstakingly through scene after scene. Then, at night, when cast and crew expected to wince through dailies, everyone was blown away by the poignancy and depth of her performance.

Believing a director's main function was to preside over accidents, Welles knew Lucas was a lucky accident in that she was one of those people the camera loves. And because she didn't have the ego to question what she was asked to do, she simply did what Orson told her. As a result, Marshall said, "she was perfect."

During one scene with Lucas, Welles also showed how he tailored his methods to Huston.

Welles wanted him to look at Lucas with a measure of lust in his eyes, but each time they shot the scene, the way he ogled her came off as vulgar. However, rather than reinstruct Huston as to how he should play it, Welles took a much subtler approach. Stopping the action, Orson spoke as if he'd just been struck by a delightful thought.

"John," he said, "do you know who you remind me of in this scene?"

"No, Orson," Huston replied, "who?"

"Your father!" Welles told Huston, who absolutely lit up at the mention of his father, whom he adored, admired, and regarded as a fantastic actor.

"Really, Orson, why?" Huston asked.

"Well, because he had that kindly, paternal air—but nobody ever had a higher score," Welles said, knowing how much Huston would be charmed to hear his Walter recalled as both a father figure and a charming ladies' man.

Nailing it on the next take, Huston removed the leer from his glance and evoked the right balance of masculine desire and graybeard gravitas that Welles had been seeking.

On the set, Welles encouraged Huston to drink throughout the day, either because Jake Hannaford was an alcoholic or out of some belief that it would release his friend's inhibitions and bring out darker tones. Perhaps it was both, but without question, Huston began his day around six A.M. with breakfast and an "eye-opener" in his room at the Desert Forest, where he'd study his lines before heading to work with a bottle of vodka that he'd drain by nightfall.

As the day wore on, Huston would often ask Welles what page they were on, to which Welles would reply, "What the hell difference does it make?"—to which the bemused Huston would gamely respond, "I want to know how drunk I'm supposed to be!"

Using the drinking to his advantage, Orson often filmed Hannaford's most emotional scenes when Huston was intoxicated as a way of accessing greater depth in the lead performance. On the downside, however, Huston was sometimes too far gone to be of much use after six P.M. and would be driven back to the motel, where he'd refuse assistance before stumbling to his room. Then the next morning he'd be showered, hangover-free, and sitting in his bathrobe when an assistant arrived with breakfast and a fresh bottle of Stoli.

Although he seemed impervious to all hazards and difficulties, Huston's drinking and unraveling marriage clearly had an impact on him during the shoot. His condition made it possible for Orson to get

beneath his skin and evoke the "loneliest man in the world" quality—
something that occurs most vividly in his scenes with Bogdanovich that
are intercut through the latter part of the film. Forming the emotional
core of the movie, their interactions are filled with power and subtlety.

The first scene takes place in Hannaford's gun room after he's discovered that Billy couldn't persuade Max David to attend the party and
experiences the humiliation of having been set up by Dale. Embarrassed, angry, self-pitying, exhausted, drunk, and strangely bemused,
Hannaford bemoans turning seventy, grabs a gun, and points it out the
window, telling Otterlake that he'd reached a regrettable juncture in
the film and with their relationship.

Skipper . . . Otterlake finally says . . . *that forty million that was
mentioned* . . .

Hannaford responds: *I know, kid, let me finish your line for you.
It's still a distant hope, how's that for dialogue.*

Shot in shadows and light cast through shutters, the scene reveals
that Jake is so broke that he sold his boat, leaving him exposed and humiliated.

That conversation ends at the drive in, as does their relationship,
culminating in a moment where Otterlake quotes Shakespeare while
Hannaford's movie flickers on the screen.

"Our revels now are ended?" he asks Hannaford, stealing the dialogue from *The Tempest.* In a tone that is cold and arch, Jake simply
says, *You bet your sweet cheeks.*

Later that spring, Welles reshot the scene, reading the lines himself in Huston's absence and telling Bogdanovich, "Play it to me."

"He wanted me to think about him and to play it like we were talking about our relationship," Bogdanovich told film writer Peter Tonguette.
"At one point he's being very cold to me and dismissive, and I say, "'Our
revels now are ended"?' . . . He had me say it many times."

Those scenes show Huston and Bogdanovich playing on two levels. First,
their public personae are on full display, as Huston is manly, seductive,

and witty, while Bogdanovich is smart, glib, and almost too eager to please. But in little moments, they are weak, alone, in pain, and unable to resurrect the tenuous balance that held their relationship together. Now surpassed by his protégé, Hannaford is left with only the hollow power to steal Otterlake's girlfriend and banish him from the kingdom.

For his part, Welles directed and manipulated their performances in ways that made each reveal their hidden vulnerability. This was demonstrated poignantly during a scene when Hannaford sits under the swordfish in his den, half-asleep and very drunk. As he is interrupted by McCambridge, telling him that the screening is about to start, a shaft of light shoots through the door and startles Hannaford, who walks across the room, where he is supposed to bump into a wooden Indian and spit in its face.

When Welles called, "Action!" the scene played as intended, with Huston running into the Indian as he stumbled toward the door. Unexpectedly, however, Huston reared back and angrily tossed a drink in the Indian's face, creating a halo of water, ice, and light above its head.

Loving the image and the surprise of it all, Welles asked, "Why didn't you spit?"

"My character wouldn't spit," Huston replied.

As March turned to April, there were signs that money was becoming tight, as Orson began bumming Huston's smaller, milder cigars and Larry Jackson rang up $3,000 worth of gas, groceries, and plane tickets on his credit card with the promise that he'd be repaid when the European producer returned to Carefree with the money from Paris. There was even a week where Peter Jason fed the entire company with residuals from a Right Guard commercial.

Meanwhile, paychecks began slowing down and sometimes stopped entirely. One crewmember told a departing comrade to cash his check on the way to the airport, since it might bounce by the time he got home.

Despite the influx of Iranian money, somehow Orson's faucet was running dry.

Throughout this, Graver held the crew together by example. Since he hadn't relied on Orson for income, others watched him and did the same. Then, after a few weeks of waiting for money that was imminently supposed to arrive from France, Orson had a visitor.

It was late at night and raining when Dominique Antoine arrived from Paris. Hugging Orson and Oja with great affection she took them into another room while Graver and others sat nearby, nervously trying to hear what was being said.

Instead, however, what they heard was the rumbling of Orson's voice as he bellowed, "Again!!!"

The money was gone and where it went soon became part of the film's lore, told in the form of an oft-repeated tale in which one of Orson's partners is blamed for its disappearance.

In that version of the story the man had been both a source of funds and a hands-on producer who allegedly did everything from cutting checks on behalf of the production to picking up funds from Astrophore in Paris and delivering them to Orson in Spain during late 1973.

That money, Welles told his biographer Barbara Leaming, always arrived in smaller amounts than expected. The young producer, however, allegedly assured Orson that things were just moving slowly and that Boushehri would eventually come through. Until then, Welles claimed, the man said he'd provide additional funds via his own company. Yet, that investment, Orson alleged, was simply the producer passing off Astrophore's money as his own.

There are two sets of documents that support this version of events. The first is an August 1974 legal agreement dissolving Orson's partnership with everyone but Astrophore which specifies that the producer's company "failed to" provide its own investment of $150,000 and also had failed to open a production account as it had been obligated to do under a 1973 agreement. Additionally, it claims that the producer's company had *misappropriated a whole or substantial* part of the money received from Astrophore.

In 1976 and 1977, Boushehri had Coopers and Lybrand audit both Astrophore and the production of *The Wind*. In each report the auditors stated that Avenel had signed an August 3, 1973, agreement with the producer's company and with Astrophore under which Orson and Oja's interest in the film was $750,000, while the Iranians and the man's production company were each obligated to provide $150,000 toward completion of the movie. The audits repeat the accusation that the producer *misappropriated* money he was supposed to transmit from Astrophore to Orson.

It is difficult to tell, however, how much these documents were influenced by Orson and his potentially one-sided version of the events.

Additionally, several accounts from individuals who worked on the film follow some version of this story, yet there are also aspects of the tale that vary depending on the source, and important facts are difficult to pin down, including a clear sequence of events that led to the alleged theft, a motive beyond simple greed, and even the total sum that was missing—which has been claimed as being anywhere from $150,000 to $350,000.

And while there seems to be agreement on the general terms of what happened, nearly everyone got their information from Orson or from someone to whom Orson had told the story. Meanwhile Orson, the accused, and to some extent Dominique Antoine, are the only people who had firsthand knowledge of the situation. Meaning that while it may still be accurate, there are certainly several factors that cast doubt on this version of events—including the fact that the producer has consistently denied the accusations and gone on to a successful, decades-long career in the movie industry during which there have been no other known accusations of financial misconduct. Of equal significance is that no one involved in the production reported the alleged theft to authorities or took legal action to remedy the alleged wrong. In fact, the producer has never been charged with a crime, nor been subject to a civil suit in connection with the accusation.

There are also other reasons to doubt the accusation, not the least of which are Orson's abysmal accounting practices and inability to manage money. Though he tried to do things inexpensively and tended to count the pennies, the dollars were usually a problem because he didn't always know where they went and funding for one film might be used on another project and vice versa.

Compounding matters further is that—on *The Wind*—Orson was living in the homes where he filmed, usually because it would represent an overall cost saving to the production. It also, however, made for a murky situation where it was difficult to tell which money was for rent, cigars, and other living expenses, and which funds were being used to pay for items directly related to filmmaking, thus bringing new meaning to the term commingling of funds. And because of the disorganized and chaotic state of Orson's personal finances, it's reasonable to speculate as to the possibility that the use of the funds was not only undocumented, but that no one really knew where they had gone or how they'd been used. Instead, they simply knew that they needed the money— and now it was gone.

Because of this, the disappearance of that money ultimately remains a mystery and creates more questions than it provides answers.

What is certain, however, is that Antoine headed to Los Angeles and met with a lawyer who was able to get Orson out of his prior contract, something she did while Astrophore was beginning to experience its own financial problems due to escalating political tensions in Iran. But, difficult as this made her job, Antoine realized two things about Orson. First, he had a character defect when it came to money, often trusting crooks and scoundrels, while being deeply suspicious of those who genuinely had his best interests at heart. Equally important, however, was her sense that beneath his own masks, Welles was confused and out of his element in Carefree. Beset with money problems and with no idea how he'd finish his film, Orson, like Hannaford, was lost.

"Orson was at his best, which is a hell of a big thing to say," was how Huston described the shoot. "I'd like a movie of him making [that] movie."

Indeed, the film had been an adventure shared by desperate men; the only question was whether or not it would come to nothing. And although the journey had been everything Huston had hoped for, the circumstances of his friend's final weeks and eventual departure from Carefree were nearly inconceivable and deserving of their own movie.

Though the details are jumbled, several things seemed to coincide that sent the production back to Los Angeles. One factor was a right-wing neighbor who concluded that someone was making a porn film after seeing the blacked-out windows, camera equipment, and steady stream of young people coming and going from the house. Finally fed up, the man called the police, but his efforts were thwarted when Welles, Huston, and McCambridge greeted the officers and explained what they were doing.

The neighbor, however, remained unhappy and vented his rage one day, screaming, "I don't care who you are, get the hell out of Carefree, Arizona!" in the middle of a scene.

"Keep that in the shot!" Orson said to Graver.

But the man had been absolutely right—Orson needed to get out of Carefree. Huston was soon gone, off scouting locations for *The Man Who Would Be King*, while the neighbor allegedly called the Slingmans to complain and found out he wasn't the first. Apparently, they'd already heard from the phone company about an unpaid bill for thousands of calls placed from their home. In response, they'd cut off the line.

After that, production assistant Rick Waltzer's room at the Desert Forest became the base for all communication with the outside world, until they ran into problems there as well after the owner saw that Orson's phone bill had reached $1,433.83, which—along with room charges—brought the unpaid portion of the motel bill to $2,500. Waltzer paid $800, but after they checked out, the owner claimed he'd had the local prosecutor file grand larceny charges against another member of the production who'd written some rubber checks to the motel.

Still owed nearly $1,800, the motel owner sent Marshall (who'd booked many rooms and handled most bills) a letter stating: "I suppose

I can afford to be screwed for the room charges, but the phone thing is something else. . . . I realize that you are having financial problems. I also realize that you are gambling on the success of the motion picture for your personal recovery. But, when I got the motel built it was no small gamble either. I thought my gambling days were pretty much over."

Were that not enough, the check for equipment and rent at Southwestern Studio (likely over $25,000) bounced and remained unpaid, despite the efforts of its manager and his lawyer. Tom Brodek, who ran Southwestern, said, "It just became more disappointing and heartbreaking because it was Orson Welles."

With his finances in ruins, Orson was in no danger of becoming too comfortable. Consciously or not, he'd sought maximum discomfort and found it yet again.

Upon his return to Los Angeles in April, Welles moved into the Bogdanovich mansion at 242 Copa de Oro in Bel Air, where he worked twenty-hour days rewriting, shooting, and editing *The Other Side of the Wind*.

At the time, Bogdanovich was preparing for the release of his ill-fated *Daisy Miller* adaptation, in which he'd directed Cybill as the title character. Although the film was not an unmitigated disaster, the reviews were generally negative, and some critics savaged the director and his star as well as the movie itself. Now that Peter was no longer invincible, *Daisy Miller* became a cathartic release for negative feelings that couldn't be expressed when he was on top.

Meanwhile, Orson took over the house as if he were Sheridan Whiteside and began shooting the weekend he returned from Carefree. Though without Huston, he had Strasberg, as well as much of the cast and crew, so they worked on party scenes, including the one in which Riche sums up her understanding of Hannaford.

"I know why he does these insane things," she says. "Casting midgets, discarding actors . . ."

"Why?" ask a group of devoted cineastes.

Directed by Orson to stare at the camera and deliver her line in a flat, emotionless tone, Strasberg says one word: "Perversity."

Later, Strasberg wrote, she thought about that line and tried to decide if it was fiction or taken directly from Orson's life story.

Anyone encountering Orson that winter or spring was aware that he wasn't in good health. Those entering his bedroom saw the ten to twenty bottles on his night table, containing medicine for pancreatitis, high blood pressure, gout, and other ailments caused or exacerbated by his weight.

Orson's condition even began to show in his work. Although he was still a superlative cameraman, his footage was frequently shaky because his chest heaved up and down as he searched for breath. His energy remained unflagging, however, and he continued pushing with the usual intensity.

More encouraging was the frequent arrival of money from Paris, as well as a May 6 letter from Weissberger, explaining that the young European distributor and his production company had been severed from the film and that Orson's agreement with both had been officially extinguished.

Before summer ended, the Hellwig brothers and their company Janus Films (which had invested in the film as well) became collateral damage and forfeited their ownership rights so that the terms of the deal could be reset with Avenel and Astrophore as sole partners. Orson had already invested $750,000, so Boushehri and Astrophore were on the hook for completion funds. All wire transfers and checks for that purpose would arrive from Paris and were immediately converted to cash by Orson's assistant, who (knowing there were frequent dry spells) would immediately take her salary and Graver's off the top before stuffing the rest in a drawer for use by the production, which continued at both Bogdanovich's home and Producers Studio.

At Producers, Welles filmed whatever he needed with whomever was available, including several matching shots from other locations. For one drive-in scene, Lou Race was asked to envelop the set in a blanket of fog made with a handheld smoke machine that would create a haze floating near the screen as Hannaford's movie is shown.

After walking front to back, then back to front, Race finally put the machine on the ground, where it continued belching misty smoke that caught a gust of air and floated upwards, where it was dramatically illuminated by colored lights in the background.

Staring at the magnificent display of multihued fog, Welles turned to Race and deadpanned, "Too baroque. Even for a Welles film."

A more telling moment occurred after a day of shooting on the rotting floors of a broken-down soundstage at Producers. Someone slid open a massive stage door during dinner so they could get much needed fresh air, only to reveal a gorgeous sunset set against a magnificent golden-red sky—all framed perfectly by the massive warehouse-high opening.

Taken by the incredible transition from day to night, cast and crew walked toward the light, marveling at the sky. Moments later, Orson walked over and saw the kind of vista he would ordinarily have rushed to shoot.

Taking it in, Welles said, "Hmmm. It looks fake," and walked away.

In July, Orson went back to France, where he planned to assemble the footage with Deschamps and his crew, then return to Los Angeles and film whatever was missing.

Early in the month, however, he did shoot two sequences in his backyard at Orvilliers—both intended to complete the sex scenes involving Kodar and Random. One of those sequences had the pair making love on a spring bed while Hannaford humiliates Dale, causing him to walk off the film. The other shots were part of the car scene they'd first filmed in September 1970.

Since Welles hadn't spoken to his John Dale in nearly four years, he needed a stand-in. And for this he turned to Graver, whose build and blond hair could approximate Random's if shot from behind.

This request, however, was too much for Gary, who drew the line at appearing naked on a bed while being filmed by the all-female crew he'd assembled in France. "Orson, don't ask me to do this," Graver pleaded.

"You've gotta do this, Gary," Welles told him. "There's nobody else."

Relenting, Graver stripped down to his pants for the car scene, which was shot at night by a bizarre crew that included not only Antoine, Deschamps, Oja, Gary, and Orson, but the conductor of the London Symphony; Orson's accountant, Bill Cronshaw; and Cronshaw's two dinner companions, a pair of Australian baronesses who remained in their expensive outfits while one of them worked as an electrician's assistant and the other made it rain with the garden hose.

With this group assembled, Orson put Oja in a Volkswagen Beetle and had her repeat what she'd been doing long ago with Random in a Mustang on an empty lot in Beverly Hills.

"What look should I have?" Kodar asked.

"The same one as four years ago," Orson said.

Still trying to re-create the moment, Kodar asked for more direction, and Orson responded, "Your animal look, darling. That's all. Your animal look."

Projecting footage Gary had shot of cars and Paris streetlights onto three movie screens they'd set up in the yard, Orson continued using poor man's process to finish what they'd started nearly half-a-decade earlier on a different continent with a different man making love to an actress who herself was now four years older.

Welles's living arrangements and expenses in France were based on a set of conditions, rather than a fixed sum. As spelled out in a July 24 memo, his day-to-day lifestyle would be funded in "accordance to those standards which are normal to his way of life." This meant luxury accommodations, office space, three meals a day (for himself and a guest at first-class restaurants), the use of a large car to accommodate Orson's size and a recurring leg condition, a driver, and laundry and other expenses.

All personal items (cigars, drinks, various other luxuries) would be taken care of by Welles, while administrative, telephone, and other charges were to be included in the film's forthcoming budget. But Welles's personal compensation as a director remained undecided, as he wanted between $3,500 and $5,000 per week and at least $75,000 for twenty-five weeks of work.

Yet while his salary remained flexible, a July 26 memo left little doubt regarding the most important issue on Orson's mind: artistic control.

"Mr. Welles is to be considered the artistic producer of *THE OTHER SIDE OF THE WIND*, throughout the entire period of time required for its completion," the memo read. "His judgment as to what shall constitute the complete form of the film shall be accepted by all parties concerned as residing solely in his professional and artistic discretion."

Explaining that he'd make all possible efforts at economy, with Astrophore committing "the fullest resources available," the memo closed with Orson reiterating dominion over final cut: "All decisions . . . in any way relating to the quality, stature and importance of the film shall be made solely by Mr. Welles, after due consultation with Astrophore and Avenel and within the limits and qualifications heretofore stated."

Emphasizing good-faith efforts, and vague as to actual dates, rights, and responsibilities, Welles wanted it to be crystal clear that he wouldn't relive his experiences on *Touch of Evil, Ambersons*, and *Mr. Arkadin*.

Then he went back to doing what he loved the most, editing. Orson and Deschamps took up where they'd left off in 1973, and the collaboration began well, despite the fact that Welles's top assistant still had neither a script nor the ability to view footage in continuity.

Working at LTC in an editing room containing three 35mm editing tables and two for 16mm footage, Welles resumed cutting multiple scenes at once, whittling them down slowly and forgoing final judgments until inspiration struck and he saw how one could lead into another in a way that enriched the material.

Editing with Welles, Deschamps found himself totally immersed and likened the experience to "being in a monastery where you have to serve God every fucking minute." Working for a lesser salary, as was his colleague Arnaud Petit and the assistants under their direction, Deschamps remained fascinated with how Orson approached footage, most notably the confrontation between Otterlake and Riche.

Standing in the center of a circle formed by camera-wielding film nerds fighting one another to get shots of Hannaford, Riche, and Otterlake, Bogdanovich's character turned frequently so that everyone could film his monologue, all done in a complex and subtle style that added deeper meaning to the shot. Deschamps was stunned.

"It gave a vertiginous sense of space and movement," he said. "The video freaks were turning in an anarchical way and the camera was turning in the opposite sense so that it was as if Peter were turning on himself."

Given the scene's intricate choreography, Deschamps assumed Welles would select the best of the eleven takes at his disposal. The director, however, cut every one of them into tiny pieces and reconstituted the monologue in a way that amplified the already incredible footage.

"It was so perfect," Deschamps said. "Only he could do that."

Welles also followed the same pattern with the footage for each sequence, reducing each take into little bits of film and then creating a new continuity within each scene.

Then the trouble began, inspired by the meaningless revelation that Deschamps had once been romantically involved with Antoine. Though the relationship ended before he met either, Welles felt betrayed because it hadn't been disclosed. And now, as a result, he suspected that Deschamps was spying for Boushehri, whom he always feared might try to steal his film just as others had in the past.

He wrote a memo at the end of July, reflecting his new attitude toward the entire editing staff, which had been working endless days without a break and would continue doing so for the next several months:

> *While it is perfectly true that the staff of film editors working on* THE OTHER SIDE OF THE WIND *are under salary to Astrophore, it is also true that in the practical day to day sense of the word, this staff must regard itself as working for me and that such instructions as I may give are to be carried out without them referring to Astrophore.*

Though Welles may have simply been reiterating his artistic control, the memo announced the return to a familiar pattern in his career. Always needing an enemy, real or perceived, with whom he could create conflict and distrust, Welles had acquired a new Judas. First it had been his new production partner. Now it was Deschamps.

After *Paper Moon* made a profit of nearly $20 million for the Directors Company in 1973, Bogdanovich's partners took $300,000 apiece in accordance with the terms of their agreement. By August 1974, two more films had been made under their production company's banner: *Daisy Miller* and Coppola's critically acclaimed *The Conversation*, which turned a profit of only $2 million. Friedkin, meanwhile, was making *The Exorcist* at Warner Bros. and hadn't produced a thing.

This wasn't what Bludhorn imagined. Everything Yablans had predicted was now becoming a reality. Before the year was over, the Directors Company was dead, undone by infighting, ego, and greed.

While Bogdanovich learned about artistic suffering, Welles was in Paris formalizing his agreement with Astrophore and accepting a deal in which they would cover the missing $150,000 and deposit it (as well as an additional $150,000) in an account to which Orson and Avenel, his Liechtenstein-based partnership with Oja, would have access. Meanwhile, in accordance with their levels of investment, it was determined that Avenel would receive 74 percent of any profits from the film, with the remainder going to Astrophore. Finally, Welles consented to submitting a production budget to his partners by September 1, 1974.

With financing in place, he briefly softened toward Deschamps, telling Antoine that the editing team had worked "heroically" in the face of woeful understaffing and insufficient equipment. He had even developed empathy for Deschamps and Arnaud Petit: In a memo to Antoine written on August 11, he requested more editors, expressing his concern that "it might be impossible to get assistants—really good ones—at short notice at this time of year, unless we are prepared to pay money to them which will represent an embarrassment to Yves and Arnaud who are chief editors and are working for low salaries."

In that vein, Welles closed the month in good humor and self-awareness, sending Antoine another memo that began:

> *Whatever cause I may give you for complaint, I am certain that you cannot object to a lack of interesting diversity in the subject matter of these memos. I am addressing you now, not on the subject of toilets [as he'd done in prior memos] but on dwarves and midgets.*

Welles had meant it back in Carefree when he said he would need midgets, but now he wanted dwarves for Hannaford's entourage. Most of them would be shot in Los Angeles and Spain, but he might need a few in Orvilliers. So he asked Antoine to price out the cost of hiring three or four French dwarves while being careful to define the qualities that differentiated them from midgets.

"I prefer dwarves to midgets (for movie purposes, I mean)," Orson wrote. "A dwarf in the English language means a distorted, short legged creature. . . . A midget is perfectly formed but simply very small in size."

Norman Foster had been right. There always was a purpose.

Things became less lighthearted by mid-September, as the insomniac Welles sent memo upon memo complaining about the editing crew.

Incensed, he bitched about their work ethic, even though they'd been logging twelve-hour days and working weekends for nearly three months.

But the die was cast, and Welles began sending memos to Antoine and Boushehri detailing Deschamps's supposed failures and asking that he be fired. Simultaneously, he was writing memos to the editor explaining the work he wanted him to complete.

Finally cutting off all direct communication, Welles had a secretary sit between him and Deschamps at LTC so she could transmit messages from one to the other, despite their physical proximity. Although Deschamps initially thought, "If he wants to work that way, okay," he quickly found it unbearable.

"It was very difficult," Deschamps recalled. "Because he was the master of the game."

Despite the tension, however, Deschamps continued staying late to watch footage so he could knit together some coherent narrative and understand the film. At the same time, Welles continued sending memos to Antoine asking for his editor's head.

Believing that Welles was just blowing off steam, Antoine remained calm as he spent nine pages venting frustration about his lack of progress and the ways Astrophore had failed him. It was this, he claimed, that had created his current predicament: living in a cold, wet home with no hot water and—worse still—unable to find some of the Lilli Palmer footage.

"[This] makes me feel like a fool," Welles wrote. "In fact, to the extent that I have allowed the spirit of cooperation to blind me to the realities of the case, I am indeed a fool. What is worse, I am very nearly bankrupt." Ultimately, however, he still cared deeply about the work, writing that his "interest and excitement in our film remains, in spite of everything, intense enough to see me through these dark days."

Taking his lament in stride, Antoine didn't believe Welles wanted to fire Deschamps. So while he continued providing direction to his editor through memos and intermediaries, Welles also sought his dismissal via letters to Antoine and Boushehri. Yet each time they asked when he'd like Deschamps to leave, there was no reply.

The dysfunction continued until Welles upped the ante by taking an editing table to Orvilliers so that he could work at home while sending a courier to LTC with instructions for the cutters, creating yet another barrier between himself and the editing team.

Then, in October, Deschamps received a memo intended for Antoine and Boushehri that asked, "Yves is still there?" He called Antoine and asked, "What's the story? Orson fired me and you didn't tell me?"

"Oh, it's just a game," she explained.

"For me it's not a game," Deschamps replied, and headed to Orvilliers on a cold fall day with plans to confront Welles. He arrived only to be told that Orson didn't want to see him, but Deschamps wouldn't leave. Staging a sit-in, he plopped down in the doorway and refused to move until he could speak to Welles.

As the day turned colder, a concerned Oja brought Deschamps hot soup and implored him to leave. "You can't stay," she said sympathetically. "It's too cold."

"No," he replied. "I will stay until he talks to me."

Then, as night fell and turned into early morning, Deschamps heard the door open and saw Orson in a white robe.

"Yves, go back to Paris," Orson pleaded. "Please, please, please go back. I beg you, go back. I beg you, please."

"But, Orson, I have to talk to you," Deschamps said.

"I understand," Welles replied. "You see me. I talked to you. Now go back to Paris."

Still master of the game, Orson closed the door and Deschamps returned to Paris, where he continued working on the film and sent a letter addressing each of Orson's complaints. After offering his resignation, Deschamps told Welles he'd enjoyed working together and was sorry the feeling wasn't mutual.

Soon after he finally left, Deschamps realized it was impossible to stay angry at Orson. "He was an adorable person," the editor recalled. "He was able to look you in the eyes and tell you something he perfectly well knew was untrue; that you knew was untrue; and that he knew you knew was untrue. But he was saying it as the absolute truth and you had to believe it. If you didn't, you would look like a perfect jerk, because you can't know what his eyes were like at that moment. He was a poor little boy, four or five years old, trying to make you believe his story."

Over the time he worked for Welles, Deschamps had stayed late and watched enough footage that he now felt he understood the movie—perhaps all too well. One of the evenings when he'd remained at LTC to view a few reels—and while still embroiled in his drama with Welles—he saw a scene in which Cameron Mitchell's character, Zimmie, is fired but told he still needs to attend the party and help arrange dummies around Hannaford's ranch.

Watching that scene alone in the editing room, Deschamps had a revelation. "Oh, my God, it's exactly my situation," he thought. "He fires me, but he wants me to keep working."

Editing with Orson, Deschamps had met an artist for whom there weren't any limits at a time in his own life when he believed he had no limits either. It was hard to leave the excitement of that environment, even when it was toxic, as it expanded his world. But in nearly nine months with Welles, Deschamps also learned something that Orson couldn't accept. In life and film, there actually are boundaries.

"I had seen the limit to madness, or my limit to what I thought was madness," Deschamps said. "I wasn't angry, but I didn't want to become crazy."

Stafford Repp was the first cast member to die, suffering a cardiac arrest in Los Angeles on November 5, 1974. Though he was best known as Chief O'Hara, Repp's *Variety* obituary noted that he left behind a wife, five children, and two grandkids and was working on the "as yet unreleased Orson Welles pic, *The Other Side of the Wind.*"

One morning a month or so after Repp's death, the staff arrived at LTC to find everything gone: The ends, the positive, the negative, and the print had vanished. Nothing had been left behind.

Having removed them the prior evening with Graver, Welles was taking his materials to Rome, where he intended to work with Marie-Sophie Dubus, who'd helped him cut *F for Fake* and whom he trusted in the face of perceived betrayal.

In Italy, they put together a number of sequences Orson intended to show in Hollywood at a February 1975 AFI Life Achievement Award ceremony in his honor. The scenes, he believed, could be used to sell the picture to a room that would be filled with producers, studio execs, and other financiers.

Though she'd worked with Welles before, Dubus said their time in Rome was the most important editing experience of her life. The footage, she said, was already so "smashing, rich, and abounding in detail" that Dubus felt as if they were starting with something that was ready to be shown in a theater.

But Orson was never happy with a cutting before he'd tried every option. With Dubus, he passed through endless takes of each sequence and shot. One day they'd cut a scene together only to undo it the next, always seeking new and better ways to construct the visuals and narrative.

Eventually informed of his whereabouts, Antoine visited Orson toward the end of his stay in Rome, where he'd edited in privacy, without the paranoid distractions that had overwhelmed him in France. Free of producers and working with a single cutter, Welles knew his efforts in Italy were critical. Though he'd scoffed at the 1971 Oscar, he had every intention of attending the AFI's ceremony for its third annual Life Achievement Award, which had been previously given to a dying John Ford and an elderly, semi-retired Jimmy Cagney.

Though Welles may have seen it as another attempt to retire him, the showman in him knew the value of having a captive audience in the ballroom and on national television (CBS). He would utilize the show for his own purposes, which would include revealing his comeback film and attracting end money that would solve both his professional and his personal problems. After that—as he'd hoped in 1970—Orson could reclaim the kind of career he so richly deserved.

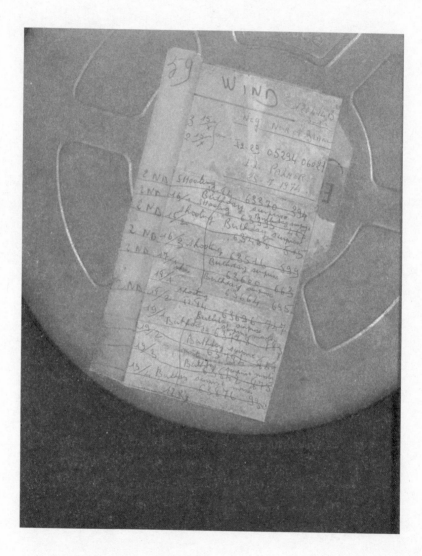

ACT THREE

1975–1985

Who do I have to fuck to get out of this picture?
　　　　　—ORSON WELLES, DURING A MOMENT
　　　　　　　OF ON-SET FRUSTRATION IN 1975

1975

He was always respectful of the crew, right up until he fired us.

　　　　　—CREW MEMBER JACK EPPS JR.

━━━━━━━━━━━━━━━━━━

The beginning of the end, as is sometimes the case, wasn't a moment of darkness or impending doom. Rather, it was a time of hope.

It was the beginning of an end that would come neither swiftly nor in a gigantic explosion. Instead, it came gradually and continued into eternity.

The end began when a small committee from AFI met at the Beverly Hills Hotel to choose the recipient of their third Life Achievement Award. The options included everyone who wasn't Ford or Cagney. The group chose Welles because they believed his artistry had been superlative and that with the selection, they were making a significant statement about their organization.

"It was a way of saying we were serious about this award and that it wasn't going to be a popularity contest," said AFI founding director George Stevens Jr. "We made the choice on the grounds that it was a choice of great integrity."

Though the committee was pleased with its decision, others were not, including several AFI members and certain factions of the Hollywood press. Kirk Douglas was outraged, and his indignation was seconded by everyone from Henry Hathaway to columnist Marilyn Beck and one of the editors at *Variety*, where McBride was now a reporter. All shared the belief that Orson's body of work boiled down to *Citizen Kane* and a bunch of films that might have been.

Joining the chorus of dissent was *Patton* producer Frank McCarthy, who expressed his feelings to the event co-chairs in a letter stating that he couldn't understand why Welles was receiving the award, when one compared him with Darryl Zanuck, Jack Warner, and other deserving Hollywood titans.

But then there was William Wyler, a potential recipient who went out of his way to congratulate Orson, as well as many staunch defenders, including Charlton Heston and Frank Sinatra, the latter of whom acted as master of ceremonies for the February 9 award show, which aired a few days later on CBS. And of course there was Bogdanovich, who fielded the call from Stevens asking if Welles would even accept the award.

Though he was excited about the opportunity afforded by the AFI ceremony, Welles had initially been deeply conflicted when the honor had been offered the prior year. Ultimately, however, he relented when Bogdanovich assured him that Stevens's goal was to show that Orson was still making pictures and not headed out to pasture.

It's hard to be the king.
(Courtesy of Mike Ferris)

John Huston, as Hannaford,
shooting at dummies of his
leading man. (Courtesy of
Mike Ferris)

Mercedes McCambridge, who said she'd jump off the Empire State Building if Orson told her to. (Courtesy of Mike Ferris)

HAPPY BIRTHDAY JAKE

Joe McBride staring into the bus that takes everyone from the studio to Hannaford's party. (Courtesy of Mike Ferris)

The Slingman House, built directly into the rocks of Carefree, Arizona. (Courtesy of Mike Ferris)

A bread truck that Orson used to create a forced perspective shot. (Courtesy of Frank Marshall)

Gary Graver, Orson, and Oja Kodar in Carefree (Courtesy of Frank Marshall)

"He wanted me to . . . play it like we were talking about our relationship," Peter Bogdanovich said. (Courtesy of Larry Jackson)

Three great directors at the same table. (Courtesy of Larry Jackson)

Welles shooting on the old MGM backlot. (Courtesy of Frank Marshall)

Orson by the pool with Gary, Oja, and Peter. (Courtesy of Larry Jackson)

Old hands Stafford Repp, Dan Tobin, and Norman Foster standing; seated are Huston, Orson, and local teenager Cathy Lucas, who turned in an unexpectedly wonderful performance. (Courtesy of Larry Jackson)

The rumors that there was "no script" were untrue. However, ever-changing dialogue had script supervisors tearing their hair out. (Courtesy of Larry Jackson)

Huston, Welles, and Bogdanovich at Southwestern Studio. (Courtesy of Larry Jackson)

Bogdanovich as a young director like himself; Gregory Sierra as Jack Simon (based on John Milius), and Susan Strasberg in back, as a critic similar to Pauline Kael. (Courtesy of Larry Jackson)

The embodiment of a legendary director in the high style of a great adventurer. (Courtesy of Mike Ferris)

Despite agreeing to the honor, Orson wasn't cooperative. Spending nearly all of January in Europe, Welles had Bogdanovich act as his go-between with Stevens, who was growing accustomed to calls that began, "George, Orson isn't happy."

The biggest source of that unhappiness was the choice of film clips they'd show at the ceremony and Orson's insistence that the only unfinished work to be shown that evening would be from *The Other Side of the Wind*.

When Bogdanovich relayed the initial message from Stevens that they'd also like to show *Don Quixote* and *The Deep*, Orson immediately accused him of conspiring with AFI. "He thought I was colluding with them and attacked me," said Bogdanovich, whose *At Long Last Love* was released weeks after the AFI show. "I was trying to do something good for him. . . . [But] he thought I was being duplicitous and going behind his back."

Orson's displeasure, however, was rooted in more than anxiety over which clips to show.

After editing in Rome during December, Welles returned to Orvilliers. Though happy with the scenes he'd prepared with Dubus, he still didn't feel they were good enough. But, more significant, Welles was suffering angst over his finances—which were in a shambles and causing him to direct much of his ire at Antoine and Astrophore, as evidenced by his reaction to an innocuous January 4 telex from Antoine to which he issued a four-page response demanding that she butt out of the editing process and explaining why he went to Rome.

> *I was finally forced to realize that my judgments in these [editing] matters had, for some reason, less weight with you than your own more or less uneducated opinion and such advice as you may have been able to obtain from the inadequately experienced cutters, whom you were keeping under salary. Thus, since I could not, after repeated efforts, prevail upon you to remove the team*

*from the film, I had no choice but to remove the film from the
cutters.*

When Antoine read the telex she phoned "in a state of extreme indignation." This caused Welles to write again, explaining that it had all
been a misunderstanding based on a bungled call between Oja and an
assistant. "I was certainly wrong to reproach you for something you had
not done," he admitted. Then he went on to detail all of his *legitimate*
complaints, most of which resulted from Antoine's apparent lack of attention when reading his memos and concurrent failure to decipher their
"precise meaning."

"When, to quote myself, 'I record my distress,' it should be obvious
that I mean what I say: I am quite simply recording my distress," Welles
wrote. "I do not see how you can possibly translate that into a personal
reproach."

Yet the actual cause of the distress had less to do with editing and
Antoine's inattentiveness than it did with the fact that Welles was nearly
broke and deeply concerned about what might happen because of his
tax problems. He had hoped to refill his coffers that winter with an eight-
day acting job on a film shooting in Athens. However, the financing for
that movie fell apart at the last minute, leaving him low on funds and
still in fear of revenue agents.

"I am worried sick about the California tax situation," he wrote Arnold Weissberger in January. "This will have to be paid some day, but
just as obviously that cannot begin to happen until I earn some money. . . .
[There is] no possible question of my paying even a token sum."

But, worse yet, Orson's feared that he might be confronted by a tax
agent or process server some time during the AFI event. As a result,
he offered Weissberger several options as to how they could deal with
that possibility, including private detectives hired to head off anyone
with a subpoena; telling AFI that he was being whisked away to a film
set immediately after his speech; or faking a "diplomatic illness" that
made him unable to appear but seemed likely to "a) create a scandal;
and b) create the rumor that I am dying."

To some extent, Orson had played a large part in his own dire financial situation because of his continuing refusal to sign a final contract or agree to the terms of his own compensation. This was compounded in late January, when he threatened to not attend the AFI ceremony as a way of pushing back against a recent contract offer and asking for money without any formal obligation on his part.

"Surely you understand by now that I'm becoming seriously convinced of the fact that my commitment to my own work and loyalty to it has been, and is being, exploited," Welles wrote to Boushehri. "What is seriously needed right at this moment is some solid proof of goodwill on your part."

Two days later, Boushehri's Paris bank transferred $100,000 into an account held by Avenel.

Orson didn't arrive in Los Angeles until three days before the AFI show. Also in attendance were Antoine and Boushehri, the latter being hosted by 20th Century–Fox producer Elmo Williams, his partner in the newly formed Ibex Films.

Ibex and Astrophore were both part of the shah's multiple efforts to modernize Iran. In the case of the film industry, the goal was to turn the country into an Eastern Hollywood. With Ibex in Los Angeles and Astrophore in Paris, Boushehri was set to produce a screen version of James Michener's *Caravans* that would be shot in Iran, and he was in talks to make films with John Boorman and Elia Kazan.

Boushehri's visit received significant attention in *Variety*, where he'd also placed a full-page ad trumpeting Orson's two most recent films. "Ready" was *F for Fake*, while *The Other Side of the Wind* was billed as "Nearing Completion." This, they hoped, would set the stage for distribution and financing deals after the AFI ceremony. Antoine had already scheduled a number of postshow screenings, and Universal wanted to see footage the following Monday.

Meanwhile, on the day of the event, Huston and Stevens were supervising preparations in the ballroom at the Century Plaza Hotel, where they were receiving frequent calls from Bogdanovich with last minute demands from Welles. They honored each of Orson's desires until Welles himself phoned with a request (the details of which Stevens cannot recall) that was unreasonable under most circumstances and impossible with the show just hours away.

Using his magnificent voice to ask a favor and also express his disappointment, Welles said something about how they were giving him an award for his accomplishments as an entertainer but seemingly believed they had better instincts about how to put on a show than their honoree. Underlying every word was the implicit threat that Welles might not show up if he didn't get his way.

But in the middle of the conversation, the electricity in the ballroom went out, leaving Stevens in darkness with a dead phone in his hand, thinking, "Oh, God. Now we've really done it."

During the few minutes they were without power, Bogdanovich had been calling desperately, only to receive no answer. When the lights came back, another call rang through.

"George, why did you hang up on Orson?" Bogdanovich asked.

The power failure had removed Orson's bargaining power, and the tables were turned. Talking directly to Stevens, Welles quickly agreed to the arrangements, lest they decide to forgo honoring him that evening.

Twelve hundred people gathered for the $125-a-plate dinner. There had been trouble getting several anti-Welles stars to attend, but that didn't matter, as the crowd included Rock Hudson, Groucho Marx, Jack Lemmon, Natalie Wood, Ryan O'Neal, Janet Leigh, Rosalind Russell, Jack Nicholson, and many other Hollywood legends and power players.

The ballroom itself was decorated with giant blowups of Orson that hung behind the stage. Rendered in black-and-white, they showed Welles in different roles; at different ages; and at vastly different sizes. There he was, huge, bearded, and hearty as Falstaff; then young and handsome as Michael O'Hara in *The Lady from Shanghai;* domineering as Charles Foster Kane; and despicable as the bloated Quinlan in *Touch of Evil*.

Before that backdrop, Charlton Heston delivered a wonderful introduction, after which the Nelson Riddle Orchestra played the theme from *The Third Man* and doors at the back of the room opened to reveal a smiling Orson, who entered to a standing ovation before taking a seat on the dais between Paola and Beatrice. Oja was nowhere to be found.

Settling into a specially made, black velour–covered chair constructed of two-by-two-inch steel tubing (designed for fear a normal chair might collapse), Welles watched as the lights dimmed and they showed a montage that included *Citizen Kane, The Lady from Shanghai, The Third Man,* and, ironically, the scene from *Touch of Evil* where Marlene Dietrich tells Quinlan that he doesn't have any future.

Then there were the tributes: Johnny Carson, Ingrid Bergman, Joseph Cotten, Edgar Bergen and Charlie McCarthy, Peter Bogdanovich, and Frank Sinatra, who sang a schlock version of "The Lady Is a Tramp" that began:

There's no one like him,
Nobody at all.
There have been legends,
But none quite as tall.
What if his girth,
Is—like—wall-to-wall;
That's why this gentleman is a champ.

As he listened to that dreadful song, and throughout the evening, whenever the camera caught Orson he was either bursting into laughter, looking on thoughtfully, or showing heartfelt emotion—whatever the moment required. Because on the evening of February 9, 1975, Orson Welles had come to play ball.

After Sinatra, George Stevens introduced Welles with a speech contextualizing the predicament of Orson's career and the thankless stature of *an artist*. After telling the crowd that movies are too often judged by profit rather than cinematic quality, Stevens said the award was for films that had stood the test of time—films such as Orson's, which were frequently made under difficult circumstances and in the spirit of creative expression rather than for the purpose of making money.

"Tonight you have seen inspired films that have met that test, and remembering the stormy seas Orson Welles has weathered in his career, hear what the writer John Ruskin said a hundred years ago, in noting that many of the most enduring works in art and literature are never paid for," Stevens said. "'How much,' he asked 'do you think Homer got for his *Iliad* or Dante for his *Paradiso*? Only bitter bread and salt and walking up and down other people's stairs.'"

But tonight Orson would be repaid with more than bitter bread. Instead, he was to be recognized for his "courage and the intensity of his personal vision."

Welles "reminds us that it is better to live one day as a lion than a hundred years as a sheep . . . ," Stevens said before closing with, "A great man never reminds us of others—Mr. Orson Welles. . . ."

Orson rose from his seat and steamed toward the stage like a locomotive and arrived at the podium nearly breathless. Genuinely moved, he stood, smoothing his beard and pushing his hair back while everyone applauded. And when they sat, Welles launched into a clever, emotional, and risky speech.

"My father once told me that the art of receiving a compliment is of all things the sign of a civilized man. And he died soon afterwards, leaving my education in this important matter sadly incomplete. I'm only glad that on this, the occasion of the rarest compliment he ever could have dreamed of, he isn't here to see his son so publicly at a loss. . . . My heart is full. With a full heart—with all of it—I thank you."

Then he spoke of contrarieties, quoting Samuel Johnson and applying the word to himself, yet not explaining that contrariety was at the center of his life and work. Contrariety was the tension that fed his art. It was Falstaff and Hal; the many facets of Charlie Kane; and both the magnificence and the obliviousness of the Ambersons. Everyone, he believed, was made up of polar opposites—and living between them made us who we are.

He used Johnson's comments to explain that while he might be considered difficult or temperamentally unlike other directors, that was also one of the qualities that made him Orson Welles. He was a dying breed, the man and filmmaker who chose to "trudge stubbornly along the lonely rocky road" in a "conglomerated world," in which he compared himself (and others like him) with a family farm that is unable to keep up with corporate agriculture.

"What we do come up with has no special right to call itself better. It's just different," Welles said. "No, if there's any excuse for us at all, it's that we're simply following the old tradition of the maverick . . . This honor I can only accept in the name of all the mavericks. And also as a tribute to the generosity of all the rest of you—to the givers—the ones with fixed addresses."

In just a few minutes, Welles had turned himself into a humble, handmade filmmaker who would suffer for his art because he was the most American of all human archetypes—the independent; the rebel; the maverick. Oh, and he tossed a bone to the money people with bogus sentiment that was still somehow disarming.

Explaining his maverick ways, Welles said that "some of the necessities to which I am a slave are different from yours. As a director, for instance, I pay myself out of my acting jobs. I use my own work to subsidize my work. In other words, I'm crazy."

The room exploded in laughter. He continued.

"But not crazy enough to pretend to be free. But it's a fact that many of the movies you've seen tonight could never have been made otherwise. Or, if otherwise—well, they might have been better. But certainly they wouldn't have been mine. . . ."

Offering a toast that sought to unite the artists and the money people, he said, "[Let's] drink together to what really matters to us all—to our crazy and beloved profession. To the movies—to good movies—to every possible kind."

That was where he probably should have stopped, in a moment of triumph, brotherhood, and goodwill. In six minutes he'd engendered sympathy for himself as an elderly orphan, starving artist, and misunderstood maverick genius. He'd proudly given Hollywood a subtle but firm kick in the ass while showing enough humility and charm to set himself up for the afterparty, where he'd have a few drinks, smoke cigars, and gather a rapt audience to whom he could casually mention needing end money for his remarkable new project. That's what many asked him to do, including Jaglom, who said to just accept the award. Welles, however, responded by saying that he would "throw himself on the mercy of everyone in attendance."

Which was why Orson continued. Despite having already shown two scenes from *The Other Side of the Wind* (including Hannaford's arrival at the party) he was setting up one more, which would be the final image of the evening.

During the party clip—where Pat McMahon introduces himself to Hannaford as Marvin P. Fassbender—the audience's laughter matched the rhythm of the scene. But now there was a sense of arch intent—as Orson's mood, voice, and eyes all seemed barbed somehow. This time the humor would be specific and uncomfortable, as he showed the two-minute scene with Billy and Max David watching Hannaford's film.

"The scene that you're going to be seeing takes place in a projection room. And waiting there is the capital 'B' big studio boss . . . [And] one of Jake Hannaford's stooges is trying to sell the unfinished movie that Jake is making, for which he needs 'end money.'" Welles looked up, smiling. "[The stooge] is supposed to explain the plot, as far as he can remember it, and incidentally to sell the movie to Mr. Big, who is a handsome young studio head, a former actor, who by the way bears no resemblance to anyone—unless you insist."

The fact that the studio boss was supposed to be Robert Evans was lost on no one. Worse, however, the sequence reflects the chaotic state of Hannaford's film and finances in a way that could be seen as eerily autobiographical, given that Orson also had an unfinished comeback movie for which he was seeking end money.

After the ceremony ended, Welles and Sinatra hopped on an elevator to the party, where Jack Lemmon was playing piano and everyone was eagerly anticipating the honoree's arrival. Then, almost poetically, as they waited for the doors to close, a man in a tuxedo reached his arm inside the elevator and slapped a subpoena on Orson's chest, just as he'd feared. In response, Orson casually stuck the piece of paper in his pocket and went to the party.

What happened in the days following the award show is hard to pin down. Two Welles biographies quote Dominique Antoine saying that Astrophore received one offer of end money but turned it down, confident there would be better deals. But there weren't. And by the time she left Los Angeles, it was clear that her post-AFI meetings had been fruitless.

The identity of whoever made the offer has never been revealed, and there is much reason to believe there may have been no offer at all. More recently, Antoine said she was unable to generate interest of any kind and doesn't recall anyone who considered providing end money.

"We thought we were going to have offers, and none came," she said. "None."

Orson, however, always claimed that there had been an offer, a good one worth $2 million, which allegedly was made by legendary agent and producer Freddie Fields.

And although the offer from Fields may well have been real, its potential existence was mentioned primarily by Orson in the early 1980s and contradicts not only Antoine, but also Bogdanovich, who can't remember a single person or studio expressing the desire to put up end money.

"That was the horrible irony of the whole thing," he said. "Everyone applauded wildly, but no one came up with a cent."

Setting up temporary headquarters in a suite at the Westwood Marquis, Welles hired new personal and production assistants, whom he'd summon to do everything from photocopying script pages and taking dictation to purchasing cases of Cuban cigars in the back of a restaurant and bringing him food from Kentucky Fried Chicken and Señor Pico.

Among the new hires was Cindy Steinway, who knew almost nothing about Welles when she arrived on his floor at the hotel to find the hallway filled with smoke, the door ajar, and Orson waiting for her in a stained bathrobe.

After that, Steinway was thrown headfirst into the chaotic whirlpool of his life and began suffering a condition she called "Welles anxiety" brought on by her boss's habit of never telling her when work would start each day. Instead, he'd just call at whatever time he deemed appropriate and say, "It's seven A.M.! Where are you!?"

Once she received the call each day and stepped into Orson's world, Steinway was completely his. But, unaware of his legend, she recalled seeing a different man from the director who was worshipped by so many, including her husband, Jack Epps, who joined the crew around the same time. The Welles that Steinway worked for seemed enormously lonely and stuck in his own head. As best as she could tell, he was putting on an endless performance in the role of "Orson Welles," which seemed to be taking a colossal toll.

"It was like he pulled the wool over everyone's eyes at all times," Steinway said. "He was just continuing the show. It was how he survived."

Then, one evening, however, Steinway saw what happened when the show stopped. While delivering a staggeringly large amount of takeout food to his room, Steinway stopped for a moment and noticed the table, every inch of which was literally covered with pills and bottles of medication. Holding the gigantic dinner and staring at the medication, Steinway couldn't hide her astonished expression. Noticing this, Orson became embarrassed and vulnerable, dropping the façade for just a moment and screaming, *"Do you think I want to live like this!?"*

But he had no choice. Living that way, putting on that show, and being larger than life was what people expected. It was what allowed him to check into luxury hotels with no money and request that all bills be sent to Weissberger. Playing Orson Welles made it possible for the crew to tromp in for lunch at the hotel buffet and rack up a huge tab before he was finally asked to leave. Simply put, being "Orson Welles" was his currency.

Welles's next move was back to Bogdanovich's house, where he'd lived the prior spring and which was available while Peter promoted *At Long Last Love,* a six-million-dollar musical at Fox starring Cybill Shepherd and Burt Reynolds, in which they performed several Cole Porter songs. Seeking the look and feel of a 1930s film, Bogdanovich shot in color on hugely expensive sets where his actors wore black-and-white costumes and performed their musical numbers live.

Released March 1, the film took a critical and financial beating which in turn gave journalists the opportunity to bash Bogdanovich, who subsequently became the subject of articles asking how and why it had all fallen apart.

With the house to himself, Welles spent much of March and April shooting party scenes. He brought in extras from local film and art schools, placing them in an Altmanesque setting in which a camera was always rolling but no one was quite sure where it was or when they were being filmed. "I felt like, 'Wow, this is Hollywood.' Similar to the Hollywood of *Shampoo,*" said director Cameron Crowe, who was still in his teens and had just moved to Los Angeles. "We all felt like we were part of something special—perhaps a new masterpiece."

In the morning, Orson could usually be found at a table on Bogdanovich's lawn, cranking out new scenes and dialogue for that day's shoot. Welles, it appeared, was constructing and reconstructing the film in his head, despite having written to Antoine in mid-April to explain that through "a tour de force of truly gigantic proportions," he was about to complete principal dialogue photography. But at the same time, he was adding new characters, including one named Osawatomie Duluth, a gay friend of Zarah Valeska's (based, in part, on Truman Capote) who despises Jake.

Shooting day after day, Welles churned through innumerable extras, and one day the group that answered the cattle call included Bob Random, who hid from the director by blending in with the students and would-be actors. When they finally wrapped and the crowd grew thinner as each extra departed, Random stood, waiting for Welles to recognize him. Then, when everyone else was gone, Welles finally noticed Random and walked toward him with a broad smile. Giving the actor a gigantic hug, he explained that the film was nearly finished. It was almost done. They were so close.

That hug and those words dissolved any of Random's anger and disappointment, sending him home completely disarmed, appeased, and unaware that this was the last time he'd ever see or hear from Orson Welles.

In his April 12 memo to Antoine, Welles detailed the few sequences he still needed to shoot and summed up recent delays caused by the film lab, cold weather in California, the health of older actors, the misfortunes in Arizona, and everything else that held up production.

"It has meant the most exquisitely torturous labor with which I have ever been faced," Welles wrote. "The end of it all is that I am now finishing scenes begun long ago involving sometimes as many as nine characters of which never more than three or four characters were ever available to me at one time and—what is even more horrendous—having to change the cast and even the characterization in midstream, inventing new characters to take the place of actors dead or unavailable and finding totally new solutions in visual and narrative terms . . . What will be the end result artistically? Will the desperation behind this crazy patchwork be revealed for what it is? . . . Is it even possible to hope that the result has been an improvement, even an enrichment? At this juncture I can only state that I feel more hopes than apprehensions."

Wanting to shoot in Los Angeles rather than Europe, Welles quickly received $10,000 from Antoine, who wanted to know how much more would be needed to complete filming.

Thus began a series of correspondence that demonstrated the financial disarray and confusion within the production, including an April 16 telex from Welles telling Antoine that his request for $25,000 made earlier that day was under the mistaken assumption that it would be enough to complete principal photography. Graver, however, had just informed him it was sufficient only to cover outstanding salaries and debts.

A huge problem, according to one crew member, was that the film was a "cash business" that became crippled every time Astrophore asked for a budget or receipts. This was exacerbated by a) the fact that money from Iran, via Paris, never seemed to arrive on time, and Welles was constantly forced to ask for the same funds over and over and b) Orson's apparent lack of a bank account, which meant that he relied on Graver and others to receive transfers, deposit them into their accounts, convert everything to cash, and then put that cash in a drawer wherever Welles was living.

Though the money would eventually arrive, Welles was constantly juggling things to keep the production going. As a result, they shot at Bogdanovich's house and Producers Studio with the tenuous financial state of the picture always in the background and an atmosphere in which Steinway said that "we never knew if we'd have film the next day."

That desperation could lead to inventiveness, and Welles thrived on creating out of necessity, such as when he instructed Graver to lie on a rug with his camera while being pulled around Bogdanovich's living room to execute a tracking shot of Paul Stewart and Tonio Selwart. Welles called it "the poor man's dolly" and said he'd learned it from Jean Renoir.

At another point, however, a florist refused to leave Bogdanovich's house until Welles paid him in cash.

Thus, in late April, Welles wrote Antoine that they would be completely finished in three weeks, but he was "presently most embarrassed by lack of cash."

Welles finished shooting the extras in late April but suffered a setback when Graver was hospitalized for exhaustion, brought on by working sixteen hours a day six days a week, while spending his other time either trying to earn a living or keeping Orson company. But he loved to shoot, he loved Orson, and he'd given his life to this movie. It was the project that would get him out of biker films and pornos—and because of this, Graver kept going until one day his body simply gave out while filming a scene near Bogdanovich's pool. Graver literally collapsed, tipping over while his camera kept rolling. Meanwhile, in the spirit of the production, Stringer instinctively caught the expensive camera while his close friend crumpled to the ground. It's exactly what Gary would have wanted.

Describing the situation to Antoine, Welles said Graver was under pressure from work on another production and suffering financial hardships that Welles hadn't known about until "[Gary] was taken in a state of coma to the hospital." By the end of the year, those hardships would include Graver's arrest on a felony charge related to unpaid production expenses (Orson got him off) and, eventually, the stress of another broken marriage.

Recuperating from extreme exhaustion in the hospital, Graver was deluged with calls from Orson, which alternated between sympathetic, paternal inquiries about his health and questions about when he'd be released, when he could come to work, and what needed doing once he was back. And though he was supposed to continue resting after leaving the hospital, Graver, still quite weak, was back on the set almost immediately.

In late April, Bogdanovich rented director William Wellman's Beverly Hills home at 628 North Hillcrest for Orson, who moved in and quickly set up an editing operation while he also continued shooting on a soundstage at Producers Studio, where his work seemed precise and purposeful. Meanwhile, still filming at Bogdanovich's, which Orson continued using as a location, there was a casual, almost haphazard atmosphere that evoked the feeling they might be shooting an endless home movie.

"It was like a faucet got turned off and it didn't feel like we were making progress," said Jack Epps Jr., now an associate professor at USC's School of Cinematic Arts. "There was no 'What are we doing next?' He kept building it and building it—just to keep his mind occupied."

Welles's mood became worse, however, on May 6, when he turned sixty and spent the day hiding in his room after the crew presented him with a birthday cake. That same day, he also received word that Boushehri would soon be taking several weeks off due to health problems and was leaving $60,000 with Antoine, who could send it to Welles at her discretion.

That figure had been determined without the benefit of a budget from Welles, who was still working without a final contract or director's fee. Since the prior September, Astrophore had been operating off Welles's rough estimates and with no projected completion date. According to Antoine, the refusal to agree on a salary was linked directly to Welles's need for complete autonomy, even if that need left him in financial trouble.

"If he agreed to his fee, then he had to agree to deliver the picture on a certain date," Antoine said. "He never agreed to any money because he wanted to keep his freedom."

Welles waited six days to respond to Boushehri, telexing him just as he was about to leave:

> *Deeply worried about your departure for six weeks. . . . There are fundamental issues to be solved between us all . . . If your plans cannot be changed, imperative that Dominique be given full authority to resolve all questions, otherwise there is no choice but to close down all work and await return. I would regret this*

even more than you since I have refused more than three hundred thousand dollars in jobs in order to keep working.

The following day, Boushehri responded that he'd be visiting Los Angeles in early June, but in the meantime Antoine was empowered to make financial decisions. "There is no question to think of stopping your work," he wrote. "The work you are doing is much too important . . . We are eager as you to finish *The Wind* and so close to the end."

Despite Boushehri's faith and the fact that Astrophore had sent him nearly $78,000 since February, Welles was feeling enormous pressure and released his tension early one morning at Bogdanovich's after an all-night shoot.

Wrapping around four A.M. and faced with two hours of cleanup, everyone groaned when Welles told them to be back at noon. Graver realized this was impossible and approached Welles to request a few extra hours for his overworked crew. The director's response came to be known as "the Friday Night Massacre" after he fired the entire crew, screamed, *"I can't work like this with everyone against me!!"* then stomped off, threatening to leave for Europe.

Welles never left, of course, and a few days later he began shooting again with Graver, Jacobson, Stringer, Race, and other stalwarts. But many who weren't full-time Welles people, such as Steinway and Epps, never came back and felt a sense of relief, while still retaining admiration for Orson as both an artist and a man. As Epps recalled, "Just having him look at me had been exciting."

Antoine arrived in Los Angeles a few days ahead of Boushehri for their June 3 dinner with Welles. Having transferred another $20,000 before leaving Paris, she was still asking for a budget as well as receipts to account for roughly half of the $98,000 provided by Astrophore since February.

Instead of a budget, Welles provided an itemized list of "Astrophore's indebtedness in Hollywood for various goods and services," much of which had been paid by Graver. The total of $53,186.10 included $15,000 in salaries, $15,000 for equipment rental, and $14,490 for location and living expenses owed to Bogdanovich, who paid Orson's rent on Hillcrest.

The bill also included $200 for one evening's rental of two dwarves.

What happened at the dinner died with Welles and Boushehri, but one thing is clear: Orson delivered yet another memo that required his partners' full attention and consideration before he would discuss it with them. The next day, he followed through, declining to meet until they'd had time to "study the memo with some care."

A few days later, Boushehri departed, leaving Antoine behind to meet with Welles. She was still there on June 16 when Welles sent a letter to her hotel explaining that he'd been editing in the garage, where there was no telephone. "So it occurs to me that I may have been missing some of your calls," he wrote, adding that unanticipated delays had "upset our latest budget calculation." Thus, he would need some time to get things in order and told Antoine she didn't need to wait around Hollywood.

Accustomed to this by now, Antoine was unfazed and knew she was being kept on hold for a budget that would never arrive. "He kept me waiting for weeks and weeks. It wasn't the first time," she said. "It was a mixture of games and to see how far he could go with me. It wasn't perverse. For him shooting a picture was like a dream, and why should he be asked to interrupt his dream for meetings?"

When she finally returned to Paris in late June, Antoine wrote Welles that producer Ray Stark had shown interest and implored him to come to France during the next ten days—since she believed that any delays by Welles could ruin a possible deal. "We are waiting for you," she told Welles, who'd mentioned his imminent departure in several letters. "We hope at the end of this week."

But he didn't arrive at the end of the week, the month, or even the summer. Instead, he disappeared.

———

"The moment my father thought something looked like it really would never happen, he'd walk away from it completely. That's how he dealt with his life," Beatrice Welles said. "If he hadn't dealt that way, the movie business would have killed him. It was his mode of survival. He'd move on to the next thing and never looked back. It was his way of excusing himself from something he couldn't deal with anymore or that he had had no control of."

And that, Beatrice recalls, is exactly what he did with *The Other Side of the Wind* during the summer of 1975. Though, in this case, he was simply excusing himself to regroup, rather than walking away. Because deep down, Orson knew that there was no way he could ever truly abandon *The Wind*.

Orson always had several projects either cooking in his mind, in discussion and negotiation with others, or otherwise floating in the ether. His mind couldn't handle a moment of being unoccupied, and since he never slept there was a great deal of room to think about what else he could be doing at any given time. Exhausted, confused, and not sure of his next move, Orson spent much of that summer focusing on one of those *other* projects, while he continued editing *The Other Side of the Wind* with a team of cutters at Wellman's home in Beverly Hills.

The project was *Sirhan Sirhan* (or *RFK Must Die*) and, according to Welles scholar Matthew Asprey Gear, a lead role in that film "could have been an easy $125,000 for two weeks' work, the kind of job Welles often accepted to bankroll his barely differentiated life and filmmaking." But, as Gear notes, "It didn't turn out that way."

Instead, the story of Orson's involvement with *Sirhan Sirhan*—which ran from roughly April 1975 until some time in November of the same year, when he officially removed himself (though his interest reemerged a few times thereafter)—reads like a brief, action-packed summary of the many aborted and unfinished projects (both known and unknown) with which he was engaged during the last two years of his career.

Slated to begin shooting in September 1975, the film was to co-star Welles, legendary running back turned actor Jim Brown, and Bogdanovich's close friend Sal Mineo as Kennedy's assassin, Sirhan Sirhan.

Documented thoroughly by Gear's lengthy article on the subject, this simple acting job became extraordinarily complicated over the summer and early fall, during which Orson: insisted on a complete overhaul of the script and dismissed the screenwriter's attempt at a quick rewrite; began working on his own version of the screenplay; sought and received approval over who would direct the movie (his choice, Joseph Sargent [*The Taking of Pelham One Two Three*] rejected the project over his doubts about its quality); offered to direct the film as a last resort and even had Gary hired as the cinematographer.

Then there was Oja, whom Welles introduced to the producers as a "newly emerged European star," in great demand across the pond, but unknown, at the moment, in the United States, where "she has no one else to speak for her." Without even remotely suggesting that she was his mistress, Orson said he was representing her out of necessity but was absolutely not her agent, nor was he connected to her in any way—other than the fact that she was the female lead in his film *The Other Side of the Wind*.

In an almost preposterous scene, Welles at one point "casually" showed the producers some footage of a naked Oja, after which she came downstairs "as if by coincidence" dressed to the nines.

Even after they discovered the true nature of Oja's relationship with Orson, the producers hired her for the part.

And finally there was the money. Orson's initial acting salary of $100,000 grew to $125,000. Then, according to producer Michael Selsman, when Orson went to work on the screenplay and offered to direct, it swelled to "$500,000 and twenty-five percent of the film" only to wind up at a "full fifty percent . . . and $700,000" when combined with Oja's salary. By that point Welles and Kodar's fees represented one third of the film's total budget.

For this reason and others, the film fell apart. Yet when all was said and done, nearly everyone involved had the same experience of being associated with Welles on a failed project.

"Naturally I was flattered that the great man wanted to work with me," said Selsman. "He was difficult but I really thought I was going to produce what would be Orson's last film—the only one he would complete before he died. I had a great time just being around him."

As noted, his involvement with *Sirhan Sirhan* didn't stop Welles from continuing to cut *The Wind*; however, that work was somewhat complicated by his efforts to avoid Antoine, Boushehri, and anyone else from Astrophore or Iran. At one point, according to production assistant Howard Grossman, he was told to send everyone home, unplug the phones, and buy a month's worth of supplies, after which Grossman and Oja desperately went through drawers of receipts, trying to account for their expenditures. Welles, meanwhile, peered through the blinds every time a car drove by, just to make certain that nobody from Iran was in the driveway.

Simultaneously, changes were taking place in Iran that had a significant impact on Astrophore. With the need to quell unrest among his subjects, the shah's modernization plans became less important—and as a result, Boushehri and Antoine were no longer working without supervision. Though they'd always been operating under the auspices of government agencies, Astrophore was now being overseen by Iranian bankers and the Film Industry Development Corporation of Iran (FIDCI), where director and producer Bahman Farmanara was particularly interested in *The Other Side of the Wind*.

Recalling the summer of 1975, Farmanara said, "[Orson] disappeared for forty days in the middle of the shoot. When he reappeared, he claimed he was ill and couldn't publicize it because no one would insure him on future films."

Not knowing how to find the director of their high-profile project did little to enhance Boushehri's and Antoine's credibility with the financiers back home.

By late summer or early fall, Welles was once again living at Bogdanovich's, where he was shooting Japanese whiskey commercials for roughly $10,000 a day while continuing to work with three assistants on several sequences he'd been editing for months.

One scene, from Hannaford's movie-within-the-movie, had Oja changing her wet clothes in the bathroom of a bar. Walking through the door, down a hall, and past some mirrors before entering the washroom, Oja goes to the sink, takes off her raincoat, undresses, and then reaches into a duffel for dry clothes. Seeing the hands and feet of a couple having sex in a stall, she puts on her clothes and leaves.

Given that the scene had been shot several times over the course of five years, one editor, Steve Ecclesine, said that Oja's age changed depending on the footage they were working with. As they cut it together, she might enter the bathroom at thirty-two, walk past mirrors at twenty-nine, pick up her clothes at thirty-three, and then be twenty-nine again standing at the sink.

Strange as that was, Orson's perfectionism guided the way he cut this fairly mundane scene by using five hundred edits in a four-minute sequence. He was breaking all of the rules and ignoring the idea that a cut had to be motivated. Instead, he was going from wide to close for no reason and employing a completely new method of putting a scene together.

"I remember thinking, 'This is so innovative, I've never seen anything like it,'" said Rick Shore, who edited another scene for Welles at the time. "It was like a Picasso painting where you just had to look at everything differently."

Shore said Welles worked like Ansel Adams in the darkroom, where the goal was to get everything you could onto the negative and create the richest-possible image. Sitting behind Shore, Welles had him make cut after cut, breaking down the footage into bits and pieces but not placing them in any order until the end.

Still, brilliant as he was in the editing room, Welles was taking things that could be done simply and making them more and more complicated, with elements and nuances that only he would ever notice.

"To 99.99 percent of the audience or anybody looking at twenty-four images [per second] flickering by, it didn't matter at all," said editor

Steve Ecclesine. "It was only for people who would stop the film and watch it frame by frame."

And whenever the editors thought they were done with a scene, Welles would frequently come back a month later and say, "Let's go back to reel number one again, I can fine-tune that and make it better."

He was doing amazing things that hadn't been tried, let alone executed, by other filmmakers, yet he also seemed to be working compulsively on shots and scenes that should have been finished long ago, seemingly unable to make up his mind and put them to bed.

"It was a psychological deficit on his part," Ecclesine said. "He never wanted to finish."

Reemerging in mid-September, Welles explained his mysterious illness to Antoine and Boushehri.

"I was suffering the most agonizing pain," he wrote. But "after a whole series of cures and therapies the English and Swiss would seem to have reprieved me from a serious rheumatic condition and the strange rheumatoid fever."

There's little doubt Welles was in poor health, but there is also no available record or independent account (aside from his letter) that he was acutely ill during the summer of 1975 or that he'd received medical treatment in Europe. According to his then secretary, Lynn Lewin, Orson didn't visit a hospital or seek specialized therapies in England and Switzerland. The worst illness Lewin recalled was a recurring liver problem brought on by the pastrami sandwiches he ate for lunch.*

Despite this, Welles thoroughly detailed his maladies for Antoine and Boushehri before asking: "Where do we go from here? Forward— that, of course, is the direction. The means of getting on the march

---

* Lewin's account is supported by Beatrice Welles, who said that her father suffered no serious illnesses or significant health problems (aside from those he lived with constantly) during that period of his life—and the ailments of which he complained were undoubtedly used as a way to explain away his desire to escape from the project during the summer of 1975.

again and the speed with which we'll reach our destination depends to a very large extent on you."

Now claiming he'd had less than a week of employment since 1973 and could document having turned down at least $1 million in work during that time, Welles complained about Astrophore's decision to hold off on money transfers until he met with them. A situation, he said, that put both himself and Graver in dire financial circumstances. Reimbursing Gary and paying off debts, he explained, was a necessity to their ongoing relationship.

"Clearly if we can't trust each other about that," he wrote, "we can't trust each other at all."

Antoine, meanwhile, understood Welles enough to appreciate his motivations. "He was escaping, you know?" she said. "He was a cat and we were trying to put a hand on him, so he disappeared. And he always thought that you were going to put a hand on him. He'd come to you and ask for a caress. You would give him the caress and then he would escape."

Writing back on September 19, Antoine expressed relief that Orson was back in good health and gently asked for a final budget and delivery date as soon as he felt well enough—explaining that the task took on some importance, as she'd recently received a "rather tough" letter from the Iranian bankers. Yet she still afforded him great latitude regarding creative control.

"<u>You</u> will have to decide (without any pressure of any kind from us) <u>your date of delivery</u>," she wrote.

Though Astrophore had now put more than $750,000 into the picture, Antoine proposed a new agreement under which they'd retain fifty-fifty ownership after Astrophore recouped its additional $166,811 from the profits. Her tone throughout was encouraging and almost apologetic, but she also made it clear that she was dedicated to the film, which they really, really had to finish—for everyone's sake.

Mehdi and I . . . are profoundly convinced that: 1) "THE WIND" will be a masterpiece. 2. It will also be a "money" masterpiece.

We are now approaching the end of your tremendous work. We must battle against any event (or person . . .) which would stop us or kill the picture. . . . I am ready to fight with all my strength. May I be totally frank? Even against you if needed— but I know that shall not be the case at any moment.

At the end, she asked Welles to finish the film in Paris so they could reduce communication problems, speed up money transfers, and reassure the Iranians. But despite insisting that he was heading to Paris several times since the AFI dinner, getting Welles there would prove a difficult task.

Two things are certain about the first major falling-out between Welles and Bogdanovich. First, the trigger for the events was Bogdanovich's film *Nickelodeon*. Second, Orson had pushed their relationship past making art that imitated his life; now his life was imitating his art, as the breach was seemingly foretold by its thematic resemblance to the breakup between Hannaford and Otterlake. And although there are several versions of the story, it was clear that—at least for the moment— their revels had ended.

Sometime in October, with Orson still occupying his home, Bogdanovich was casting *Nickelodeon*, a comedy about the early days of Hollywood. Having given Orson a copy of the script and hoping to cast him as studio chief H. H. Cobb, Bogdanovich said he was awakened by his houseguest in the middle of the night.

"Get up!" Orson yelled from the bottom of the stairs. "Wake up!"

When Bogdanovich came to the stairway, Welles explained how much he loved the screenplay and wanted to discuss the picture immediately.

Over the next few weeks, the pair continued to talk about the film and how to shoot it, with both ultimately agreeing that it should be in black-and-white. Bogdanovich, however, said that he didn't think Columbia executive David Begelman would ever go for it.

Claiming it was a battle worth fighting, Orson told Bogdanovich, "Just go to Begelman and tell him you can't do it unless it's in black-and-white. Trust me. It'll work."

Bogdanovich decided to follow Orson's advice and had a confrontation with Begelman, who promptly called his bluff and shut down the picture. Devastated, Bogdanovich told Welles that the plan hadn't worked. Rather than offering solace, Orson bemoaned his own fate, saying: "That's the end of my career in Hollywood."

Soon, however, Begelman put the picture back in production, but with a substantially reduced budget. As a consequence, Bogdanovich allegedly had to tell Orson that Columbia wasn't willing to pay his going rate of $15,000 a day for ten days' work. Instead, he'd have to do the job for $10,000 a day.

Welles explained that although he wanted to act in Peter's film, he couldn't agree to be in a studio picture for less than $15,000 a day. If it were just for Bogdanovich, he'd do it for free. But if executives knew he'd work for $10,000, he'd never get $15,000 a day again.

Bogdanovich decided to remedy the situation by talking to the film's stars—Ryan O'Neal and Burt Reynolds—who gladly gave up $25,000 apiece to supplement Orson's paycheck. In telling Welles that he could get him $150,000, Bogdanovich made the mistake of explaining how he'd solved the problem. This caused Orson to bow out, insisting that he couldn't take money from other actors.

"He had too much pride," Bogdanovich said. "But there was more to it than he just didn't want to take money from Burt and Ryan. I also had a feeling that he was afraid to do the part because he wasn't very good at remembering lines, and I think he didn't want to embarrass himself in front of me by not knowing the words."

A letter Orson wrote on October 22 after an argument with Bogdanovich supports the idea that he had real doubts about his ability to handle the role and also raises the question of whether he even wanted the part:

At this moment the obligation is yours: you must hear me out when I define my own limitations. Tactically at this state, a director is better advised to entertain any ideas which may be offered. I say <u>entertain</u>. What you <u>accept</u> and <u>decide</u> will come later, when you are functioning as the maker of your film. Then it will be time for me to satisfy you. Now it is for you to satisfy me.

Is what you expect me to give the character of Cobb what I believe I can deliver? Is it even—to put it rather less pleasantly— what I want to attempt? . . . A star (however dim) of forty-five years' standing cannot help but regard himself as an expert on the subject of what he cannot do . . . This means, quite simply, that I must be satisfied on my own terms; and not just yours.

What you are offering will do miracles for my professional career, but for me, our friendship is more precious than Oscars. And if, during the shooting of your picture, there is the slightest reason to anticipate any real difference between us, let us please settle right now for what is really valuable.

In other accounts, however, Orson had never wanted the role and didn't know how to refuse Bogdanovich, whose friendship and generosity had been truly exceptional. He'd taken the role because he had no choice. But when Bogdanovich lost the deal with Columbia, Orson allegedly saw a way out, which only became more frustrating when the project was reinstated on a reduced budget.

According to this version of events, Orson simply refused to accept the offer from O'Neal and Reynolds in order to escape, blaming it on the principle that he wouldn't take money from the pocket of another actor. Now, having gone to the trouble of arranging things to see that Orson got paid, Bogdanovich stood his ground and said he had to play Cobb.

When Bogdanovich left the following morning, Welles reportedly gathered his crew. After telling one of them to hand-deliver thank-you notes to Reynolds and O'Neal, he told the rest to strike the set and have everything out by the time Peter returned.

Knowing Bogdanovich would search for him at luxury hotels and restaurants such as Chasen's, Welles had a crew member check him into a Holiday Inn at the corner of Sunset and the 405 freeway—the one place Peter would never look. He registered under an assumed name, entered through the service elevator, and lived there for several days.

Meanwhile, Bogdanovich (who saw Orson as a surrogate father) ran around Hollywood searching the usual haunts for Orson until he received a call a week later. It was Welles. He said he wouldn't be appearing in *Nickelodeon*.

Bogdanovich, however, said it ended much less dramatically. After the letter and the buildup of tension over the role, he told Orson that his mother was coming for a visit in a while and that he needed the spare room. Welles was gone within twelve hours.

Although the truth was possibly somewhere in between the two accounts, there was unquestionably a breach in their relationship as evidenced by a letter sent on November 23, at which point Welles was out of Copa de Oro and no longer able to receive and send telexes via Bogdanovich's production office, as he'd been doing for some time.

Meanwhile, on that date, Bogdanovich, who'd been so generous, sent a letter to Astrophore seeking $17,000 as payment for his acting work and to recoup loans he'd made to Orson. "I cannot wait for payment any longer," he wrote. "Unless I receive immediate and complete recompense . . . I will have no other alternatives but to turn matters over to my Paris attorneys."

The following day, Welles informed Astrophore that he no longer could receive correspondence at Bogdanovich's office—and nearly two weeks later, he received a firm but respectful letter from his former protégé:

Dear Orson, Let me assure you that despite any disagreements or controversies with your producers, my original understanding with you concerning my compensation for acting in The

Other Side of the Wind *is still in order . . . I leave it in your capable hands to work out the arrangements.*

By late October, Welles was also having trouble with Astrophore, as Antoine had grown increasingly testy because Welles didn't appear to be doing anything that would help move things forward. He hadn't finished the film, nor would he come to Paris for meetings. He wouldn't even sign a piece of paper indicating that Astrophore owned a share of the film's negative.

Welles complained that he was being strong-armed via telex, when what he really needed was encouragement. Antoine, however, was desperate and wrote to Welles after he'd accused her of blackmail, explaining: "As I warned you and Arnold Weissberger, since the last three months Astrophore is now part of a new Iran in which Iranian banks have taken a percent of the shares." And now that Boushehri was no longer the film's only financial backer, she said, the bankers had advised him not to send Welles any more money until he formally acknowledged their part ownership of the negative.

At the end of her memo, Antoine added a personal note, indicating that Orson's word was good enough for her and Boushehri, but that they couldn't continue with "business as usual." Asking for a letter confirming Astrophore's interest in the negative, she said, wasn't such a taxing request, and it would go a long way toward pacifying the bankers.

"For the moment I am the one (and Astrophore with me) who is receiving from Teheran ultimatums and threats," she wrote. "And more definitive than I shall ever send you. I am trying to save the whole venture."

Her pleas continued throughout the fall. Having repeatedly asked for a delivery date and a meeting with her, Boushehri, Weissberger, and possibly Farmanara as soon as possible, Antoine found that Welles wouldn't commit to anything. Each time she tried to pin him down, he was either working on the picture or would reveal another crisis, such as Graver's arrest, which Welles believed wouldn't have occurred had Astrophore paid their debts.

Taking her plea to Weissberger in late November, Antoine said she was headed to Iran for a film festival and discussions regarding the fate of Astrophore and *The Other Side of the Wind*, after which, she would be back in Paris on December 8 or 9, a time when Welles had agreed to meet with her and Boushehri.

"Arnold, you must understand that if for any reasons, Orson is postponing that trip again or [doesn't] agree for me to come over in [*sic*] the States, you can imagine that everybody will be in serious trouble," she wrote. "So I really wish that Orson will be in Paris on December 9th, as promised."

It's unclear whether Welles arrived for that meeting, but he was definitely in Paris on December 15, when he met with Antoine at the Hôtel Plaza Athénée to hash out a final budget and delivery date.

With each delay and failure to complete the picture, Orson was losing more and more of his ownership interest in the film. According to Barbara Leaming's biography, his and Oja's share had dwindled to less than 20 percent by the time he sat down with Antoine. Intent on doing anything to make sure the movie was finished, Antoine needed an agreement that would solve Welles's problems as well as Astrophore's—which required a budget. But the first order of business was setting a completion date but Welles wouldn't commit because, Antoine said, "he thought he was becoming a prisoner again."

To make Welles comfortable, Antoine offered two proposals. First, Astrophore would restore his share of the film as proposed earlier and—after recouping their $150,000—would share equal ownership of the film with Avenel. Her other proposal was a tactic to put Welles in control: "You choose the date to deliver the final picture," she told him.

Welles first said he wouldn't be responsible for delays if the workers at LTC went on strike, and Antoine agreed to this. They would change the dates if the lab suffered a walkout. "Okay," she said. "Put a date on it."

Welles said he'd finish in April or May 1976 (accounts vary), giving him four to five months to complete the film. After agreeing to this date,

Antoine protected Astrophore from late delivery by having Welles agree to give up 10 percent of his share for every month it took to complete the film after his self-imposed deadline.

Though the decisions they made were financial, Antoine says there was a larger issue guiding the talks. "In the moment he was sure [of the dates] and very happy," she said. "Because the money was never the problem for him. He never made a decision because of money. Like always, it was regarding his freedom."

They arranged for an agreement to be drawn up so Welles could sign it in Los Angeles the following month.

Joe McBride's December 16 interview with John Huston ran in *Variety* two days before the premiere of *The Man Who Would Be King*. In the article, ironically titled "John Huston Finds That Slow Generation of 'King' Has Made It a Richer Film," McBride talked to Huston about the making of a brilliant movie that was shot in an exotic location, then scored, edited, completed, and released in less than two years' time.

At the conclusion, McBride mentioned Huston's role in *The Other Side of the Wind*, inspiring the man who'd embodied Hannaford to say: "I'll have to find out where Orson is. I'm going to call him up and say, 'Why the hell don't you finish it?'"

1976–1978

You can't put an ultimatum on an artist.

—Gary Graver

During his nearly forty-year rule, Mohammad Reza Pahlavi, the second shah of Iran, had managed to alienate a remarkable group of opposing forces whose combined discontent would give rise to the Iranian Revolution of 1978–1979.

There were many reasons Iranians had problems with the shah, beginning in 1941, when Allied forces selected him to replace his own father. He was immediately seen as a tool of the West, a belief that was strengthened in the early 1950s when American and British forces quelled a brief revolution for him. Thus, he'd now been placed in control twice, not by his own people, but as the result of decisions made by other nations.

The Western influence wasn't necessarily a bad thing for Iranians, as the shah's 1963 White Revolution conferred voting rights on women; allowed non-Muslims to run for office; and created economic, health, and educational programs in a genuine attempt to improve the lives of Iran's lower classes. But despite his Western social policies, he was a brutally oppressive ruler and maintained power through a ruthless secret police force. Then there was the way he lived, which was opulent even by imperial ruler standards. In 1971, to celebrate the twenty-five hundredth anniversary of the Persian Empire at Persepolis (in honor of which Orson had narrated a documentary entitled *The Shah of Iran* [1972]), the shah spent nearly $100 million to entertain foreign dignitaries at the same time many nearby residents starved in the streets.

The biggest problem, however, was a Muslim cleric who'd declared the White Revolution to be "the destruction of Islam in Iran," because it broke Shiite tradition by allowing the use of tobacco and alcohol, freed women from having to wear veils, and allowed citizens to go to the movies. The cleric was Ayatollah Ruhollah Khomeini, whose 1963 arrest by the shah's forces set off protests that required a period of martial law. The following year, at age sixty-two, Khomeini was exiled and wound up in Iraq, where he spent the next fourteen years sending back manifestos that turned him into a near deity among conservative Shiites and fueled the uprising that toppled the shah's regime.

In 1975, as pressure mounted from right, left, and center, the shah created a new, unopposed, monarchist political party that required the membership of all citizens. The next year, he unilaterally replaced the Islamic calendar with a new, imperial calendar, based on the date the Persian Empire had been founded. Neither move was popular, and the protests began again, with Khomeini claiming that "freedom is at hand."

Because of these developments, the shah had bigger things on his mind in 1975–1976 than establishing his nation as a location for American films and co-producing a movie Orson Welles had been working on for six years.

Amid the turmoil, the politically savvy Boushehri had retained considerable power within the regime, but not enough to prevent Astrophore from being turned over to others who simply wanted the film finished and off their books. And though he possessed great wealth and influence, Boushehri found himself in an immensely difficult situation in which he still maintained his firm belief in both Welles and the film. Antoine felt the same way, and the two would do everything in their power to make sure the seeds of a revolution wouldn't destroy *The Other Side of the Wind*.

Welles received at least three drafts of the contract while back in Los Angeles at the beginning of 1976. The first one reiterated the terms of what they'd agreed to in Paris, but Welles wanted a few changes. Next came a new contract—in French. Welles wrote back requesting an English version, which he received but with which he still had issues. Thus, with the April/May deadline still in place, there was no signed agreement and the feeling remained that everything was up in the air.

Because of this, Antoine sent Welles a January 15 telegram conveying Boushehri's urgent need for him to submit a budget and delivery date for the work print. All other problems could wait—they needed those two items before anything could happen.

Meanwhile, Welles was living and editing at the Beverly Hills Hotel, where he was paying triple scale to editors who were available to him whenever he wanted to work, which was often after midnight and into the early morning. To help with this work, he requested that Antoine purchase a $13,000 editing table in France that could be deducted from his director's fee whenever they'd settled on what he'd be paid. Antoine responded that if he sent a letter agreeing to the current terms, the equipment would be shipped immediately.

By late February, however, the editing table hadn't arrived, because Bahman Farmanara was unsure that Welles would commit to a delivery date. A filmmaker himself, Farmanara was taken with Welles the artist, fully appreciating his work and the manner in which he'd transformed cinema with *Citizen Kane*.

"He was a genius," Farmanara said. "And as fascinating as anyone could be."

But as head of production for FIDCI, he was also responsible for a film that he believed was being poorly managed. And since he was an experienced director and producer, Farmanara could remove the stars from his eyes and view Welles as someone who'd needed to finish a film long ago.

The pair met only once, earlier in the winter, when they shared a four-hour lunch in Paris. Viewing himself as a producer with a problem on his hands, Farmanara was unwilling to be taken in by Welles's attempt to charm him out of more money. "He'd already received many times the $150,000 he'd asked for, and there was still no end in sight," Farmanara said. "All I wanted was a delivery date and he refused to give me a date."

When it became clear that he wasn't going to get any more money, Welles abruptly got up and left, sticking Farmanara with the lunch check.

With that as the basis for their relationship, Welles rejected several contracts from Astrophore and then received another in March that had been drafted by Farmanara's attorney, Werner Wolfen. That deal included new terms in which the Iranians would retain a conditional right to final cut should Welles greatly exceed his completion date.

Perhaps inspired by the mere mention of giving a producer final cut, Weissberger began pursuing options in which Welles could buy out Astrophore for $1.15 million—money they would raise from either investors seeking a tax shelter, an American distribution company, or the presale of foreign distribution rights. Though this plan didn't appear to get very far, it clearly had been attempted on some level and might well have succeeded, according to a memo from Antoine a few months later.

"We must never forget that when Arnold Weissberger told Mehdi several months ago that you were ready to buy back the Iranian share, so as to get rid of them, Farmanara gave his instant agreement," she wrote.

But instead of buying back the shares, Welles continued his unhappy partnership with the Iranians, from whom he wanted his independence.

"For the past six and a half years, Orson Welles, the man who gave us 'Citizen Kane'—arguably the greatest American movie—has been roaring, in the sands of Arizona and in some of the more remote regions of Hollywood, trying in his own inimitable fashion to wind up a movie called 'The Other Side of the Wind.'"

That sentence appeared in an April *New York Times* feature story entitled "The Film That Orson Welles Has Been Finishing for Six Years." Its author was Charles Higham.

The article portrayed Welles as a combination of colorful genius ("Orson's like a painter," Strasberg was quoted as saying. "He's creating on film. That's why he takes years") and disorganized, semimaniacal bully who worked with imaginary midgets and was making it up as he went along.

Revivifying the "fear of completion" theory, Higham noted each of Welles's unfinished films and recounted several strange stories from the set (quoting Strasberg, Rich Little, and others) before letting Welles have the last five paragraphs to explain why *Ambersons, The Deep,* and other films had given the incorrect impression that he was a "tragically self-destructive genius," when in truth he was simply "just a poor slob trying to make pictures."

It is perhaps indicative of Higham's journalistic ethics that both Welles and Little claimed they had never been contacted by Higham (as revealed in an exchange of letters between the pair later that spring) and it seems almost inconceivable that Orson would have granted his nemesis an interview on this or any subject.

Welles wrote first, on April 22, to explain that he had no hard feelings toward Little and greatly regretted the misunderstandings that led to his departure. Giving the explanation that his European production partner had screwed them both in not coordinating Little's deadline with the requirements of the shoot, Welles took full responsibility for the situation.

"The plain truth is that what I have already called a bad 'mistake' was most certainly made—and made by me and for this I hope you will accept my apologies."

Then he turned to the real purpose of his letter, Higham's article, a "piece of character assassination" that Welles said might tank potential distribution deals "now that our film is completed." He explained that Higham had never visited the set, let alone met or spoken with him, and said that the author was creating "fantasies" about the film that made "the whole movie seem like pure lunacy with no redeeming spark of artistic interest."

After mentioning Higham's retelling of the "midgets on the roof" story, attributed to Little, Welles said he had no problem with the fact that the comedian had shared it on at least one talk show—in that it was a good joke he was entitled to tell. That said, however, putting it in print, Welles believed, made him look "positively certifiable."

In the end, Welles asked that he and Little collaborate on a letter in which the comedian explained his departure from the film and expressed the fact that he enjoyed a happy working relationship with his director. "This or something like it," Welles wrote, "would do a lot to get me off the hook."

"I'd told the story on a couple of talk shows and that's why he sent me the letter," Little said, the message of which was "Keep it funny, but don't make me look like I should be put in a home."

Writing back to Welles in May, Little lamented the fact that he'd needed to leave and couldn't complete his work on the film. "My three weeks with you was one of the most enjoyable and educational times of my life, despite the outcome," Little wrote. "I've spent many a sleepless night thinking about the work we put into each scene and the laborious task you had of doing it all over again. I loved working on the picture and I loved working with you."

After admitting that he'd told the story (as well as his version of nearly being killed by Huston's driving) while discussing Huston with Michael Caine and Sean Connery on *The Irv Kupcinet Show,* Little concluded by explaining that he'd never spoken to anyone from *The New York Times.* Enclosed with his reply to Orson was a separate letter of recommendation in which he explained that his abrupt departure wasn't caused by any problem with Welles, whom he described as "a man who possesses a great sense of humor and truly one of the great directors of our time."

With things seemingly going nowhere, Boushehri asked Welles's associate Claude Fielding to intervene as an arbitrator who could sit in on their negotiations, record any agreement, and then create a document embodying whatever resolution they'd achieved.

Writing to FIDCI attorney Werner Wolfen in early June, Fielding admitted that the request made him "a little wary." Wolfen replied by once again offering the deal in which Farmanara and FIDCI would have final cut.

None of this mattered, however, after Welles received a note from Antoine declaring that "Astrophore is dead since June 13th."

Now working for director-producer Carlo Ponti, Antoine expressed her willingness to find end money and get *The Other Side of the Wind* out of the cutting room and into theaters. Boushehri, Antoine said, felt that he could still handle the task of producing, but only on the basis of the agreement Wolfen and Farmanara had proposed, a path she believed would be a waste of Welles's time to pursue.

Antoine told Welles she had at least three solutions for buying out the Iranians and funding completion of the film. First there was Myron Karlin, president of Warner Bros. International, who'd seen Antoine in Cannes and expressed great enthusiasm when she told him about Welles's new film. Karlin said he would be open to a proposal that paid Welles, provided end money, and got rid of the Iranians. The only problem was that Warner Bros. would come out owning the picture.

Then there was Ponti, who was also interested but saw that the situation in Iran put Welles's partners in a bad bargaining position. His thought was to wait until things got so bad that the Iranians would sell their share of the film for $500,000.

The final option was James Kennedy, a young Irishman who owned Vancouver-based Ashling Multimedia, a distributor affiliated with Universal and United Artists. Kennedy was fascinated by Welles, and his "biggest wish would be to try and take 'The Wind' out of the dead situation where it stands now." His solution was to pay the Iranians $1 million over two years, while giving Orson a $100,000 advance on his next film once *The Other Side of the Wind* was in the can.

Antoine said she was sure that Farmanara and FIDCI would gladly sell out their interest and thought Boushehri would accept the deal, but she cautioned that she couldn't guarantee his agreement. In closing her letter, she reiterated her commitment to Welles and the film, telling him, "I am ready to do anything to see 'The Wind' on a screen."

And though Welles shared that desire, he didn't pursue any of these options. Instead, Orson remained in neutral, where he didn't have to deal with money and, as a result, continued his partnership with Boushehri.

On July 4, 1976, the following question appeared in *The Boston Globe:* "Is Orson Welles ever going to finish his new movie, 'The Other Side of the Wind'?"

The response was: "Although there is speculation that Welles may add this film—started nearly seven years ago—to his file of other unfinished flicks, the genius of 'Citizen Kane' vehemently denies it and says all he needs is a little more money."

Three days later, Norman Foster died of cancer at the age seventy-two, and despite the fact that he'd had a forty-year career in which he'd directed more than thirty films and acted in many others, his obituary, just like Stafford Repp's, made prominent mention of the fact that his last acting role had been opposite Huston in *The Other Side of the Wind*.

As things worsened in Iran and Boushehri began to worry about his investment, he had Coopers & Lybrand audit Orson's work on three films, the most significant of which was *The Other Side of the Wind*.

The report tracked all funds advanced by Boushehri, Astrophore, and SACI (an Iranian government film office) by the end of August 1976. The total came to $1,019,450. Of that total, Coopers & Lybrand could find that only $321,496 worth of expenditures had been both properly documented and directly related to the film.

"Due to a complete lack of budgetary or accounting control we were unable to satisfy ourselves whether all expenditures had been accounted for or whether or not [certain expenditures were] necessarily incurred on behalf of the film."

After the financial breakdown, the audit assessed that the film had no current value, as it was incomplete and work seemed to have stopped after Welles rejected Astrophore's contract proposals. Thus, for Boushehri to recoup any of his investment, the movie would have to be completed and released, which meant spending more money, an unlikely proposition given Welles's current relationship with his backers.

Meanwhile, Astrophore's ace in the hole was its possession of the negative, which was stored at LTC and could be accessed only with their authorization. Welles, however, had the work print stored in Los Angeles.

Things were at a stalemate—or, as Huston said in 1976, "It's about as complicated a situation as a picture can get into."

Largely unseen after its opening week, *Nickelodeon* was now the third film that afforded critics the opportunity to rip into Bogdanovich—again—leaving him on the defensive and in a difficult situation.

Having already forfeited $500,000 of his $750,000 fee on the film to cover delays and overruns, he now reduced his asking price to $600,000. And to make things more unpleasant, even Ryan O'Neal was spouting off about how the movie was no fun to make and how badly he thought it had turned out.

In the midst of this shit storm, one reporter asked Bogdanovich if his career bore any similarity to Orson's. What once would have been deeply flattering now seemed like just another punch in the gut.

Bogdanovich shot back with an accurate summary of their careers: "Orson's never been in a situation comparable to mine, except before he made *Citizen Kane*. I'm not as good as he was and he's never been as successful as I am."

According to David Denby's article in *The New York Times*, the loud crash of Bogdanovich falling back to earth may have had several causes. Some wondered if he couldn't judge material. Others thought he was derivative or that he'd hitched a ride on the brilliance of Mc-Murtry's novel. There were those who believed that he was isolated from anyone who might criticize his work now that he was no longer collaborating with Platt. Finally, there were some who blamed his relationship with Shepherd, claiming he was trying too hard to make her a star.

Bogdanovich, Denby said, was a victim of what made him brilliant: his reverence for and total dedication to film. His life had been lived like a "fable," where the director always hits a home run and then goes back to his Bel Air mansion with a gorgeous, smart, funny blonde.

"It has the romance of big success and the romance of big failure," Denby wrote, "and obviously it's not over. Peter Bogdanovich's career is now at a low ebb, although he is hardly 'through.'"

Possessing remarkable charm and extraordinary persuasive ability,

Bogdanovich tended to react in moments like this with a mixture of confidence and self-pity. In responding to the article, he complained that others simply hated the fact that he had such a great life. "My affair with Cybill is the reason many people want me to fail," he said. "People in Hollywood are jealous of me and envious of her."

In the face of this, Bogdanovich had begun to reestablish his relationship with Welles and would soon try again to help the man he still worshipped. And though he was about to take time away from Hollywood, movies remained at the center of his life. Thus, when asked if he was far too interested in film, Bogdanovich replied, "I've heard that since I was fifteen and I don't know what it means. Cinema is my whole life."

In an undated letter to Mehdi Boushehri written in 1977, Welles summed up where he felt he stood in relation to and as a result of *The Other Side of the Wind.*

> My own first priority, for much too long now, has been "THE OTHER SIDE OF THE WIND." Tragically very little of that time has been spent on constructive work. Overwhelmingly, it has been time lost in simply waiting for the chance to work— time utterly wasted.

That waiting, Orson wrote, had all but destroyed his career as an actor and a director, bringing both to their *lowest point* since he'd begun making films. In part, Welles explained, he blamed the decision to use the AFI award presentation as an opportunity to show clips from *The Wind.* That move, he said, had backfired, as the event *should have been a turning point* in his career, but instead had wound up as a way of publicizing a project that he'd failed to complete and thus revived old myths about his inability to finish movies and lack of interest in working as an actor for other directors.

The result, Orson explained, had been a financial disaster in which he claimed to have turned down over $2,000,000 in work on various projects simply to *keep myself free for the completion of our film . . . .*

But now, after nearly forty years in the business, Orson was *not only without income but without prospects,* lamenting that *it's not too easy—in the sixty-second year of my life—to make plans for a fresh start.*

1978

The new year did afford Welles a fresh start, and as a result, *The Other Side of the Wind* was given the opportunity for new life.

Never having had any qualms about appearing in bad movies or hawking products to fund his art, Welles was just beginning to work as the pitchman for Paul Masson wine, a job that would provide him nearly $500,000 in annual income. During the remaining seven years of his life, he would use that income to pay back many of the loans he'd received and other debts he'd incurred over the years.

Although the endeavor was clearly driven by money, Welles found himself compelled to dominate the creative process in making ads for a cheap American wine that wanted to class up its reputation with the endorsement of a well-known sophisticate.

The concept behind the ads was that Welles would begin by discussing a famous work of art, often opening with something like "Margaret Mitchell began writing *Gone With the Wind* in 1926 and she finished it ten years later" or listening to some classical music, after which he'd say, "It took Beethoven four years to write that symphony." Then he'd compare those projects to the ripening of Paul Masson wine.

Welles took this "most innocent form of whoring" seriously and tried to do his best work, giving input on lighting, scripts, and even his own makeup. Eventually, however, he would become testy or horrified by the scripts and situations with which he was faced, including one ad in which he was asked to compare the wine to a sacred form or craftsmanship.

"Stradivarius took three years to make one of his violins," Welles said. "Paul Masson took—" At this point he stopped, refusing to go forward with the ad.

"Come on, gentlemen, now really! You have a nice, pleasant little cheap wine here. You haven't got the presumption to compare it to a Stradivarius violin," he said. "It's odious."

What he would do, however, was try to take on a new project as the result of his somewhat mended relationship with Bogdanovich.

As *The Other Side of the Wind* languished and Welles seemed un-receptive to all offers that might extract him from the Iranians or pro-vide end money, he told Bogdanovich that Paul Theroux's book *Saint Jack* would make an excellent film. Agreeing to produce (with Orson directing), Bogdanovich discovered that *Playboy* owned the novel's film rights, and to secure them he dropped a lawsuit he and Shepherd had filed against the magazine for unauthorized use of a screenshot from *The Last Picture Show* in which Cybill was bare-breasted. A deal was struck and it became Welles's film to direct, despite the fact that he refused to meet with Hugh Hefner at the Playboy Mansion.

"I won't set foot in that place," Welles said.

"You won't?" Bogdanovich responded.

"I won't," Welles said, and explained his reasoning as follows:

"Never touch shit, even with gloves on," he told Bogdanovich. "The gloves only get shittier, but the shit doesn't get any glovvier."

When the deal was struck, an excited Welles said he wanted Jack Nicholson to play the lead—an expatriate in Shanghai who moonlights as a pimp and discovers that he's vastly more principled than his high-end clientele. Bogdanovich set up meetings with Nicholson, but Welles canceled, deciding he'd prefer Dean Martin in the role. This didn't thrill Nicholson, and while Bogdanovich thought Martin would make an intriguing protagonist, he also knew that Deano wasn't terribly bankable at the time. Welles, meanwhile, hadn't worked on the script and was doing nothing to move things forward with Martin.

Before long, Shepherd and Hefner (who still owned part of the picture) became antsy and suggested that Peter take over. Feeling trapped, Bogdanovich realized that the project would remain idle unless he wrote and directed the film, in which he ultimately decided to cast Ben Gazzara in the lead. It would be Peter's back-to-basics picture, made outside of the system, on a much smaller budget, and without a studio leaning over his shoulder.

The moment was symbolic. Despite what he'd protested to the media, Bogdanovich was following Orson's path on some level, in that he'd become fed up and was making a guerrilla-style movie that was much more free-form in production and technique than his previous work. Smaller and more artistic, the film would bear his personal stamp— making it the first real attempt at a "Peter Bogdanovich" movie.

For Welles, the symbolism was much deeper, as it hit on one of his most profound themes. "Orson thought I betrayed him," Bogdanovich said. "That was the end of our close relationship."

The new breach between the pair was confirmed during one of Welles's appearances on *The Tonight Show*, which was being guest hosted by Burt Reynolds. Sitting at home, Bogdanovich watched Welles make fun of him before a national audience as he was joined and egged on by Reynolds, who apparently disliked Bogdanovich. The feeling was mutual.

"They both spent a few minutes putting me down. Publicly," Bogdanovich said. "So I sent Orson a note saying, 'I saw you on *The Tonight Show* last night. I'm wondering how you're feeling. I guess I know now.'"

Welles responded quickly, sending Bogdanovich a single envelope containing two notes, with the explanation "I've sent you two answers. You can use the one you like."

The first note was an abject apology, where Welles confessed to betraying Peter's friendship and expressed deep regret. Then there was the second message.

"It was a shorter note saying I deserved it," Bogdanovich said.

The shah spent 1978 barely clinging to both his power and his life. Secretly diagnosed in 1974 with a form of non-Hodgkin's lymphoma, he hadn't been faithful in taking the anticancer drugs prescribed by his French doctors, and his condition was worsening—though only his wife and physician knew that he was ill.

Having spent his entire reign as the regime's sole decision maker, the shah found that his ever-worsening health had compromised an already questionable ability to handle difficult situations, in particular the looming threat of revolution. Thus, while his cancer spread, the fifty-eight-year-old shah grew more and more depressed; but he still managed to fan the flames of anger among Shiites by demanding that his information minister write a newspaper article accusing Khomeini of numerous transgressions—including homosexuality.

Published in January, the story hastened the shah's downfall as his forces clamped down on a student protest, killing as many as seventy demonstrators. This not only inspired rage, it also broke the "barrier of fear" among his opponents, who were now ready to take on their ruler and his military no matter what the cost.

A winter and spring of demonstrations followed, with police and military forces attacking more protestors, which in turn escalated the protests and led to more deaths among the shah's foes. Then, in May, a group of commandos raided the home of a liberal pacifist cleric who'd long opposed Khomeini. But when Ayatollah Kazem Shariamadari watched commandos kill a member of his flock, even he turned against the shah, who began wiping out moderate clerics for their weakness.

And as time ran out on the shah's empire, it was also running out for his former brother-in-law's attempts to strike an agreement with Welles that would either return his investment or get things back on track. Then an opportunity fell from the sky.

Between 1972 and 1977, James George had been Canada's ambassador to Iran. A World War II veteran and son of a wealthy Toronto physician, George had enjoyed a long and successful career in Canada's foreign service, which included ambassadorships in Sri Lanka, India, and Nepal. Iran had been his final post.

Valued as an astute observer, George was easygoing and able to connect with people at all levels of society wherever he was stationed. Bright and perceptive, he mixed easily with locals and politicians and always knew the score, often before anyone else. Which was apparently the case in 1976, when he concluded that the shah would be overthrown. "It was just obvious what was going to happen," George told *The Globe and Mail*. "It was clear there would be a revolution. The only question was how much blood the Shah would be willing to spend to keep his power."

Leaving Iran in 1977, he became involved with a philanthropic organization (the Threshold Foundation) that was made up of wealthy individuals who shared core humanistic beliefs and engaged in a wide range of endeavors that were in keeping with Eastern spiritual values.

George was sixty years old, and acting on behalf of his foundation and his close friend actress Suzanne Cloutier, when he met Welles in 1978. The ex-wife of actor Peter Ustinov, Cloutier had played Desdemona in Welles's *Othello* and had the kind of admiration and warm feeling for him that made cast and crew come running whenever he set up a camera.

Having heard about Welles's struggles with *The Other Side of the Wind*, Cloutier went to George, whom she'd known for years, and asked what he thought about financing the film as a favor to Orson. "It sounds like an interesting project," George said. "Orson's film will be tremendous."

So they went to Los Angeles and had several dinners with Welles, who told one wonderful story after another. The worldly George did not find himself taken in by Orson's charm or celebrity; rather, he said, "I came away with a wonderful impression of his subtlety and his brilliance."

Believing he could provide a solution to Welles's problems, George began negotiating a contract under which his organization, the Threshold Foundation, and Cloutier could fund the film's completion.

By May, George had approached Boushehri, laying out a plan in which his group and Astrophore would join together as a Dutch corporation and co-produce *The Other Side of the Wind*. As part of the deal, Astrophore would be paid more than $800,000 in order to equalize the ownership interests in the film and the Dutch company would own 60 percent (30 percent for Astrophore and 30 percent for their new partners) of the film, with Welles's percentage dropping from 50 percent to 40 percent. And as a final benefit to Boushehri, the new holding company would take over all negotiations with Welles.

Boushehri responded quickly and said he'd take the deal to the bankers in Iran after he and Welles mulled it over.

Via Weissberger, Welles came back with a counteroffer in which ownership remained at fifty-fifty and he was guaranteed final cut. But, most important, Weissberger explained, the entire objective of signing on with George and Cloutier was to get Boushehri completely out of the picture. They might be willing to budge on ownership percentages—but final cut and the elimination of Boushehri were non-negotiable.

In August, ten days after he'd promised free elections the following year, the shah declared martial law to quell violence and demonstrations. Later in the month, nearly five hundred people died in a fire at the Cinema Rex movie theater. When the cause was revealed to be arson, each side blamed the other for the tragedy.

As things deteriorated, Khomeini moved to a home outside Paris, where he held court with journalists and prepared for his return.

Desperate, the shah went on television in November and proclaimed that as an Iranian citizen he'd heard and approved of the revolution. Promising change, he even arrested important members of his regime. But it wasn't nearly enough.

The day after the shah made that speech, George wrote a letter to Welles from his suite at the Beverly Wilshire, where he was staying as he attempted to close the deal:

"I am sorry that because of the situation in Iran (and for no other reason) my negotiations have taken longer than we both expected," George wrote. "However we now have everything put together and are ready to proceed as soon as you are ready. If you have any concerns regarding money being available when due, let us discuss ways and means of reassuring you on this."

Sent on November 6, George also enclosed a letter from Mehdi Boushehri.

Dear Orson,

I should like to confirm [to] you personally and to Avenel that to my deep regret, Astrophore Films have sold to Mr. James George's group all our rights in your film *The Other Side of the Wind* . . . We hope to have everything signed and turned over to Mr. George on his return to Paris from California about mid-November. Naturally all this is conditional on Mr. George completing his contract with you.

With my continuing best wishes for your film, which I am sure will be an outstanding success.

Warmest Regards (hope to see you soon)—Mehdi

George's letter also reaffirmed two agreements that had been reached—but not signed—on August 3, one with Astrophore and another with Welles.

Under those agreements, George's group (as Liechtenstein-based Gatineau Films) would pay Boushehri $1.18 million to acquire his company's rights. The renegotiated deal with Welles guaranteed final cut and gave him ten months to complete the film—with the clock not ticking until all materials had been provided to Welles and properly organized and cataloged. There were also very generous financial terms.

Gatineau agreed to deposit $500,000 in a Los Angeles bank account for Welles and Avenel to use in paying off any entity to whom the film was in debt. To complete production, they would also provide "not less than $400,000 nor more than $750,000." This brought Gatineau's total investment to nearly $2 million.

Three days after confirming that he'd cleared all roadblocks to an agreement, George was still at the Beverly Wilshire, where he penned a handwritten note to Welles seeking his approval of the deal as soon as he was willing to sign. "My only concern is that we complete our deal and I then get Boushehri's final signature while he can still legally sign," George wrote. "[Boushehri] has promised to be in Paris for this purpose on November 16th."

George's attorney, Richard Kaplan, wrote a letter on November 13 agreeing to several changes to the contract required by Weissberger. Two days later, he sent another letter to Weissberger indicating that George would agree to more changes regarding the release of funds from the bank account that held the $500,000. With Boushehri waiting in Paris, George was ready to go there as soon as Orson signed the papers, which they needed him to do very soon.

"Each day's news only underscores the very real concern we both share," Kaplan wrote. "Without a final agreement with Avenel, Mr. George cannot conclude a final agreement with Astrophore."

Yet there was still no signature.

Finally, on November 22, in a letter marked "Personal and Private," George wrote to acknowledge Welles's apparent reluctance to make a deal with him and Cloutier. In addition to assuring Welles that he wouldn't even consider involving himself unless he was firmly convinced that he could handle being producer, George revealed his true purpose:

"I am not in this venture for any other reason than the simple, initial impulse of Suzanne, who felt that together we might facilitate the birth of an authentic masterpiece . . . ," George wrote. "The truth is normally simple. She is doing this for you. I am doing it for her. I have waited here nearly three weeks to tell you that."

Welles and Weissberger continued to ask for more changes. Each time there seemed to be an agreement, another alteration of the terms or wording became the linchpin of the entire enterprise. Meanwhile, the closer they got to a deal, the more Welles backed away from George and Cloutier. He became harder to get in touch with and missed meetings until the situation was beginning to feel impossible.

As George tried to please Welles and Weissberger, his partners at the charitable foundation began to lose patience. But George kept at it and tendered a new contract in 1979, a year that began with the shah's departure and Khomeini's return to Iran.

In the end, George, the foundation, and Cloutier simply gave up, concluding that they should leave movie financing to people in the film industry. "The resulting contract [proposed by Weissberger] and all of the conditions attached to it seemed to be too much for a nonprofit charitable institution," George said. "We eventually backed away because Orson became too difficult for the board of our foundation."

All of this left Welles in the same unhappy circumstance of wanting to finish the film but remaining partners with the one person this side of John Houseman he'd least like to be working with—Boushehri, who despite everything still believed in Welles and *The Other Side of the Wind*.

Welles, however, had no such faith in Boushehri. At the end of 1978, via Avenel, he asked a French court to issue an injunction that would essentially forbid LTC from giving Boushehri and Astrophore access to the film into which they'd sunk more than $1 million.

As the dispute over ownership of and access to the negative began, Joe McBride attempted to save the day by going to Roger Corman and asking him to buy out Boushehri. Corman said he'd love to but couldn't out of fear that he'd be the defendant in innumerable lawsuits the day they released the film.

1979–1985

As Khomeini took over in Iran, the American Film Institute decided to offer a multisession workshop called "Working with Welles," whom they chose to honor because he was a well-known filmmaker, actor, and celebrity who could help them reach a wider audience. This meant that the director whose films never made a buck was being honored because he was marketable.

But they also chose Welles because he was an artist and a rebel whose movies were studied and had now become the subject of film school dissertations. "It's a tragic story," said AFI's Michael Webb. "A story of missed opportunities and unfulfilled promise."

Charlton Heston, Peter Bogdanovich, Tony Perkins, Gary Graver, Roddy McDowall, Burgess Meredith, and Stanley Cortez had all agreed to participate in the sessions that would take place at the Directors Guild Theater. Welles, however, hadn't committed to participate because, according to Webb, "[he] makes up his mind from one week to one hour prior to the event."

But Welles did show up for some of the programs—just as he would have shown up at his own funeral, if possible.

During one session, with McBride moderating a panel that included Skipper Hill, Welles said that he'd become involved with theater at Todd because he'd wanted to become the focal point of Hill's life. Though he'd been interested in art and dramatics before entering Todd, Welles used them, he said, as a way to insert himself into the Hill family and the forefront of Skipper's mind.

To capture the essence of his feelings, he turned to Hill and said, "I'm the boy you could have had . . . If he had been gay, I would have been gay."

For anyone who'd seen the clips of Bradley Pease Burroughs (whose dapper, harried, foppish schoolmaster seemed at least partially modeled on Skipper), the comment would seem to have added a new autobiographical element to *The Other Side of the Wind*. Welles, however, issued a strong denial that the film was based on his own life.

"You mustn't look for keys," he said, then paused before adding, "I never even went sledding."

In an article about the AFI sessions, Charles Champlin of the *Los Angeles Times* talked about clips Welles had shown from *The Other Side of the Wind*, which he described as "Orson Welles's almost legendary movie about a legendary Hollywood director."

Welles's direction, Champlin wrote, showed that he was "creatively as light on his feet and tireless as the 25-year-old who made 'Citizen Kane'" and had created scenes that involved "blizzards of very fast cuts, dramatically and even luridly lighted and full of extreme closeups." It was "Welles at his most flamboyant."

During that session, Welles talked extensively about the film and claimed it was 96 percent finished, but that the negative was stuck at LTC, while alleging that the Iranians had charged $1 million of their own expenses to the film.

"The end of it all is that when the telephones work again and the banks open again [in Iran], it may be possible to detach this film from the Iranians," Welles said. "You can imagine with what interest I watch the evening news. The chant 'death to the Shah' does not come solely from the Iranians."

Jack O'Brian and Marilyn Beck were both syndicated columnists covering the entertainment industry. And though Beck had expressed her displeasure over Welles receiving the AFI award in 1975, both she and O'Brian seemed compelled to write about the director during the late 1970s and early 1980s.

On March 8, 1979, O'Brian ran the small notice that "Orson Welles hopes to finish *The Other Side of the Wind*, which has run out of capital twelve times in almost as many years. Its co-star John Huston hopes to live as long."

But three years later, in July 1982, Beck's column told a different story. "Orson Welles is finally close to completion of *The Other Side of the Wind* after 12 years of toil and trouble," she wrote.

After explaining that Welles had originally self-financed the film, she quoted Bogdanovich, who said *The Wind* had been "a stop and go situation ever since." Bogdanovich incorrectly contended that the Iranian government had seized the film and placed it in the vault at LTC after the shah's departure, adding that Welles had possession of his materials and "has only a few scenes left to complete."

And indeed, twelve years after beginning to work on *The Other Side of the Wind*, Welles was still seeking end money. But the question of who owned the negative wasn't as clear-cut as it had appeared.

Welles still had the work print, and the negative remained at LTC, but the idea that the Iranian government had seized the film was only partially true. They had indeed come to Paris in 1979 and attempted to take back the movie on the grounds that both the picture and Astrophore were the property of the Iranian people.

Having anticipated something like this, Boushehri had added a level of remove that made it legally difficult to claim Astrophore as an Iranian asset. To do this, he'd named one of his French employees the company's new managing director. With that change, Astrophore, formerly an Iranian-financed company headquartered in Paris, became something murkier. Now it had a French principal as well as a Paris location; as a result, the only Iranian attachment to the project was Boushehri's arm's-length financial interest. Although this might not stand up legally, it made any attempt to grab the company's assets more complicated than simply bullying an Iranian citizen and saying, "This belongs to the people."

This maneuver, however, wasn't what ultimately saved Astrophore and *The Other Side of the Wind* from being subsumed by the new Islamic regime. Instead, it was a remarkable stroke of luck that took place shortly before the ayatollah's people came to Paris.

What occurred was that Françoise Widhoff (who'd worked on the film in Carefree and had long been with Astrophore) had received a letter from the French tax authority, mistakenly indicating that the company owed roughly 600,000 francs (around $115,000) in back taxes. And although she'd resolved the issue with the French government, Widhoff still had the letter when the Iranians (who were very courteous) arrived and told them how glad she was that they'd come to rescue

Astrophore. Handing them the tax bill, that was due in three days, Widhoff explained that they were welcome to seize the company.

It was enough to keep Khomeini's regime out of the filmmaking business.

Sometime in 1979 or 1980, Welles had filed an injunction to prevent Astrophore from having control over the negative. And between 1979 and 1982, Astrophore attempted to have the injunction removed on several occasions.

Among their numerous efforts was a January 1981 motion asking a French tribunal to dismiss the entire matter and order the parties to reach a new agreement in order to complete the movie. When that didn't work, they petitioned the court to rule in their favor against Welles, charge him a penalty of 500,000 francs (roughly 75,000–100,000 dollars), and allow them to finish the movie with another director. Their primary argument was that Welles had refused to complete the film.

In March 1982, however, the court ruled in Welles's favor. Their conclusion: Astrophore had failed to secure adequate financing, whereas Welles had given every indication that he'd wanted to finish his movie. The tribunal maintained that he'd been justified in not signing the amended 1976 contract tendered by Farmanara, in which the producers would have final cut if *The Other Side of the Wind* had not been completed within a reasonable time period.

There were two immensely ironic aspects of this ruling. The first was the ultimate resolution, in which the court concluded that Welles and Boushehri could not terminate their agreement, as the former had moral and artistic rights that couldn't be taken away and the latter possessed a clear financial interest in the film. The court ordered the two parties to complete the film as soon as possible, under the guidance of a judicial administrator.

But the real irony was the basis for that decision: the legal concept of *droit d'auteur* ("the right of the author"), which, under French copyright law, conferred "moral rights" upon the author of a work of art.

Among the rights afforded artists under *droit d'auteur* are the right of publication, which allows creators to decide when their work can be released; the right to protection of their honor and reputation; and the right to respect the integrity of the work—meaning that the piece of art in question cannot be altered by others without its author's consent.

In order to qualify for *droit d'auteur,* the artwork itself must "bear the stamp of the author's personality."

Orson Welles had been saved by the auteur theory.

At the same time, however, the negative would remain at LTC, and the auteur and his producer were back where they'd started. Welles couldn't move forward without Boushehri; and Boushehri couldn't do anything without Welles.

Between 1982 and 1985, Welles would occasionally consider ways he could finish the film. Perhaps if he could attain ownership, he would do it as almost a mock-umentary, with himself narrating.

"If I ever get it again, I'm going to do it as an extremely different film," he told writer Bill Krohn in 1982. "I'm going to stand outside of it and talk about it as myself . . . [and turn it into] a movie within a movie within a movie. It's one of those endless plots, not so much the making of it, the unmaking of it."

Thus, Welles would be putting on yet another mask and adding just one more reflection to the great hall of mirrors the film had become. Or maybe he'd just edit it together and finally get it done.

During the last three years of his life, Welles had editor Jon Braun set up footage from *The Other Side of the Wind* so they could watch it and think about ways that various scenes might be improved. He'd occasionally say he just wanted to watch it, then decide he was compelled to refine it even further. There was no sense that he was in any hurry.

Meanwhile, in 1984, Welles is said to have suffered a personal crisis when Paola allegedly discovered his affair with Oja and ordered him to stay away from their Las Vegas home. It is unclear, however, whether this was actually the case, as there had been rumors about Orson and Oja for at least fifteen years. Because of this, there is a decent chance that Paola may have known about the affair, but it is absolutely clear that Beatrice did not, and that revelation may have been the real issue.

Extremely close to both of her parents, Beatrice had never attended a day of school because Orson and Paola wanted her to be with them and clearly viewed their company and their frequent travels as a sufficient education for their daughter, who became a model in London, yet still moved to Sedona, Arizona, with her parents in the mid-to-late 1970s. Given this, having Beatrice find out about her father's affair may have allowed Paola to acknowledge and react to it more freely. There is also the possibility that Paola thought the affair was long over and the revelation that Orson was still involved with the same mistress may have been the cause of a serious new rupture in the Welles marriage.

Despite the revelation that he led a double life, however, Orson and Paola remained close, speaking on the phone two or three times every day, just as they'd done during the making of *The Wind*—despite the common assumption that Oja was his great love and that his marriage to Paola was somehow a mere formality.

"There is this misunderstanding where people think we had no [family] life and that it ended when I was about ten [around the time Oja entered the picture]," Beatrice Welles said. "We were incredibly close until the day he died."

The next year, another relationship hit the rocks when Welles accused Bogdanovich of having kept transcripts of their interviews from their unfinished book. The inference was that Bogdanovich had some commercial purpose in mind, despite the fact that he'd returned his half of the advance years before and promptly dug out the transcripts and returned them in 1985 after Welles had questioned his intentions.

In the days leading up to his death that October, Welles did the voice-over for an episode of Cybill Shepherd's television show *Moonlighting* and provided the voice for the planet Unicron in the animated film *The Transformers: The Movie*. His last appearance, however, was on October 9, 1985, the afternoon before he died, when he was a guest on *The Merv Griffin Show*.

Introduced by Griffin as someone who "captures our attention with every word he speaks," Welles emerged from behind the curtain, walking with a cane, looking both sage and wan. The pair discussed the women in Welles's life and moved on to modern television and his career, during which Welles described being a "star" in Dublin at sixteen and how he was an old pro by age twenty-two.

Summing it up, he told Griffin, "I had a tremendous streak of luck; I really think it has everything to do with anybody's life."

After the taping Orson had dinner with his biographer Barbara Leaming and his long-time friend Alessandro Tasca. The latter then drove Orson home and the pair talked together at the home on Stanley Avenue for several hours.

The next morning Welles was found dead, wearing a bathrobe and slumped over his typewriter.

He was seventy years old.

Just like Jake Hannaford.

Among the many things that I said over the years, another that people like to quote, is this: "If you want a happy ending, that depends, of course, on where you stop your story."

Well, perhaps you thought our story might end here—where it started—with my death. Maybe you thought that The Other Side of the Wind *would disappear with me, forgotten by everyone except those who made it, and even then, only as a fond memory of a unique film-making experience. And who would doubt you? Truly? Have you ever heard about efforts to complete von Stroheim's five-hour* Queen Kelly *or Eisenstein's* Que Viva Mexico!*—much less the release of Jerry Lewis's* The Day the Clown Cried? *Have you? No, of course you haven't.*

But the story of The Other Side of the Wind *doesn't end with my death, or the funeral and memorial service that followed. It doesn't* end with the laudatory obituaries and critical reevaluations that validate something I liked to say as the years wore on: "They're gonna love me when I'm dead." They did. Yet still I died alone—survived by my wife, three daughters, Oja, and The Other Side of the Wind.

Because many of those who were involved with the film [and others who'd loved me during my seventy years] remained committed to me in death. They were committed to my memory, my legacy, and the film that defined the last fifteen years of my life.

So forgive me for the false ending at the start of this story. Because if you know nothing else about me, the technique of opening with the main character's death is just that—a technique. A little surprise that shouldn't surprise you all that much—given that we all wind up in the same place, don't we?

Our story goes past my death and past those of many others. And it takes up again with what began happening after they lifted my body off that typewriter and carted me out of my house at 1717 North Stanley Avenue, just a few miles from Roxbury Drive.

AFTERLIFE

Artists aim for something timeless . . . and that's what he got.

—PRODUCER JENS KOETHNER KAUL

Even by funereal standards, the official service in Orson Welles's memory was a depressing affair that took place at a Hollywood funeral home Christopher Welles described as looking like "a hot sheets motel." Attended by a small crowd that included Paola, Welles's daughters, and a few close friends such as Gary and Skipper, the short, bleak ceremony ended with Beatrice receiving her father's cremated remains in a pine box.

Out of the country when he died, Oja didn't attend the funeral—though she did take Beatrice up on an offer to view Orson's dead body prior to its cremation. Arriving at the funeral home, Oja walked silently past Orson's daughter, went to the body, and then left without saying thank you or acknowledging a moment of kindness during an awkward and painful situation.

Oja, however, got her chance to remember Orson on November 2 during a public memorial at the Directors Guild Theater. Hosted by

Peter Bogdanovich, the event drew such a large crowd that many were turned away due to a lack of seating.

In addition to Janet Leigh, Geraldine Fitzgerald, Charlton Heston, and other celebrities, the crowd included Gary, Skipper, and many who'd known, admired, or worked with Welles over the years. Paola, Beatrice, Rebecca, and Christopher, however, weren't invited. This was Oja's event.

The ceremony began with Orson's voice filling the auditorium, as everyone was treated to his discussion of the director's role in the film-making process—recorded four years earlier at a Hollywood Foreign Press Association event during which he'd pointed out that "the trouble with movies today . . . is that all of us are too much in love with them and there's no damn cure for it."

This was followed by eulogies from several friends and colleagues, all leading up to the moment when Oja, clad in black, took the podium and changed the tone of the entire event.

Oja was angry. She was angry at the terrible fact that Orson was dead, but there was much more than that. She was angry at Beatrice and Paola; angry at the Iranians; angry at the Hollywood system; and angry at the French. She was angry at those who'd betrayed Orson in life and those who'd never sought to truly understand him. Orson, she said, was too generous and kindhearted to have been filled with self-pity or angry at those who'd tried to constrain his brilliance.

Then, after recounting her version of the story about finding Orson weeping while he watched *Ambersons* on television, Oja read a telegram from French president François Mitterrand, who lamented that "a genius of cinema has gone forever."

But even those words gave way to a sarcasm-laced tirade against Mitterrand and the French minister of culture, both of whom, she believed, had failed Welles. "I am sorry that Monsieur Mitterrand, even at this sad hour, had to still play politics and defend his establishment," she said. "I must explain that after long negotiations [over a French-financed, Welles-directed film of *King Lear*], Orson started to suspect that [the]

French government and their government-owned television never sincerely intended to make the film."

Welles, she claimed, was being used to provide cover for an imprudent comment the minister of culture had made about American society and why the generously funded *King Lear* had fallen through—even after Orson had voluntarily given up his $300,000 directing fee just to make the project a reality. This, apparently, was how Mitterrand treated the "genius of cinema."

Ending her comments with a quote from Orson's unfinished film *The Dreamers,* Oja read the following:

"There are only two things it is ever seemly for an intelligent person to be thinking. Yes—one is: What did God mean in creating the world? And the other: What do I do next?"

What happened next involved coping with the fallout of Orson's last will and testament, into which he'd woven the seeds of *The Other Side of the Wind*'s afterlife.

Drafted in 1982, the will left Paola the bulk of Orson's estate, including cars, works of art, jewelry, personal effects, and their Las Vegas home. Oja got the house on North Stanley Avenue and all of its contents. Each daughter received $10,000.

It also contained the following provision:

Except as otherwise provided for in this Will, I have intentionally and with full knowledge omitted to provide for my heirs. If any person obtains a determination that he is one of my heirs-at-law, and if by reason of such status he would otherwise share in my Estate or any portion thereof, then I give them the sum of ONE DOLLAR and no more to such person.

Using the word *he* to describe other heirs may have meant nothing. Alternatively, it could have meant there was more going on than Welles worrying about some unknown, alleged heirs trying to poach off his estate. Always wanting a son, he had filled that hole in his life with people such as Gary and Peter—all while there was the possibility that he may have had one, or more, male offspring.

The eldest of them was director Michael Lindsay-Hogg. The son of actress Geraldine Fitzgerald, Lindsay-Hogg was born in 1940, not long after his mother worked with Welles. Sharing an affinity for cigars and some of Welles's facial features, Lindsay-Hogg bore no resemblance to his aristocratic British father.

Although long suspecting that he might be Welles's son, Lindsay-Hogg never received confirmation from Fitzgerald, who, like Orson, always denied the rumor. But shortly after her death, his mother's close friend Gloria Vanderbilt allegedly told Lindsay-Hogg that Welles was indeed his father.

Another possible male heir was Tim McIntire, a beefy, often bearded actor whose mother, Jeanette Nolan, had known Orson since their radio days in New York and played his on-screen Lady Macbeth. Though Nolan was happily married to actor John McIntire from 1935 until his death in 1991, there remained allegations that she'd had an affair with Welles that resulted in the 1944 birth of Tim, who died in 1986 and whose physical similarity to Welles was remarkable.

Then there is the curious case of Oja's nephew Sasha Devcic, who was born in the mid-1960s and appeared as a young boy in *F for Fake*. Raised in Los Angeles, he grew close to Welles, with whom he spent considerable time that included postproduction and editing work on *The Other Side of the Wind* in the early 1980s. A dead ringer for Welles, at some point Sasha ceased using the name Devcic, and has long been known as Sasha Welles.

Welles's will also clearly stated that he would disinherit anyone who challenged his division of assets, particularly those bequeathed to Oja. This issue was important enough for Welles to add a codicil shortly before he died, leaving her his ownership rights in a number of unfinished projects. That confirmation of her ownership interests specifically explains that the story, screenplay, positive, and negative of *The Other Side of the Wind* would become Oja's property upon his death.

Between the will, the codicil, court decisions, alleged conversations, and sheer time commitment to the film, several parties now claimed some ownership of the project or a right to be involved in its completion.

First there was Astrophore, which owned half of the picture after investing more than $1 million in the production, supplemented by substantial loans that Boushehri, had allegedly provided Welles for use in making the film.

Oja owned the other half as the sole living partner in Avenel and also possessed other rights that were more difficult to define than those of Astrophore, with whom she shared ownership of the negative. She was coauthor of the script, lead actress in the movie, and the person who had the work print and many other elements of the film, some of which were physically located in the home she'd inherited—along with its contents—from Orson. (There are claims that the title to the home on Stanley Avenue was already in Oja's name, making Orson's bequest redundant.) Finally, Oja could possibly argue that she was heir to Orson's perpetual and inalienable moral rights under *droit d'auteur.*

As his widow and Orson's direct heir, Paola arguably had the standing to make a claim challenging Oja's interest in the film and asserting that it belonged, at least in part, to her.

Gary Graver, meanwhile, was forty-seven years old and had given fifteen years to both Welles and the film, investing his entire career, personal life, and financial future in *The Other Side of the Wind* despite not owning a percentage of the picture. Additionally, he would seem to have known as much about the movie as anyone alive. And if the film were never released, all that knowledge, time, and dedication would become as significant as the echo of a man screaming into an empty canyon.

The final interested party was Peter Bogdanovich, who'd suffered immensely since the release of *Nickelodeon,* during which time his re-lationship with Shepherd had ended and he'd fallen in love with Dor-othy Stratten, a kind, innocent, and beautiful twenty-year-old *Playboy* centerfold. Casting her alongside Audrey Hepburn in his next film, *They All Laughed,* Bogdanovich wanted to show the world that Stratten was as talented as she was gorgeous.

Stratten, however, was still married to a deranged hustler named Paul Snider, who'd brought her to Los Angeles from their native Van-couver after submitting Dorothy's naked pictures to *Playboy.* Unable to accept the end of his marriage, Snider hired a private eye to follow his ex-wife, and on August 14, 1980, Snider killed Stratten in an un-speakably gruesome murder-suicide that left the forty-one-year-old Bog-danovich devastated.

In the months that followed, Bogdanovich repurchased *They All Laughed* from its producer, Time Life Films (which was getting out of the business), and paid to distribute it himself, spending nearly $5 mil-lion to release it as a tribute to Stratten. When the film failed at the box office, he wrote the book *The Killing of the Unicorn: Dorothy Strat-ten 1960–1980.* This only brought about further financial woes, as he was sued by Snider's private eye, who felt he'd been portrayed as an accomplice.

When Bogdanovich declared bankruptcy in December 1985, the *Los Angeles Times* reported that he had $6.6 million in debts against $1.5 million in assets and "only $21.37 in the bank and $25.79 in his pocket."

Against this tragic backdrop, Bogdanovich maintained that he'd been asked to finish *The Other Side of the Wind* if anything happened to Welles and also that he was owed $200,000 to $250,000 in return for money he'd lent Welles, his own acting work as Otterlake, and the use of his home as a location.

And with each party holding on to his or her financial, personal, pro-fessional, or emotional interest in the film, the stage was set for things to get *really* complicated.

Given their roles as wife and mistress, it's no surprise that Paola and Oja didn't care for each other. Under most circumstances, they could have arranged their lives so as to never cross paths again.

But in truly Wellesian fashion, Orson's will did not leave things in a tidy state. Instead, the two women in his life found themselves in conflict over "who owned what," which raised the potential for continued and unwanted contact between the pair. Because of this, both agreed to meet at a Nevada attorney's office in mid-August 1986 to settle their disputes and resolve all ambiguities related to overlapping ownership rights in Orson's projects, after which they could get out of each other's lives for good.

On Tuesday, August 12, 1986, Paola left her Las Vegas home in a car driven by her thirty-nine-year-old friend Bill Kurasz. By some accounts, she was on the way to meet with Oja. In others, the meeting was scheduled for August 14 and Paola was heading to do an interview with a crew that was making a documentary about Orson.

But wherever she was headed, Paola was in the passenger seat when, according to news accounts, Kurasz drove into the path of another vehicle, resulting in an accident in which Paola suffered injuries that required her to be rushed to Desert Springs Hospital in Las Vegas, which was where she died a few hours later, with Beatrice at her side.

In the space of less than two years, thirty-year-old Beatrice Welles learned that her father had been cheating on her mother for two decades and then lost both parents within a ten-month period. But despite this pain and upheaval, there were still matters that needed to be resolved with Kodar.

What spurred the need to settle things was the existence of two documents Welles had signed in the three weeks prior to his death: 1) a promissory note stating that he would pay Oja $130,000 by the end of January 1986; and 2) another promissory note (written six days before he died) giving Oja half ownership, with Paola, in his pension and benefit plans.

With Paola gone and Beatrice left to handle things, an agreement between Orson's family and his mistress was signed on November 7, 1986. In that contract, Beatrice accepted Orson's codicil granting ownership of *The Other Side of the Wind* to Oja, who agreed to relinquish her interest in the retirement funds after recouping the $130,000 Orson had owed her.

Now there seemed little doubt that Oja owned 50 percent of *The Wind* and was artistic heir to Orson's moral rights as its creator.

With the negative locked away in Paris and the (alleged) nearly finished version edited by Welles nowhere to be found, Oja and Gary showed the work print to John Huston, hoping he'd agree to put the finishing touches on the film. Now eighty and attached to an oxygen tank, Huston met the pair one morning in 1986 at the home of television producer Norman Lear, where the host offered Huston a drink.

"No, no, no, no," the frail-looking director said to Lear.

But when asked a second time, Huston relented, telling Lear, "Well, perhaps a little tequila."

After the group watched the footage, Huston said he wasn't sure what to do with the film and suggested that his twenty-four-year-old son, Danny, could oversee its completion. Oja scoffed and asked John to reconsider.

Not long after, however, any chance of Huston finishing *The Wind* evaporated when Danny innocently told a reporter that his father might take the job and the information wound up in Marilyn Beck's December 6 column: "It looks as if Orson Welles's *The Other Side of the Wind* will finally be finished by John Huston."

Believing the revelation would cause Boushehri to ask for more money, Oja called Huston in a state of distress and interrogated him—despite the fact that he had no idea how word had gotten out until later, when Danny confessed his mistake.

That was the end of any talk that Huston would finish *The Other Side of the Wind*, but it was not the end of his directing career. The following August, a very sick Huston shot *The Dead,* an art house adaptation of a short story by James Joyce that seemed difficult, if not impossible, to capture on film. But Huston tore into the project (written by his son Tony and starring his daughter Anjelica), directing the film from a wheelchair and still smoking despite the oxygen tank.

Released in December 1987, four months after Huston's death, *The Dead* (as well as his 1985 film, *Prizzi's Honor*) was exactly the kind of film Orson had bemoaned the lack of twenty years earlier when talking to Bogdanovich on the set of *Catch-22*. But, as he always did, Huston defied the odds and left the world with two great films and also with as unconquerable a spirit as the sickly boy who crawled out the window and learned to ride waterfalls.

With Huston out, Oja and Graver showed *The Other Side of the Wind* to several prominent directors, including Steven Spielberg, Oliver Stone, George Lucas, and Clint Eastwood, hoping that one of them would take on the project.

After striking out with Stone, Lucas, and Spielberg, Oja found out that Peter Jason had recently appeared as Eastwood's commanding officer in *Heartbreak Ridge* and called him, insisting that he take the film to Eastwood, who had a reputation for rescuing obscure and offbeat projects from the scrap heap. Jason told Oja that she should write a letter that he'd drop off at Eastwood's Malpaso Productions on the Warner Bros. lot. When he read the handwritten note in Oja's somewhat broken English, however, Jason retyped the letter, fixed the grammar, and took it to Eastwood's office.

Expecting nothing, Jason was back at home when he received a call from a secretary at Malpaso who asked him to wait on the line for Eastwood.

"Pete?" the *Dirty Harry* star said when he came on the line. "It's Clint. What is this?"

"It's Orson Welles's last movie," Jason replied.

"Can I look at it today?" Eastwood asked.

Jason quickly called Graver, and they grabbed reels of two scenes (the rain-car-sex scene and Hannaford's arrival at his party) and drove them to Eastwood's office, where they showed the footage to Clint and his associates Tom Rooker and David Valdes.

At one point Valdes said, "There's nothing here we can use," and left the screening, which Rooker said everyone had come into anticipating a lost treasure, only to see a film that "was all over the place and kind of a mess."

Dejected, Graver and Jason stuck their film cans back in the trunk and began driving off the lot when Rooker ran out and told them Eastwood was intrigued by some of what he'd seen. "He couldn't figure out how you did the rain on the window," Rooker said, adding that Eastwood was leaving the next day but would love to see a script or have the film put on tape so he could try to figure it out when he returned from Africa, where he was portraying a fictionalized Huston in *White Hunter Black Heart*.

While Eastwood was gone, Jason and Graver took footage to Eastwood's editor five reels at a time. But when *White Hunter* didn't do well at the box office, it extended Eastwood's financial losing streak and left him with less clout at Warner Bros., which Jason said made any chance of a deal evaporate. Rooker, however, said the reason was that Eastwood's team simply couldn't figure out how to resolve the financial and creative problems the film carried with it.

Regardless, Eastwood certainly was influenced by what he'd seen of Hannaford when developing his own characterization of Huston for *White Hunter Black Heart*—including a scene when an overzealous man introduces himself and Clint's character, John Wilson, replies, "Of course you are."

The next opportunity for the film to be completed came not long afterward, in the late 1980s, when Graver showed some footage to *Mississippi Burning* producer Fred Zollo in a seedy Hollywood flophouse straight out of Raymond Chandler.

Arriving first, Zollo waited uneasily for Orson's cinematographer, whom he'd anticipated would be a dashing "old Hollywood" type. When Graver arrived, however, he looked beaten down by life. Immediately sympathetic, Zollo sensed how years of hope had given way to a midnight rendezvous in a creepy, half-empty building where, for the millionth time, Graver was going to show a film he'd made with Orson Welles.

When the pair entered the dark apartment and Graver turned on the lights, it confirmed Zollo's instincts. "You just knew it was a tragedy beyond tragedies," he said. "You knew it was *Sunset Boulevard*."

The whole thing felt illicit, as if Graver feared someone would find out he had the film and might take it away during the screening. Likewise, as he viewed the combination of edited, partially edited, and raw footage, Zollo was blown away to the point where he feared going to the bathroom, because he worried that he'd come back only to be told that he'd seen enough.

What he watched in that dingy room, Zollo said, was a set of visually spectacular scenes that embraced the style of 1960s directors such as Arthur Penn, mixed with sequences that signaled a completely new version of the razzle-dazzle you expected from Orson Welles.

After that screening, Zollo began working with his attorney, Jay Harris, who happened to be Arnold Weissberger's partner. In collaboration with Graver, Zollo and Harris discussed making an end run around Astrophore by seeing if there was enough footage to reconstruct the film from what they already had. When that approach didn't work, Zollo chose a simpler path.

"We had the money," Zollo said. "So I asked, 'How much money will it take to buy them all out?'"

Told by an intermediary that each party would go away for a few million dollars, Zollo offered exactly what they'd asked for. Then, however, he received a counteroffer—now everyone wanted more, so he offered more, after which everyone wanted more than that. Ultimately, the total buyout price, according to Zollo, grew to exceed $10 million, at which point he decided the situation was too ridiculous even for Hollywood and walked away.

Between 1988 and 1997, Graver toted a battered work print around the world, doing anything he could to find a buyer. At one point in 1991, Frank Marshall told a reporter that all the elements of the film were available and simply needed to be gathered together. Yet nothing happened and the footage remained where it had been, until 1997, when Michael Fitzgerald came along.

Fitzgerald had arrived in Hollywood in the 1970s with his brother, attempting to sell a screenplay based on Flannery O'Connor's novel *Wise Blood,* whose rights they were able to obtain because their father was the literary executor of her estate. Finding there was little interest in the southern gothic tale, the brothers received rare encouragement from Huston, who told them he'd direct if they could line up sufficient financing for even a bare-bones production.

By 1979, with a budget of $190,000, Huston shot the Fitzgeralds' *Wise Blood* script on location in Macon, Georgia, in less than two months. The cast included Ned Beatty, Brad Dourif, and Harry Dean Stanton—all working for almost nothing. Even Huston took a role in the film so they could save money.

Maintaining his relationship with Huston, Fitzgerald and his wife, Kathy, also produced *Under the Volcano* and knew Welles through their attempts to make a film version of *The Cradle Will Rock* shortly before Orson death.

Then, in 1997, after watching several reels of *The Other Side of the Wind* at Graver's home on the San Fernando Valley side of the Hollywood Hills, Fitzgerald was so taken with Huston's performance that he decided to see if he could get the film finished as a way of honoring the two great filmmakers.

To make this happen, Fitzgerald went to one of Hollywood's foremost film preservationists and asked if he'd finance the project. With substantial resources, the man had no interest in financial gain, only the desire to preserve the unseen work of a certified cinematic genius. He was the perfect producer and agreed to put up the money, but he wished to remain anonymous.

In late April 1997, Fitzgerald wrote a letter to Boushehri, introducing himself as the representative of an unnamed but deep-pocketed foundation that wished to take out a sixty-day option at $20,000 and would guarantee $500,000 upon completion of purchase. If he accepted, Boushehri would also receive 20 percent of the gross until he'd earned an additional $750,000—at which point his percentage would drop to 10 percent. Twenty-four years after he'd first paired up with Orson Welles, Mehdi Boushehri, now in his early eighties, would finally have the chance to recoup his investment.

Having been through many convoluted negotiations, Boushehri was wary of the anonymous funding source and sought reassurance that the money was real. After an exchange of letters that summer, however, he became convinced of the producer's legitimacy and ultimately requested a "simple deal" but also added that no real talks could begin until Fitzgerald could prove that he had access to the work print, which represented the only expression of Welles's vision and "must be respected."

He wouldn't participate in a film that was anything less than what Welles would have wanted.

Fitzgerald lined up the funding and the print, then met with Boushehri in Paris. He was surprised to find that the man who'd been portrayed as a villainous character intent on blocking Orson Welles's film was actually a gracious, elegant, and intelligent man who'd been behaving cautiously after being burned so many times in the past.

Once he'd agreed to a deal with Boushehri, Fitzgerald returned to Los Angeles and set up a dinner with the financier, Graver, Marshall, and Bogdanovich, who'd supervise the creative efforts. The group gathered at Madeo Ristorante on Beverly Boulevard, where (before the preservationist arrived) Fitzgerald explained that he was leaving for Cannes the following day and one ground rule would have to be observed in his absence. No one, he said, was to contact the financier while he was in France. He was to remain the sole intermediary, to avoid any possibility of jeopardizing the deal. Everyone agreed.

But when he arrived in Cannes, Fitzgerald received word from the preservationist, who told him that one of the parties had called that morning, insisted on seeing him immediately, and then had asked for a $250,000 personal loan. In response, the preservationist asked the man to leave, then called Fitzgerald and told him, "I'm out."

After that, the deal simply evaporated.

Despite winning the Palme d'Or at Cannes for his 1985 film *Mask*, Bogdanovich was unable to revitalize his career over the remaining years of the 1980s. Even his success at Cannes had an unhappy ending, as Bogdanovich sued Universal for $19 million for using Bob Seger's music (rather than Bruce Springsteen's—as originally planned) on the sound track. Since then, he'd directed and produced *Illegally Yours*, *Texasville* (a *Last Picture Show* follow-up), *Noises Off*, and *The Thing Called Love*, as well as a handful of television projects.

He'd also aroused controversy by marrying Stratten's younger sister, Louise, in 1988, when she was twenty and he was forty-nine. Taking fire from every direction, he was even subjected to claims of immorality from Hugh Hefner. And by the summer of 1997, Bogdanovich was filing for bankruptcy a second time when he found himself on the wrong end of a $4.2 million verdict after being sued by a couple with whom he'd contracted to buy a $1.9 million house.

During the hearing it was revealed that Bogdanovich had been taking $50,000 vacations; spending $6,000 a month on rent; and buying roughly $70,000 worth of clothes a year. These expenses, his attorney argued, were essential to Bogdanovich's career and financial future, because living less extravagantly would indicate that he was no longer of consequence. The horrible truth was that Bogdanovich had to keep up appearances by living way beyond his means just to have the possibility of securing work that would afford him the chance to rebuild his career.

"It's somewhat like riding a tiger," his attorney said. "If you fall off, you get eaten, and if you stay on, it's a rough ride."

Nobody understood that better than Bogdanovich.

In 1958, Universal's hijacking of the final cut on *Touch of Evil* had been the last straw that proved to Welles that the studios were impossible. Now, forty years later, the same studio was going to rerelease the same film after a restoration performed by preservationist Rick Schmidlin and Academy Award winner Walter Murch, who based their work on Welles's fifty-eight-page memo and editing notes. As much as possible, they were restoring *Touch of Evil* to Welles's vision but made no claim that it was a "director's cut."

And this is where Beatrice Welles reentered the story. Over the preceding thirteen years, Beatrice had come to view herself as Orson's artistic executor and guardian of his legacy, an understandable position given that she was heir to Paola's estate and the only one of Orson's children who seemed interested in the position.

On the advice of representatives she'd hired to protect her father's legacy, Beatrice became a central figure in the *Touch of Evil* restoration saga when her artistic rights consultant Thomas A. White told the press that Schmidlin and Murch's work was anything but an "artistic homage." Instead, he claimed, "Universal just wants to make more money from their film library." Amid that controversy and some ensuing threats, the Cannes Film Festival cancelled the debut screening it had scheduled for May 1998 and Beatrice became a lightning rod for criticism from those in the Welles community, including Charlton Heston, who reacted to the situation by telling a newspaper, "Beatrice Welles is not a filmmaker. She's not qualified. Universal didn't consult me, or Janet [Leigh]. Why should they? We were all working for salary. If you don't have a share of the picture you have no control over it." Heston continued his campaign by calling Beatrice "an idiot" on television and inferring that she would shut up and go away if Universal offered her $35,000.

The dispute over *Touch of Evil* would ultimately define the two opposing views of Beatrice Welles, who had done her own restoration of *Othello* in 1992. One camp believed it was her job to protect Orson's legacy and that she was doing so appropriately, while detractors characterized her as a villain who filed lawsuits in the name of her father's art and then was paid off to remove her opposition.

After *Touch of Evil* received much critical praise, McBride and Schmidlin created a detailed proposal to complete *The Other Side of the Wind*, which they showed to Universal and other studios. There was some interest, but not enough to make a deal.

Then Matthew Duda, a Showtime executive, decided he wanted to take on the project.

A Harvard film major in the late 1970s, Duda spent an enormous amount of time at the Orson Welles Cinema and was in the audience one evening for a showing of *Othello* and a subsequent Q&A with Welles. At one point, someone asked a question about *The Other Side of the Wind*. Becoming intrigued by the film, Duda maintained his interest when he took a job with Showtime in 1981.

While at Showtime, Duda became friendly with Graver (whom he'd met in Boston and at Orson's memorial), who often shot B movies that ran on the cable network and frequently pushed Duda to complete *The Wind*.

In 1998, that cajoling finally paid off, and Showtime decided to finish the movie with Bogdanovich overseeing the final edit and postproduction. Using McBride's budget of $3 million, they moved ahead and pursued rights. Meanwhile, Oja and Bogdanovich allegedly cut McBride out of his role as a producer because he'd budgeted a salary of $50,000 for the eighteen months of work that he'd commit to the project. With Oja claiming his involvement was "ridiculous," McBride walked away, while Bogdanovich, who'd called him "greedy," asked Showtime for the money he was allegedly owed by the production.

Duda's plan to complete the film revolved around three issues: Boushehri's rights as an investor; Oja's underlying rights to the material; and Beatrice's ability to disrupt things in her role as executor of Orson's estate and the person with power over how he was portrayed. Handling matters in an orderly fashion, Duda pursued options with Boushehri and Oja, who had possession of the physical materials and ultimately owned the film.

Like Fitzgerald, Duda was surprised upon meeting Boushehri at Showtime's Los Angeles offices. Having taken Welles's side from the beginning, he'd always envisioned the shah's brother-in-law as some shadowy figure. But once Boushehri was sitting across from him, Duda realized things weren't so clear-cut.

"He was a very calm and lovely man," Duda said of Boushehri. "A real gentleman."

Sharing his Coopers & Lybrand audits, Boushehri indicated that he simply wanted to get his money back, or at least some return on his investment. Showtime, however, was unwilling to pay him $1 million for fear Oja would want the same. Nevertheless, Duda was able to sign options with both parties.

The next step was to get a release from the Welles estate, not because it had any rights, but in order to eliminate the fear that Beatrice would block distribution.

In meeting with Beatrice several times, Duda found that, like Boushehri, she defied his expectations. Charming, bright, and clearly loyal to her father's legacy, Beatrice held one legitimate concern—namely, that someone other than Orson would complete his movie.

"Everyone wanted to shoot me," Beatrice said of long-held fears that she would block the film's release. "But, I wasn't sitting there saying, 'nobody can have this movie.' I was trying, in my way, to be able to preserve his work and its integrity and still have people see it."

To deal with her concerns about the integrity of Orson's movie, Duda told her they could possibly add some documentary elements to the film that would let the audience know which portions had been edited by Orson and which had been completed by others. The idea satisfied Beatrice, who claimed that "the last thing I ever wanted was for this movie to sit in a vault in Paris."

Suddenly, it appeared that Matthew Duda was close to solving the problem.

Four years later, Showtime still hadn't seen the negative but had continued extending its options with Boushehri and Oja, when the appearance of trouble with Beatrice reemerged—this time via an August 2002 article in *The Telegraph* where Thomas A. White, allegedly speaking on behalf of Orson's daughter, brought Kodar's interests into question.

"Oja Kodar has nothing to do with the estate of Orson Welles," White said. "I don't accept that she is the partner of Orson Welles in any sense of the word. Partnership is a relationship based on equality. How can she be equal to one of the world's greatest film talents?"

He was right, but, then again, there was nobody making the argument that Oja was Orson's equal, and the manner in which White had taken down Orson's mistress injected a new tension into the background of any discussions about completing the film.

Graver also had his own complicated relationship with Beatrice and her representatives, believing that she was jealous of the "moviemaking family" Orson had established with himself and Oja. This, Graver said, had been the motivation when she'd taken him to court to block his attempt to sell Orson's *Citizen Kane* Oscar at auction in 1994—at a time when he desperately needed the money. During court proceedings attorney Alan Gutman successfully argued that Orson never intended for the Academy Award to be a gift—an allegation that seemed to invalidate much of Gary's professional life.

Rebecca, Orson's daughter with Rita Hayworth, died in 2004, leaving only Beatrice and Christopher. Nearing seventy, Christopher was no longer disappointed that Orson hadn't been the father she'd wanted, and was of the opinion that all of his films "should be shown at every opportunity. Even his unfinished work." It all should be shown, she said at the 2005 Locarno Film Festival, "because everything is valuable."

Since her father's death, Christopher had also formed a relationship with Oja and had come to like her. Thus, the pair greeted each other happily at Locarno that year, where McBride and Antoine were in attendance, as was Gary, who was wearing a collar around his neck. Graver told everyone that it was nothing. But, sadly, that wasn't true. Graver, neither a smoker nor a heavy drinker, had throat cancer.

Thrice divorced, he had been through enormous stress in his personal and professional life. Then in 1985 he'd found happiness with his fourth wife, actress Jillian Kesner, who not only tolerated his lifestyle, but supported his dreams. This had given him stability for the past two decades while he'd traveled with reels of footage in an effort to find end money for *The Other Side of the Wind*. He'd even written a letter to Donald Trump, explaining that the attention-seeking millionaire could become the man who finally finished Orson Welles's last movie.

"I'm still working with Orson," he told McBride at Locarno. "I never stopped."

Graver, who was in his early teens when he lost his alcoholic father to liver disease, had turned to the movies as a source of comfort and paternal influence. They became everything to him, just as they had for Bogdanovich. Then Orson came along and filled the void, taking over Gary's life and maintaining his grip even after his death.

Growing up with Welles as a major presence in his life and the dominant force in his father's, Gary's eldest son, Sean, said that Orson's charisma and presence took over a room even when he was silent. "I used to think that he had power because his name was Orson Welles," Sean Graver said. "But I really believe the power wasn't in the fact that he was Orson Welles—it was that he had the type of personality people couldn't say no to."

Even Sean was unable to say no when, in the late 1970s, Gary would have him cash $10,000 checks and take the money to Orson in an envelope. "Everyone was always in service to Orson and the project," Sean said. "And nobody ever said no."

Ultimately, that inability to say no took a toll on Graver. Orson was an addiction, and there were times when Gary realized that it could often be bad for him. But he couldn't quit and he never did, even up until his death in November 2006, when he was working on a book about his career with Welles. He'd shot and directed hundreds of films, but in the end, all of his allegiance belonged to Orson Welles and *The Other Side of the Wind*.

"To his death, I believe he felt that *The Other Side of the Wind* was the best project he'd ever worked on," Sean said. "He'd always dreamed of making the kinds of movies that Orson made, and he thought this was the great work of his life."

Though few had seen it, there were many who agreed with Graver that the film was undoubtedly "the work of a genius . . . and beyond doubt one of the outstanding specimens of Welles's incredibly innovative oeuvre," as Stefan Droessler of the Munich Film Museum said. According to one critic, *The Wind* was a film by "a creator at least twenty years ahead of his time."

And in 2005, as Gary's health deteriorated, there was a sudden burst of hope when Beatrice reached an agreement with Showtime, leading Duda to believe that the film he described as "a Picasso in the attic that needs a frame" was about to come down the stairs.

Now it was Paul Hunt's turn to complicate the situation.

A hard-living B-movie producer and director who'd worked as an editor, soundman, camera operator, and gaffer on *The Other Side of the Wind*, Hunt was described by Graver's son as "the strangest, weirdest guy you ever met." Though he'd worked with Welles numerous times, Hunt rarely came up in discussions of those who'd been close to Welles or made major contributions to *The Wind*.

In 2006, however, Hunt, film distributor Sandy Horowitz, and their partner, John Nicholas, began talking to Boushehri about an option, with the underlying claim that it was Paul—not Peter or Oja—who'd been entrusted to oversee the film's completion. "I spoke to Orson on many occasions about how Peter and Oja saw their roles and how Orson saw them," Hunt said. "Orson's point of view was substantially different than [Peter's and Oja's]."

By February 2006, the group had signed a letter of intent with Boushehri, promising him $400,000 if they acquired all rights to the film and another $400,000 upon release, with an additional 10 percent of profits up to $200,000. Then, without money changing hands, Boushehri granted Hunt's group access to the negative at LTC, for the purpose of making copies they could use in postproduction or to secure distribution agreements.

Beatrice quickly responded, filing a motion in French court requesting that LTC be enjoined from releasing the negative to anyone. At this point it was roughly twenty-five years since the film had been locked up in the lab. Joining her in this action, strangely enough, was Oja—who'd intervened and asked the court to uphold the injunction.

On July 7, 2006, the court upheld the injunction, thus blocking Hunt's group and protecting Welles's "moral rights," which apparently belonged to Beatrice.

Were this not complicated enough, Boushehri died in 2006 at the age of ninety-one. This, of course, altered the landscape: Now the players moving forward would be his widow, Jacqueline Boushehri, Hunt and his partners, Oja, Showtime, Beatrice, and Astrophore, whose status wasn't exactly what everyone had assumed during their two decades of trying to make a deal.

For years, all negotiations had taken place with the understanding that Astrophore and Boushehri were one and the same. Thus, if you acquired Boushehri's rights, you were also acquiring Astrophore's, giving you 50 percent ownership of the picture. But after his death, the parties began to see that things were a bit more complicated than that; Boushehri, it seemed, had bifurcated his rights. In reality, there were two entities: Astrophore, the production company now run by Françoise Widhoff, which owned the actual rights to the film; and Boushehri, a private investor who owned part of the company. Thus, it was Widhoff and Astrophore who owned Boushehri's half of the negative and its distribution rights, while Jacqueline had inherited production rights, allowing her to prevent others from showing the material.

Widhoff, meanwhile, insisted that she didn't own a thing. Instead, she said, it all belonged to Jacqueline. With Oja and Beatrice now on the other side, Duda said, "it was a truly Orsonian deal structure."

In April 2007, Peter Bogdanovich told the *New York Sun* that a deal was 99.9 percent done. It was not the last time he told reporters or festival crowds that the parties were close to striking an agreement that would result in the completion and release of *The Other Side of the Wind*. At the same time, however, Hunt's group continued to pursue ownership rights under the belief that they had an eternal option, based on an agreement signed by a dead man, for which they'd paid no financial consideration.

In an e-mail between Hunt's and Jacqueline Boushehri's attorneys, the latter claimed the deal with Mehdi had been intended to "light a fire under Oja Kodar" that would encourage her to make a deal with someone—either Hunt or Showtime. But, quoting prior correspondence on the subject, the attorney assessed the likelihood of a successful negotiation with Oja:

> *I think she's the problem . . . We have been waiting for many years for her to agree to a deal. . . . Showtime has told us for many years that they knew they could make a deal with Mehdi in an instant, that was easy. They didn't want to waste time on that until they made a deal with Oja. My own personal feeling (off the record) is that she is incapable of making a deal with anyone. . . . Our client has never been the problem. Kodar has been.*

By October, the attorney wrote again, upset that Hunt's group was still shopping the picture on the basis that they owned the copyright: "No one could ever interpret Mehdi's 'Letter of Intent' to somehow be a perpetual right without consideration or obligation on behalf of your clients. It doesn't say that and no rational interpretation could give it that meaning."

Soon Oja's lawyer was involved, asking Hunt's group to stop asserting rights that were "baseless and in bad faith." Claiming that Showtime wouldn't complete a deal because of their interference, the attorney said that the entire situation had caused Oja to suffer "irreparable financial harm and emotional distress that continues to adversely affect her health."

Meanwhile, in April 2008, Bogdanovich, accompanied by Sasha Welles, filmed the opening of the Los Angeles storage vault for Showtime, who'd put up $200,000, and rented an editing suite in Santa Monica where Peter could examine the work print and other materials they found.

Though he'd been anxious as to what was in the vault, Duda found remarkable footage among the reels they removed and was pleased to see that it was in far better shape than he'd anticipated. Meanwhile, the vault also contained material that he never could have imagined they'd find, such as audio of Welles himself explaining the film.

Still protected by a court order that required agreement between the parties, the negative remained at LTC and under Astrophore's control. Because of this, Showtime went to Widhoff, who said she'd sign over all rights to Jacqueline Boushehri (who was eager to make a deal), but only after they'd signed a contract with Oja. This, Duda and others saw, was a most unlikely prospect.

"Just when you thought you'd made some progress, there was always something and you'd slog back," Duda said. "The personal stuff ebbs and flows over the years. Everybody loves everyone, then they hate each other. They work together and then they won't work together."

Now, however, with Oja essential to finalizing a deal for total ownership, Showtime found out that she was also negotiating with German producer Jens Koethner Kaul, who would later join forces with Filip Jan Rymsza and his Los Angeles–based production company, Royal Road Entertainment.

Koethner Kaul had encountered Oja first, in November 2008, when a mutual friend from Los Angeles thought he might be able to help her fund the completion of Welles's film.

After several phone conversations with Oja, Koethner Kaul also spoke with Jacqueline Boushehri and came to realize that once he'd reached an agreement with them, he'd only need to deal with Bogdanovich and Beatrice in order to tie up the ownership rights and finish the movie (at an estimated cost of $3.25 million). Each woman wanted only $300,000 for her share of the film—a substantial reduction in price from the millions Fred Zollo had been asked to pay.

Koethner Kaul asked to see the movie and sat through eleven hours and sixteen minutes of footage that had been digitized by Showtime. When it was over, he believed he'd seen a masterpiece. It had to be completed.

Oja, however, was using Koethner Kaul not just as a potential investor, but also as a way of gaining leverage with Showtime by playing the two parties against each other. Thus, as Duda furiously tried to make a deal with Oja and Jacqueline so that Astrophore could finally release the negative, the Showtime executive realized that Kodar was also in talks with someone else and had doubled her price, to $750,000. Koethner Kaul and Rymsza accepted Oja's new figure, though she eventually wound up asking for a substantially larger amount, as well as total artistic control and Croatian distribution rights.

Because of this, Duda decided to explore whether Showtime could complete the film without possession of the negative by simply using all the material that had been found in the vault. That would eliminate having to deal with Astrophore or Beatrice, but they would still need Oja, who now claimed that another party had offered her a sum far larger than $750,000.

"Her price just kept changing," Duda said. "She kept going higher and higher, and then she said we'd sabotaged her [nonexistent offer for more money]."

On the verge of retirement after thirty years at Showtime, Duda still hadn't figured out a way to complete *The Other Side of the Wind*.

Then Frank Marshall stepped in.

Since his early work for Bogdanovich, Marshall had become a producer, with the *Indiana Jones, Back to the Future,* and *Bourne* franchises all to his credit, not to mention *The Color Purple, Poltergeist,* and innumerable other successful films.

And it was Marshall who helped Koethner Kaul and Rymsza pull the deal together. With Showtime stepping back, Royal Road and Koethner Kaul's only competition was Paul Hunt's group, now without Hunt, who died in September 2011. Hunt's partners, however, believed their option with Boushehri was still in effect and felt the same way about a copyright they'd registered on the film in 2007, which Horowitz ultimately threatened to sell on eBay if nobody bought them out.

Koethner Kaul, however, had gone directly to Widhoff and explained his intention to use Academy Award–nominated composer Michel Legrand and a famous, award-winning editor to follow Welles's blueprint, convincing her that the film could be completed as a feature.

In September 2012, Widhoff signed over Astrophore's rights, giving Koether Kaul control over the negative, which remained at LTC under the injunction. The transfer of ownership put Oja, who was still negotiating with multiple parties, in a corner; at one point she threatened to change her will by adding a provision that nobody could complete the film or access the negative until twenty-five years after her death.

Despite Oja's difficult negotiating posture, Koethner Kaul, Royal Road, and Marshall (all interested in getting the film completed and into theaters) continued pursuing her rights, while they now owned those belonging to Astrophore. Oja, meanwhile, still sought more money, Croatian distribution rights, and artistic control over the movie.

After retiring, Duda remained interested in the project but came to accept what he'd known all along. Oja had been the party everyone thought was essential to getting the project done. But throughout the years, she'd tried repeatedly to squeeze every bit of leverage she could out of potential investors and then would get cold feet when a deal was close, always believing something better was just around the bend. Though there had been roadblocks with Beatrice, Boushehri, Hunt, and the innumerable factors that seemed to curse the deal, it seemed that Oja had been the biggest obstacle of all preventing the completion of *The Other Side of the Wind*.

In spring 2013, when I interviewed Frank Marshall at his office in Santa Monica, he told me, "This could be the day we pull everything together. We're talking to Oja today. As you know, she owns half the movie, so we still need her to come on board and agree to sell her rights."

Just before Christmas 2013, I sent Marshall some follow-up questions, one of which regarded a rumor that Oja had made a final power play. In his response, Marshall inserted a line copied from a recent e-mail sent by Sasha Welles.

"Oja has given me her rights, which include the screenplay," Sasha wrote. "But, I am not giving anyone clearance to use it."

NOW WHAT?

Nearly eighty years after his fight with Ernest Hemingway, forty-five since he took the first shots at the house on Lawlen, and thirty since Welles was found slumped over his typewriter, the story of *The Other Side of the Wind* (like the film) remains unfinished.

The project has outlived not just Stafford Repp and Norman Foster or Orson and Gary, but also Huston, the entire Hannaford mafia, Susan Strasberg, Charles Higham, Geoffrey Land, Pauline Kael, Paul Hunt, Dennis Hopper, Paul Mazursky, and many, many other members of the cast and crew.

In addition to the hours of footage, the negative (still locked up at LTC), and the innumerable attempts to complete *The Other Side of the Wind*, one of the primary things left behind is a set of potentially unanswerable questions.

Among those questions, two of the most intriguing are these: Was the film autobiographical? And what did it all really mean?

Orson had always warned not to "look for keys," which might lead to the belief that his work was autobiographical. Yet if there are indeed answers, that is the first place one would have to look: at his career, his life, and *The Wind* itself.

To try to understand *The Other Side of the Wind*, one place to start is the beginning of Welles's filmmaking career, with the first few minutes of *Citizen Kane,* which, like *The Wind,* examines a man's true character from multiple perspectives. In *Kane,* we see the various sides of Charles Foster Kane via personal interviews and accounts of his life; while in *The Wind,* the many types of cameras and angles from which the film is shot all work to create a picture of Hannaford.

As with the rest of his films, this doesn't mean that Welles gives you real answers as to whether these men are good or bad, kind or evil, brilliant or just subject to the vicissitudes of luck. And that's the way he wanted it, because what Welles did was provide the information and show the audience that man is unknowable and complicated, made up of polar opposites, and ultimately good, bad, and everything in between.

Though *Kane* may be the most complete film ever made, its opening literally overflows with symbols of incompletion, beginning with a leading shot of Xanadu, Kane's unfinished mansion—and then leads us further into a tangled web.

As Jedediah Leland said, Kane was disappointed in the world, so he built one of his own; and it is Leland who says that Charlie Kane never finished anything but the review of his own wife's opera that his drunken friend couldn't write.

Meanwhile, the film opens with the following quote at the beginning of a newsreel being made upon his death:

In Xanadu did Kubla Khan
A stately pleasure-dome decree . . .

That line is from "Kubla Khan," the unfinished 1797 poem written by Samuel Taylor Coleridge.

Thus, Orson Welles's first and best-known film opens with images and words about an unfinished mansion that are taken from an unfinished poem—all to tell the story of a great man who has a bright mind, boundless energy, gigantic ambition, and extraordinary charisma. Yet it is that same man who fails to live up to his own expectations and those of others, in part because he can't finish anything and keeps getting in his own way.

Unlike Higham's thesis, this isn't about a fear of completion so much as a means of pointing out the strange symmetry with which Welles began and ended his career. It was as if he had an unconscious understanding of how everything would play out, long before it happened.

Leaving aside Orson's warning for a moment, the fact is that Charlie Kane and Orson Welles had much in common. Both spent essentially parentless childhoods without the mother who'd been their anchor and with someone else watching over their money. Each grew up with few restrictions on his imagination, ambition, or behavior. Neither was accustomed to hearing people say no. And as a result, neither believed in boundaries, or at least not when it came to himself, and ultimately this quality would prove to be both an enormous gift and a colossal curse.

As young men, Kane and Welles were adventurous and idealistic, taking to life with a gusto-filled, libertine sensibility. They wanted to be that rare and remarkable thing—a great man, which is exactly what they became. The trick, however, was that neither became the great man he anticipated. Kane never lived up to his bold "Statement of Principles," and Welles never repeated the perfection of *Citizen Kane*. But in the end, both men failed because of the things that affect us all— their own humanity and character flaws, not to mention the curious nature of luck.

Throughout their lives, Kane and Welles wore very similar masks that magically transformed them into larger-than-life figures. Yet beneath those masks were boys who lost their parents and their childhood. As a result, they were their own greatest creations and self-made works of art that remained the center of attention in a world of their design, in which they tried to transform newspapers, wives, mistresses, and locations—all with the vision of turning them into exactly what they wanted.

At bottom, Orson Welles and Charlie Kane were good men, with big hearts, who were compelled to betray other men who dared to grow too close to them. For Kane, it was Leland. With Orson, it had been Bogdanovich and, to a lesser—and less obvious—extent, Graver.

Then there is Jake Hannaford, who, like Orson, dies at the age of seventy while seeking money to complete the film that will bring him back in every possible way. Hannaford and Orson both lost their fathers to suicide—either real or imagined. Both were married multiple times and had a strong desire to turn their love interests (John Dale and Oja Kodar) into movie stars, just like Kane trying to legitimize his lounge-singer second wife inside of the opera house he built for her.

While Welles and Hannaford are each charming, powerful, broke, making a comeback movie, and seeking end money, each also betrays a former protégé, who—in both cases—is Peter Bogdanovich.

Wearing the mask of a man's man, Hannaford turns his life into a performance, much of which has been conceived to cover up his hidden homosexual desires. Meanwhile, the facts of his life and the making of *The Other Side of the Wind* are an almost eerie match for what happened to Welles while making the film, which leads one to the possible conclusion that Hannaford (whose manliness is quite different from Welles's) may well have been a mask Welles put on his own face.

Richard Ben Cramer wrote the following of Ted Williams:

"Few men try for best ever, and Ted Williams is one of those."

Kane and Welles were both men who were aiming for best ever.

Hannaford is who they became.

Where *Kane* was a story about the creation of a man, *The Other Side of the Wind* is about another man's dissolution and destruction;

the unmaking of a man and artist who has lost control of his creativity and is now trapped inside the brain that has made him a genius.

So, what is *The Other Side of the Wind* about? What does it mean?

There are no answers to these questions. Instead, the film is a fragment, composed of brilliance and madness; finely honed and wildly disorganized; meticulously edited but ultimately unfinished. The movie is a shot at perfection in a world where the director can no longer control his muse and is left to stumble about a maze composed of his own art and creativity. It's a world that shows Welles at his best and his worst, bringing together his polar opposites—but leaving him unable or unwilling to recognize that his art and life have become one and the same. What was real hasn't become just confused. After a fashion, it ceased to matter.

Creating a narrative that kept changing along with his life, and the making of his own film, at some point Welles stopped inventing his story and began recording impressions of his world as it evolved around him. The result was a film that could never be finished. Because to finish it might have meant the end of Orson's own artistic story—and that was impossible to accept. So he kept it going and going.

Aiming for something so creative, clever, and impossible to execute, *The Wind* would become the photographic negative of *Kane*, refracted through the fun house mirrors in *The Lady from Shanghai* and frequently filmed with the degree of difficulty required to pull off the tracking shot in *Touch of Evil*.

But in the end, remarkable men such as Welles, Kane, and Hannaford can't control their own self-destructive impulses. This doesn't make them bad. In fact, it's quite the opposite. These frailties are what make them real.

In between the time he made *Citizen Kane* and *The Other Side of the Wind,* the man for whom everything seemed possible had been around the world and shot it all, just like Hannaford. Though he still believed in his own magical and artistic abilities, while also possessing a remarkable passion to create, Welles may have literally shot it all dead.

And by this time, no matter how brilliant or enthusiastic he was, perhaps one thing might have changed. Because maybe, just maybe, by this point, Orson Welles had come to think that, just like the beautiful sunset as seen through the studio doors, it all looked fake.

ACKNOWLEDGMENTS

When I began looking for people to interview, the first thing I learned is that everyone keeps *The Other Side of the Wind* on their résumé and in their bio for eternity. And nobody does it for lack of accomplishment. Rather, *The Wind* remains part of their lives for reasons that range from the uniqueness of the experience to devotion to Welles to sheer pride in having been involved in one of his films.

Indicative of this is a story about CBS chief executive Les Moonves, who was approached by a Showtime (CBS subsidiary) executive with a proposal to complete *The Other Side of the Wind*. The man assumed that Moonves probably didn't know much, if anything, about this unfinished Orson Welles film. He was wrong. Not only had Moonves heard of the film—he'd actually been an extra during one of the shoots in Carefree, Arizona.

Fortunately, Moonves wasn't the only person like that—as the process of working on this book was one of eternal discovery and surprise. People had forgotten many things, but nobody ever forgot being part of *The Wind*. And I was enormously fortunate to be able to work on this book about a great man and one of his remarkable projects.

Trying to understand (much less apply order to) the history of *The Other Side of the Wind* isn't something you can do alone. Like any book,

it requires that many people who have their own lives to deal with offer their wisdom, patience, and time to a stranger who is poking around
into a never completed film that began shooting forty-five years ago.
In the case of *The Other Side of the Wind*, I received much, much more
than I gave from the generous and knowledgeable group I met and spoke
with.

Among them, the first and most important individual I must thank
is Joseph McBride, who wrote extensively about the making of the film
in his wonderful book *What Ever Happened to Orson Welles: A Portrait of an Independent Career*. From the moment I first contacted him,
Joe went above and beyond to make sure he offered me every resource,
insight, and contact that he could. Many of the revelations I came upon
were the result of following a lead Joe had given me. Not only that, he
opened his home to me and has been extremely supportive of this project in every possible way—there are no words to express my thanks
for the debt I owe to him.

The community of Welles scholars (of which Joe is a member) has
also been valuable beyond measure. In particular, I would like to thank
Jonathan Rosenbaum, Matthew Asprey Gear, Peter Tonguette, and
Peter Bogdanovich. Each was incredibly helpful in his own way—and
each was gracious with his time and insight. I cannot thank them
enough. The same goes for Brian Kellow, who helped me gain a deeper
understanding of Pauline Kael.

This book could also have not been written without the help of Dominique Antoine, Beatrice Welles, Filip Jan Rymsza, Mike Ferris, Françoise Widhoff, and Jens Koethner Kaul, who allowed me to question
them endlessly about all aspects of their involvement, both large and
small. Similarly, Frank Marshall, Larry Jackson, Glenn Jacobson, and
Peter Jason were all invaluable—not to mention enormously enter-
taining in their descriptions of life on the set.

In terms of entertainment, I must also acknowledge Rich Little and
the late Paul Mazursky. The former spent much of our interview con-
ducting conversations between Orson Welles and John Huston in dead-
on impressions of their actual voices. The latter spontaneously described

the opening scene of a movie about the making of *The Other Side of the Wind* in which Ayatollah Khomeini and a council of mullahs watch footage from the film and offer their surprisingly educated opinions on how to edit the final cut.

Each interview yielded something, but in particular I would like to thank Matthew Duda, Lou Race, Fred Zollo, Eric Sherman, and Michael Stringer for their stories, their observations, and their honesty.

At the University of Michigan's Special Collections Library, which houses the Orson Welles–Oja Kodar Papers, Kathleen Dow and Peggy Daub were unbelievably helpful, as was David Frazier at the University of Indiana's Lilly Library, where I was able to look at Peter Bogdanovich's papers. Special thanks to Rob Elder for telling me about the Bogdanovich collection at Indiana and to Ray Kelly at Wellesnet for being immensely supportive and helpful at every turn.

Aahba Rathee did a huge amount of research and copied things that I would still be copying were it not for her efforts. Don Sjoerdsma tried to help me put this all into a time line. Layton Ehmke did things that only Layton Ehmke can do.

Sadly, several people I interviewed have passed away, including Marie-Sophie Dubus, Paul Mazursky, Lyllah Pennachio, and the fantastic Rift Fournier. All will be missed.

My eternal thanks to Daniela Rapp at St. Martin's Press, who gave me the opportunity to do this book and the extra time I needed to complete it (on several occasions). I couldn't ask for a better editor. I feel the same way about Jonathan Lyons at Curtis Brown Ltd., who is not only a great agent, but an even greater guy who has supported me every step of the way. I cannot say enough good things about both Daniela and Jonathan. Also at St. Martin's, allow me to thank production editor John Morrone, designers Rob Grom and Steven Seighman, and the copyeditor, Sona Vogel.

My wife, Susan, not only has been a patient, hilarious, encouraging, and loving partner through all of this, but also is the best resource I have whenever there are creative roadblocks—and even when there aren't. In terms of noncreative roadblocks, my four sons, Will, Leo, Teddy, and Francis, are the best distractions in the world.

Finally, one of the most interesting interviews I conducted was with film editor Yves Deschamps, who helped me understand the magic of Orson's editing process, as well as a fact that was borne out in conversation after conversation with everyone who worked on the film: Orson Welles was many things—brilliant, difficult, charming, imperious, hilarious, a little paranoid, and talented beyond measure—but more than anything else, he was a man of enormous personal magnetism who also had a childlike quality that made him irresistible. In the end, no matter what had happened, it was impossible not to love him.

Thus, the last person I need to thank is Orson Welles: the most fascinating and brilliant person I will ever write about. His complex personality, remarkable artistry, and incredible life are an inspiration. Not only did he direct several of the best films ever made, but he was absolutely right about so many things, including the fact that everyone would love him *after* he was dead. He deserved better.

NOTES

BACKSTORY: BEFORE THE BEGINNING

p. 8 "anything seemed possible": Joseph McBride, *What Ever Happened to Orson Welles?: A Portrait of an Independent Career* (Lexington: University of Kentucky Press, 2006), p. 163.

p. 9 "Here are the faces of men who are close to death": Mark W. Estrin, ed., *Orson Welles Interviews* (Jackson: University of Mississippi Press, 2002), p. 144.

p. 9 "infantry" . . . "like a cocksucker swallowing": Peter Viertel, *Dangerous Friends: At Large with Hemingway and Huston in the Fifties* (New York: Doubleday, 1992), p. 46.

p. 9 "Mister Hemingway . . . how strong you are": Estrin, p. 114.

p. 10 "get to be like Hemingway": McBride, p. 176.

p. 10 "It's about both of us": Viertel, pp. 45–46.

p. 10 "I will play the part": McBride, p. 180.

p. 10 "At the end of his life": Ibid., pp. 182–83.

p. 11 "about death, the portrait of decadence, a ruin": Ibid., p. 183.

p. 11 "Back to New York": Albert Maysles, author interview (hereafter referred to as "AI"), 10/29/10.

p. 11 "Why don't you come spend a week with me": Ibid.

p. 11 "We spent day after day": Ibid.

p. 11 "a tragedy in three acts": *Orson Welles in Spain*, directed by Albert and David Maysles (unreleased film viewed at Maysles Films offices, New York, N.Y., 2010).

p. 11 "their death in the afternoon": Ibid. This is a clear allusion to Hemingway's 1932 book about the traditions and practice of bullfighting, entitled *Death in the Afternoon*.

p. 11 "El Americano": Orson Welles and Peter Bogdanovich, *This Is Orson Welles* (New York: HarperCollins, 1992), p. 44.

p. 11 "a pro" . . . "time of [his] life": Ibid.

p. 12 "living and dying second hand": Michael Parkinson, *Parkinson: The Orson Welles Interview*, BBC, 1974.

p. 12 "about the love of death": *Orson Welles in Spain*.

p. 12 "pseudo-Hemingway, a movie director": Ibid.

p. 12 "a confrontation between my hero": Ibid.

p. 12 "We're going to shoot it without a script": Ibid.

p. 12 "Have you ever done that" . . . "Nobody's ever done it": Ibid.

ORSONOLOGY: WHAT YOU MUST KNOW

p. 15 "What he hated was the responsibility": Clinton Heylin, *Despite the System: Orson Welles Versus the Hollywood Studios* (Chicago: Chicago Review Press, 2005), p. 356.

p. 15 "the desire to take medicine": Barbara Leaming, *Orson Welles: A Biography* (New York: Viking Penguin, 1985), p. 8.

p. 16 CARTOONIST, ACTOR, POET AND ONLY 10: *Capital Times*, Madison, Wis., February 1926.

p. 16 "the old masters": Ibid.

p. 16 "At times when Orson": Ibid.

p. 16 "it had never occurred to me": Leaming, p. 10.

p. 18 "convinced . . . that I had killed my father": Orson Welles, "My Father Wore Black Spats," *Vogue Paris*, December 1982–January 1983.

p. 19 "He knew that he was precisely": Micheál MacLiammóir, quoted in "Orson Welles: Three Men in One," *Lincoln Sunday Journal and Star*, March 20, 1966, p. 15F.

p. 19 a rave in *The New York Times*: Leaming, p. 46.

p. 19 "Christopher—she is here": Christopher Welles Feder, *In My Father's Shadow* (Chapel Hill, N.C.: Algonquin, 2009), p. 3.

p. 19 "more littered with sensational catastrophes than mine": McBride, p. 204.

p. 22 "no madness": Orson Welles, "Twilight in the Smog," *Esquire*, March 1959.

p. 22 "[Falstaff] is the greatest conception of a good man": Bridget Gellert Lyons, ed., *Chimes at Midnight* (New Brunswick, N.J.: Rutgers University Press, 1989), p. 261.

p. 23 "Who will hear no": Simon Callow, *Orson Welles: Hello Americans* (New York: Viking Penguin, 2006), p. xiv.

p. 24 $50 million at the box office: www.the-numbers.com/movie/Bonnie-and-Clyde#tab=summary.

p. 25 sold $60 million worth of tickets: www.the-numbers.com/movies/1969/0ERID.php; www.indiewire.com/article/critics-notebook-why-easy-rider-still-matters-45-years-later.

THE GREATEST HOME MOVIE EVER MADE

p. 27 ORSON WELLES'S UNSEEN MASTERPIECE SET FOR RELEASE: www.theguardian.com/film/2011/jan/23/orson-welles-last-film-release.

p. 27 "We are in negotiations": Ibid.

p. 29 "That's the car . . . what was left of it": Orson Welles and Oja Kodar, *The Other Side of the Wind: Screenplay*, edited by Giorgio Gosetti (Paris: Cahiers du Cinéma, 2005), p. 118.

p. 29 "Hannaford's own unfinished motion picture": Ibid., p. 118.

p. 30 "sketch a film likeness": Ibid., p. 118.

p. 30 "Ohh-kay . . . Cut!": Ibid., p. 120.

p. 31 "I'm doing the book on Mister Hannaford": Ibid., p. 120.

p. 31 "just making it up as he": Ibid., p. 138.

p. 32 "What he creates": Ibid., p. 152.

p. 33 "Please, dear lady": Ibid., p. 162.

p. 33 "Man, that's all it is": Ibid., p. 198.

p. 34 "Our revels now are ended": Ibid., p. 200.

p. 34 "Cut!": Ibid., p. 208.

ACT ONE

p. 39 "Orson Welles looking very well": Army Archerd, "Just for Variety," *Variety*, July 3, 1970, p. 2.

p. 39 "I bet he's at the Beverly Hills Hotel": McBride, pp. 143–44.

p. 39 "Hello": Gary Graver and Andrew Rausch, *Making Movies with Orson Welles* (Toronto: Scarecrow Press, 2006), p. 5.

p. 39 "Let's go home": McBride, p. 143.

p. 39 With Orson, someone said, timing was everything: Dominique Antoine, AI, 8/21/12.

p. 40 he was "like a lighthouse": Callow, p. 69.

p. 40 "Get over to the Beverly Hills Hotel": Graver and Rausch, p. 5.

p. 40 "I'm about to make a movie": Ibid.

p. 41 "beautiful bootlegging sisters": www.imdb.com/title/tt0060462/.

p. 42 "I saw the actress Ruth Gordon": Graver and Rausch, p. 6.

p. 42 "Orson would be number one": Sean Graver, AI, 11/15/11.

p. 43 "Orson Welles movies": McBride, p. 276.

p. 43 "present from God": Ibid., p. 138.

p. 44 like "a fairy queen": Rift Fournier, AI, 2/14/12.

p. 44 "My father's life was his work": Feder, p. 266.

p. 45 "I like this boy": Graver and Rausch, p. xi.

p. 46 "Can you hold": McBride, p. xii.

p. 46 "Is this going to be a *feature-length movie*?": Ibid.

p. 46 "Well, I finally meet my favorite critic!": Ibid.

p. 46 "I've never been as excited by movies as movies": Joseph McBride, *Orson Welles* (Cambridge, Mass.: Da Capo Press, 1996), p. 193.

p. 47 "You've seen *Kane* sixty times": McBride, *What Ever Happened*, p. 151.

p. 47 "He made terrible movies": Nicole V. Gagne, "Where Is The Other Side of the Wind, or *Quien Es Mas Macho:* Orson Welles, John Huston or Ernest Hemingway," *Cineaste*, Winter 2003, p. 4.

p. 47 "Hannaford's underlying interest": McBride, *What Ever Happened*, p. 176.

p. 48 "I'd rather spend": Ibid., p. 151.

p. 48 "Tijuana's out": Graver and Rausch, p. 9.

p. 48 "working with Orson" . . . "Is Christ Jewish?": Eric Sherman, AI, 8/2/11.

p. 49 "You guys are playing a camera-sound team": Ibid.

p. 49 "feeding off themselves": McBride, *What Ever Happened*, p. xiii.

p. 49 "Oh, no, thank you, Eric" . . . "They make them for me": Welles, la-after-midnight-bartok.blogspot.com/2011/06/eric-sherman-2 -weeks-with-orson-welles.html.

p. 50 "this is *an auteur film*": McBride, *What Ever Happened*, p. 167.

p. 50 "three-volume novel" . . . "I know everything": Welles and Bogdanovich, p. 171.

p. 50 "I love this man and I hate him": Ibid.

p. 51 "high priest of cinema": McBride, *Orson Welles*, p. 200.

p. 51 "mother fixation" . . . "Oedipal complex": Ibid., p. 166.

p. 51 "fear of completion": Charles Higham, *The Films of Orson Welles* (Berkeley: University of California Press, 1970), p. 190.

p. 51 "an oblique reflection on the changes": McBride, *Orson Welles*, p. 194.

p. 51 "The main thrust of my argument": Ibid., p. 195.

p. 52 "C'mon now, you're supposed to be": Ibid.

p. 52 "the only beautiful thing I want in this shot" . . . "Von Sternberg": McBride, *Orson Welles*, p. 197.

p. 52 "I give [actors] a great deal of freedom": Ibid., p. 196.

p. 53 "Cut! Cut! Cut!": Sherman, AI, 8/2/11.

p. 53 "He looked at us as if to say": Ibid.

p. 53 "Is the camera a reflection of reality": Peter Bogdanovich, AI, 1/10/13; also see www.moviemaker.com/magazine/issues/45/welles.html.

p. 53 "We never had a budget": McBride, *What Ever Happened*, p. 144.

p. 54 "a minotaur in his labyrinth": Higham, p. 189.

p. 54 "He was grotesque": Ibid., p. 189.

p. 54 "sensed a feeling not directly expressed": Ibid., p. 190.

p. 55 "At the moment of encounter": Ibid., p. 191.

p. 55 "I don't know of any more fun": Orson Welles letter to Peter Bogdanovich, August 15, 1970.

p. 55 "When I left Rio": Ibid.

p. 55 "Come on, Orson": Graver and Rausch, pp. 157–58.

p. 57 "Brilliant, my boy!": Andrew Yule, *Picture Shows: The Life and Films of Peter Bogdanovich* (New York: Limelight Editions, 1992), p. 10.

p. 57 "seemed to hold on to the dream": Ibid., p. 9.

p. 58 "Because you have written the truest words": Orson Welles, quoted by Peter Bogdanovich, brightlightsfilm.com/55/windiv.php#.U3 JLuihYyxI.

p. 59 "There was in fact": Welles and Bogdanovich, p. xii.

p. 59 "I don't like it either!": Ibid.

p. 59 "Why can't I?": Ibid.

p. 59 "well-meaning" . . . "half-truths": Peter Bogdanovich, "Is It True What They Say About Orson," *New York Times*, August 30, 1970.

p. 60 "I remained cool": Bob Random, AI, 10/14/11.

p. 60 "I didn't want to do *The Beverly Hillbillies*": Ibid.

p. 60 "Oh, hi, Orson": Ibid.

p. 60 "You have the part,": Ibid.

p. 61 "For $5,000,000 they could have": Peter Biskind, *Easy Riders, Raging Bulls: How the Sex-Drugs-and-Rock 'N' Roll Generation Saved Hollywood* (New York: Touchstone, 1999), p. 125.

p. 62 "I was just an element": Fournier, AI, 2/14/12.

p. 62 "Can we read it" . . . "tell us the story": Danny Selznick, AI, 3/7/12.

p. 63 "one of my colleagues": Fournier, AI, 2/14/12.

p. 63 "The word was that you and Ned could": Selznick, AI, 3/7/12.

p. 63 "Okay, Danny, that's it" . . . "Good-bye": Ibid.

p. 63 "There's only one thing in movies I hate as much": www.wellesnet .com/?p=1606.

p. 64 "According to a young American critic": Estrin, p. 135.

p. 65 "One of the reasons I'm so bored with Antonioni": Welles and Bogdanovich, pp. 103–04.

p. 65 "an architect of empty boxes": Graver and Rausch, p. 159.

p. 65 "Antonioni never got a shot like that" . . . "You bet your sweet ass": Ibid., p. 54.

p. 67 *"Rain!"*: Robert Aiken, "Citizen Welles," *North Shore News,* British Columbia, Canada, February 8, 1999.

p. 67 "He just loved the filmmaking process": R. Michael Stringer, AI, 6/30/11.

p. 68 "Orson simply wouldn't suffer a fool": Ibid.

p. 68 "I can't believe I'm": Ibid.

p. 68 "You can't treat him like he's your pal": Ibid.

p. 68 "Mike Stringer would be good": Ibid.

p. 69 "Orson would demand a shot that was": Sherman, AI, 8/2/11.

p. 69 "a mean Santa Claus": Joel Sussman, AI, 12/9/11.

p. 69 "Am I seriously lifting": Sherman, AI, 8/2/11.

p. 70 "Each shot had something to do with": Ibid.

p. 71 "No, Gary . . . God doesn't want": McBride, *Orson Welles,* p. 200.

p. 71 "God, I'm fat": Graver and Rausch, p. 11.

p. 72 "Orson may not be the father you've always": Feder, p. 214.

p. 72 "Darling girl, very nearly my first frustration": Ibid., p. 220.

p. 74 "You'll never get it in color": Don Graham, "Picture Perfect," *Texas Monthly,* February 1999, www.texasmonthly.com/story/picture-perfect/page/0/6.

p. 75 "like a silent movie": Random, AI, 10/14/11.

p. 75 "Anything that made the shot more": Stringer, AI, 6/30/11.

p. 76 "He knew exactly what he wanted": Leslie Otis, AI, 10/18/11.

p. 77 "I wanted sandwiches": Random, AI, 10/14/11.

p. 78 "Everybody excused him for everything": Ibid.

p. 78 "Where's the lighting" . . . "That's cool, man": Graver and Rausch, p. 58.

p. 78 "god-director" . . . "in front of that camera": Dennis Hopper transcript, undated.

p. 78 "Orson Welles wants you to be in his new movie": Paul Mazursky, AI, 1/24/11.

p. 79 "Why would Orson Welles want me" . . . "party scene": Ibid.

p. 79 "Ho, ho, ho, Paul Mazursky": Ibid.

p. 80 "He needed to know it was the most important thing": Henry Jaglom, AI, December 2010.

p. 80 "Hello, Henry" . . . "Hello, Paul": Paul Mazursky, *Show Me the Magic* (New York: Simon & Schuster, 1999), p. 149.

p. 80 "Paul, I want you": Ibid., p. 149.

p. 80 "What sort of man": Ibid., p. 149.

p. 80 Hannaford has been living in Europe for some time": Ibid., pp. 149–50.

p. 81 "I'm going to bring him to my house": Jaglom, AI, December 2010.

p. 81 "But what about people who can't first make": Paul and Henry, part I, unpublished transcript, p. 8.

p. 81 "Don't condescend to me!" . . . "Let me finish": Ibid.

p. 81 "Don't say a word": Mazursky, AI, 1/24/11.

p. 82 "Are you asking him if he's a homosexual!": Paul and Henry, unpublished transcript, part II, p. 8.

p. 82 "We did this for two or three hours": Mazursky, AI, 1/24/11.

p. 82 "Mr. Welles, it was such a thrill": Ibid.

p. 83 "Hello?!" . . . "Hi, Orson" . . . "Busy, Bob": Peter Prescott Tonguette, *Orson Welles Remembered* (Jefferson, N.C.: McFarland, 2007), p. 83.

p. 83 "Orson has no friends": McBride, *What Ever Happened,* p. 160.

p. 85 "Doesn't that look like Jacy?": Graham, "Picture Perfect."

p. 85 "I thought, 'That's kind of the way'": Ibid.

p. 86 "Cybill was irresistible": Ibid.

p. 86 "I can't decide who I'd rather sleep with": Peter Bogdanovich, www.texasmonthly.com/story/picture-perfect/page/0/5.

p. 86 "That's what movies are like": Ibid.

p. 87 "Come work for me": Rachel Abramowitz, *Is That a Gun in Your*

Pocket: Women's Experience of Power in Hollywood (New York: Random House, 2000), p. 31.

p. 87 "I'm going down to do this movie with Orson": Frank Marshall, AI, 1/22/13.

p. 87 *"Frank!* Go move that thing": Ibid.

p. 87 "My God! I've been accepted": Ibid.

p. 88 "It was the most amazing thing": Ibid.

p. 88 "Visually and in a cinematic sense": Ibid.

p. 89 "Let's roll!": Michael Ferris, AI, 9/9/11.

p. 89 "the amount of dirt; the way he tossed it": Ibid.

p. 89 "Once we got used to it, we expected it": Ibid.

p. 90 "You're a picture maker": Yule, p. 51.

p. 90 "You can only feel for people on celluloid": Abramowitz, p. 31.

p. 90 "It's almost impossible to hate Peter": Ibid.

p. 91 a short but highly inaccurate piece: Charles Higham, "Orson's Back and Marlene's Got Him!" *New York Times,* January 31, 1971.

p. 92 "That was my father,": Beatrice Welles, AI, 9/16/14

p. 92 "the one great creative force": Pauline Kael, "Orson Welles: There Ain't No Way," *New Republic,* June 24, 1967.

p. 92 "It is difficult to explain": Pauline Kael, "Raising Kane," *The New Yorker,* February 20–27, 1971.

p. 93 "Mankiewicz died [in 1953] and his share faded": Ibid.

p. 93 "Why would the biggest film critic in America": Brian Kellow, *Pauline Kael: A Life in the Dark* (New York: Viking, 2011), p. 158.

p. 94 "an old enemy of mine": McBride, *What Ever Happened,* p. 191.

p. 95 According to her biographer Brian Kellow,: AI, 1/17/12.

p. 96 "Orson was shattered by it and I thought": Bogdanovich, AI, 1/10/13.

p. 96 decimate Kael's article and expose her as a fraud: Peter Bogdanovich, "The Kane Mutiny," *Esquire,* October 1971.

p. 96 "How am I going to answer this?": Kellow, p. 167.

p. 97 "like Pussy Galore": Pat McMahon, AI, 6/6/11.

pp. 97–98 "The director is interested in you" . . . "Are you free Saturday": Ibid.

p. 98 "God, I've admired you": Ibid.

p. 98 "Mr. Hannaford . . . I'm Marvin P. Fassbender": McBride, *What Ever Happened*, p. 208.

p. 98 "We've invited my friend Pat McMahon" . . . "Can you memorize these lines rapidly": McMahon, AI, 6/6/11.

p. 99 "I'm sorry to bother you" . . . "that was Burl Ives, wasn't it?": Ibid.

p. 99 "Had I known that": Ibid.

p. 99 "Oh, my God, George C. Scott in *Patton!*" Tim Purtell, "Oscar Grouch,": *Entertainment Weekly*, April 16, 1993, www.ew.com/ew/article/0,,306200,00.html.

p. 100 "two-hour meat parade": news.bbc.co.uk/2/hi/obituaries /455563.stm.

p. 100 "They're not going to get me like that": Bogdanovich, AI, 1/10/13.

p. 100 "He didn't want to give them": Ibid.

pp. 100–101 "Genius is a word" . . . "man of genius": www.oscars.org /video/watch/43rd _welles.html.

pp. 100–102 "Ladies and gentlemen, with this great honor" . . . "I thank you for it": www.oscars.org/video/watch/43rd _welles.html.

p. 102 "Happy lunacy": www.oscars.org/video/watch/43rd _welles .html.

p. 102 "Thanks, John. . . . Bring it over!": Graver and Rausch, p. 71.

p. 102 "If he calls and says, 'I need you'": McBride, *What Ever Happened*, p. 193.

p. 103 "the world's greatest living radio actress": www.nytimes. com/2004/03/18/arts/mercedes-mccambridge-87-actress -known-for-strong-roles.html.

p. 103 "He's going to cut your hair": Mercedes McCambridge, *The Quality of Mercy* (New York: Berkley Publishing, 1982), p. 117.

p. 103 "I understand you're going to cut my hair" . . . "the character you are going to play": Ibid.

p. 104 "That's what it's like to work": Ibid., p. 116.

p. 104 "If [Orson] asked me to jump off": McBride, *What Ever Happened*, p. 193.

p. 105 "Eddie is such a magnificent ruin": www.brightlightsfilm.com/55/windiv.php.

p. 106 "How was it, Gary?" . . . "Can we use it?": Graver and Rausch, p. 31.

p. 106 "Peter, I'm trying to make a movie here" . . . "can be a real shit": McBride, *What Ever Happened*, p. 196.

p. 107 "Dear Joe: We didn't get a chance": Ibid., p. 171.

p. 108 "About my part in the Welles picture": Letter from Joe McBride to Ronald Gottesman, July 25, 1971.

p. 108 "Orson Welles has one of those 'guess who' ventures": "Orson Welles Plots H'wood 'Guess Who' Pic" *Variety*, August 2, 1971, p. 2.

p. 108 "It's not a cute thing": Frank Brady, *Citizen Welles* (New York: Doubleday, 1989), p. 544.

p. 109 "To get out of film school as quickly as possible": Lou Race, AI, 10/11/11.

p. 109 "Mr. Welles, I appreciate your obligations" . . . "petty harlotry": Ibid.

p. 109 "I think you and I": Graver and Rausch, p. 152.

p. 109 "a masterpiece" . . . "since *Citizen Kane*": Biskind, p. 139.

p. 110 "all the Bogdanovich pictures have been made": Aljean Harmetz, "Peter Still Looks Forward to His *Citizen Kane*," *New York Times*, November 14, 1971, p. D13.

p. 110 "Orson was horrified by money": Jean-Pierre Berthomé, "Two Open Doors to the Labyrinth; Interview: Dominique Antoine," *Positif*, July/August 1998.

p. 111 "the weirdest great movie ever made,": Dave Kehr, www.chicagoreader.com/chicago/the-lady-from-shanghai/Film?oid=2552830.

p. 113 "He'd have a new [house]": Stringer, AI, 10/18/11.

p. 113 "the most innocent form of whoring": McBride, *What Ever Happened,* p. 8.

p. 113 "We were living at the George V,": Beatrice Welles, AI, 9/16/14.

p. 113 "It may have been chaos,": Beatrice Welles, AI, 9/16/14.

p. 118 "What made the deal possible": Nick Brown, ed., *Francis Ford Coppola's* The Godfather *Trilogy* (Cambridge, UK: Cambridge University Press, 2000), p. 37.

p. 118 "marked the zenith of director's power": Biskind, p. 206.

p. 119 "I wasn't impressed by his legend": Yves Deschamps, AI, 6/12/12.

p. 120 "Orson, it would be easier if I knew": Ibid.

p. 120 "That was the way he rebuilt the interpretations": Ibid.

p. 121 "It's impossible that you can't find money": Ibid.

p. 121 "You're working with Orson Welles and you want to": Ibid.

p. 121 "How do you do?" . . . "So for producers we stand up and say hello?": Berthomé, "Two Open Doors to the Labyrinth."

pp. 121–22 *"You bet!"* . . . "see what we do next": Antoine, AI, 6/22/12.

p. 122 "That was part of his genius": Ibid.

p. 122 "I don't wait for you to love me": Ibid.

p. 122 "That's when I understood the big baby": Ibid.

p. 123 "He was acting": Ibid.

p. 123 "Welles has shot": *Variety,* "International Soundtrack," December 26, 1973, p. 20.

ACT TWO

p. 127 "The great danger for any artist": www.laweekly.com/2000 -12-28/news/go-go-go/.

p. 127 "It was really hard to tell": Mary Ann Newfield, AI, 10/6/11.

p. 252 "Describe a typical day on the set": brightlightsfilm.com/55 /windiv.php.

p. 128 "Oh, no, no, no": Larry Jackson, AI, 7/22/11.

p. 129 "She taught me money is for spending": Jeffrey Meyers, *John Huston: Courage and Art* (New York: Crown Archetype, 2011), p. 350.

p. 129 "Because it was the wrong thing to do, kid": Meyers, p. 196.

p. 130 "I have it, darling": Marshall, AI, 1/22/13.

p. 130 "My God, he's matured!": McBride, *Orson Welles*, p. 211.

p. 130 "You've been in this picture for three years?": McBride, *What Ever Happened,* p. 21.

p. 131 "an adventure shared by desperate men": Viertel, pp. 389–90.

p. 132 "Don't worry. . . . We'll shoot": Rich Little, AI, 5/22/12.

pp. 132–33 "John, I want you to meet" . . . "Not that kind of impressionist": Ibid.

p. 133 "John, you're just causing yourself": McBride, *What Ever Happened,* p. 184.

p. 133 "Was that the line, Orson?" . . . "Well, not exactly": brightlightsfilm.com/55/windiv.php#.U3MKBK1dVn8.

p. 134 "What the fuck is this movie all about?" . . . "about us": Celeste Huston, AI, 9/28/11.

p. 134 "Orson, what does" . . . "I haven't the foggiest": Little, AI, 5/22/12.

p. 134 "You were crying": Ibid.

p. 135 "Let me tell you the true story" . . . "how beautiful Phoenix is": Ibid.

p. 135 "Who's your fat friend?" . . . "on his way": Ibid.

p. 136 "I thought he'd lost his mind": McCambridge, pp. 143–44.

p. 136 "Very good, John" . . . "Thank you, Orson": Ibid., p. 144.

p. 136 "That's the one" . . . "We'll print them all": Race, AI, 10/11/11.

p. 137 "A rat of a woman": McBride, *What Ever Happened*, p. 200.

p. 137 "What film was that?": Susan Strasberg, *Bittersweet* (New York: Signet, 1981), p. 249.

p. 137 "I'm no actor, dear": Ibid.

p. 138 "the angel within the beast": McBride, *Orson Welles,* p. 36.

p. 138 "What's wrong with you?": Viola Hegyi Swisher, "Orson Welles and Five Years of 'The Other Side of the Wind,'" *After Dark*, March 1976.

pp. 138–39 "Where's Susan?" . . . "She would never do a scene that badly": Ibid.

p. 139 "He was real and fake at the same time": Constance Pharr, AI, 9/29/11.

p. 139 "You need to do this": Race, AI, 10/11/11.

p. 140 "Idiot! Can't you see": Strasberg, p. 250.

p. 140 *"Run! Do not walk!"*: Peter Jason, AI, 1/22/13.

p. 140 "Nineteen hippies": Ibid.

pp. 140–41 "Well! Who does!?" . . . "What we need is a generator": Ibid.

p. 141 "No, I want a swordfish!": Ibid.

p. 141 "Oh, my God! . . . It's fantastic!": Ibid.

p. 142 "like they were at an Italian funeral": Ibid.

p. 143 "The person Orson yelled at most": Race, AI, 10/11/11.

p. 143 "Keep this, Gary" . . . "once we're done shooting": Graver and Rausch, p. 67.

p. 143 "The script I had was over 200 pages": Newfield, AI, 10/6/11.

p. 144 "What the hell is this about?": Little, AI, 5/22/12.

p. 145 "I'm going to need": Richard Waltzer, AI, 6/20/11.

pp. 145–46 "What should I do?" . . . "make up dialogue": Little, AI, 5/22/12.

p. 146 "I just need you until Sunday" . . . "a way to start over": Marshall, AI, 1/22/13.

pp. 146–47 "Go get Eddie!" . . . *"Peking, China!!"*: Jason, AI, 1/22/13.

p. 148 "Shoot it in black-and-white": McBride, *What Ever Happened*, p. 146.

p. 148 "You were on the phone" . . . "with Peter Bogdanovich": Marshall, AI, 1/22/13.

p. 148 "I just finished shooting with Rich Little" . . . "You just saved my life": brightlightsfilm.com/55/windiv.php#. U3MacihYyxI.

p. 148 "Now you know": Ibid.

p. 149 "My God, that's not what a successful": Charles Higham, "The Film Orson Welles Has Been Finishing for Six Years; Will Welles Finish His Film," *New York Times*, April 16, 1976, p. 45.

p. 149 "When Peter came in to play Peter, it was bizarre": Marshall, AI, 1/22/13.

p. 149 "Could you talk about the aesthetic difference": Waltzer, AI, 6/20/11.

p. 149 "It was so surreal that you couldn't": Ibid.

p. 149 "So, Peter, how many": Bogdanovich, AI, 1/10/13.

p. 150 "Mercedes knew just how to deal with Orson": Juergen Hellwig, AI, 8/17/12.

p. 150 "Okay, try it another way" . . . "Because you're a brilliant actor" Bogdanovich, AI, 1/10/13.

p. 150 "Why don't we do a shot where there's no cut?": Ibid.

p. 150 "I think Orson thought": Ibid.

p. 151 "It was all sorts of stuff": Tonguette, p. 109.

p. 151 "I was thinking about being him": Ibid.

pp. 151–52 "This is Mr. Hannaford's night" . . . "borrow from ourselves": Clip from *The Other Side of the Wind*, American Film Institute Salute to Orson Welles, CBS, February 17, 1975.

p. 152 "If anything happens to me": Bogdanovich, AI, 1/10/13.

p. 152 "Don't worry": Jackson, AI, 7/22/11.

p. 153 "The obituary won't even mention that I was here": Ibid.

p. 154 "Thanks, John, that'll do": Huston, p. 344.

p. 154 "Orson didn't want any women around": Jason, AI, 1/22/13.

p. 154 "Everything you learned in school is balls!": Cybill Shepherd, AI, 1/30/13.

p. 155 *"Turn away from the camera, Cybill!"*: Ibid.

p. 155 "My dear, why don't you": Race, AI, 10/11/11.

p. 156 "For any given scene": Ibid.

p. 156 "she was perfect": Marshall, AI, 1/22/13.

p. 156 "John, do you know who you remind me of": brightlights film.com/55/windiv.php.

p. 157 "What the hell difference does it make?": McBride, *What Ever Happened*, p. 201.

p. 158 "Play it to me" . . . "many times": Tonguette, p. 109.

p. 159 "Why didn't you spit?": Jason, AI, 1/22/13.

p. 160 "Again!": Leaming, p. 479.

p. 162 "Orson was at his best": Swisher, "Five Years of The Other Side of the Wind."

p. 163 "I don't care who you are" . . . "Keep that in the shot": Celeste Huston, 9/28/11.

p. 163 brought the unpaid portion of the motel bill to $2,500: Letter from Jim Hines of the Desert Forest Motel to Frank Marshall, May 2, 1974.

pp. 163–64 "I suppose I can": Ibid.

p. 164 "It just became": Thomas Brodek, AI, 11/15/11.

p. 164 "why he does these insane things": Strasberg, p. 251.

p. 166 "Too baroque": Race, AI, 10/11/11.

p. 166 "It looks fake": Ibid.

p. 167 "Orson, don't ask me to do this": McBride, *What Ever Happened*, pp. 188–89.

p. 167 "What look should I have?": Antoine, AI, 7/5/12.

p. 167 "accordance to those standards": Living expenses memo from Orson Welles to Dominique Antoine, July 24, 1974.

p. 168 "Mr. Welles is to be considered": Memo from Orson Welles to Dominique Antoine, July 26, 1974.

p. 169 "being in a monastery": Deschamps, AI, 6/12/12.

p. 169 "It gave a vertiginous sense of space": Ibid.

p. 169 "It was so perfect": Ibid.

p. 170 "While it is perfectly true": Memo from Orson Welles to film editors on *The Other Side of the Wind*, July 30, 1974.

p. 170 two more films had been made: Biskind, pp. 211–13.

p. 170 agreement with Astrophore: Contract between Les Films de L'Astrophore and Avenel Inc., August 9, 1974.

p. 171 "It might be impossible": Memo from Orson Welles to Dominique Antoine, August 11, 1974.

p. 171 "Whatever cause I may give you for complaint": Memo from Orson Welles to Dominique Antoine, August 26, 1974.

p. 172 "It was very difficult": Deschamps, AI, 6/6/12.

p. 172 "[This] makes me feel": Memo from Orson Welles to Dominique Antoine and Mehdi Boushehri, September 24, 1974.

p. 173 "Yves is still there?" . . . "For me it's not a game": Deschamps, AI, 6/6/12.

p. 173 "You can't stay" . . . "go back to Paris": Ibid.

p. 173 "He was an adorable person": Ibid.

p. 174 "Oh, my God, it's exactly": Ibid.

p. 174 "I had seen the limits to madness": Ibid.

p. 174 Stafford Repp was the first cast member to die: Obituary: Stafford Repp, *Variety*, November 11, 1974, p. 11.

p. 175 "rich and abounding in detail": Marie-Sophie Dubus, AI (e-mail), 11/27/11.

ACT THREE

p. 179 "Who do I have to": McBride, *What Ever Happened*, p. 207.

p. 179 "He always respected the crew": Jack Epps Jr., AI, 8/15/12.

p. 180 "It was a way of saying": George Stevens Jr., AI, 10/28/11.

p. 180 who expressed his feelings to the event co-chairs in a letter: Letter from Frank McCarthy to Charlton Heston and Howard Koch, December 11, 1974.

p. 181 "George, Orson isn't happy": Stevens, AI, 10/28/11.

p. 181 "He thought I was colluding with them": Bogdanovich, AI, 1/10/13.

p. 181 "I was finally forced to realize": Memo from Orson Welles to Dominique Antoine, January 4, 1975.

p. 182 "I am worried sick about": Letter from Orson Welles to Arnold Weissberger, January 15, 1975.

p. 182 "create a scandal": Ibid.

p. 183 "Surely you understand by now": Letter from Orson Welles to Mehdi Boushehri, January 22, 1975.

p. 183 "Ready" . . . "Nearing Completion": *Variety*, February 5, 1975, p. 31.

p. 184 "Oh, God, now we've really done it" . . . "hang up on Orson?": Stevens, AI, 10/28/11.

p. 185 "There's no one like him, nobody at all": filmmakeriq.com/2011/09 /afi-tribute-to-orson-welles.

p. 186 "Tonight you have seen inspired": www.wellesnet.com/?p=46.

p. 186 "reminds us that it is better to live one day": Ibid.

p. 186 "My father once told me": Ibid.

p. 187 "What we do come up with has no special right": Ibid.

p. 187 "some of the necessities to which I am a slave": Ibid.

p. 187 "But not crazy enough" . . . "every possible kind": Ibid.

p. 188 "throw himself on the mercy": Jaglom, AI, December 2010.

p. 188 "The scene that you're going to be seeing": www.wellesnet.com /?p=46

p. 189 "We thought we were going to have": Antoine, AI, 7/5/12.

p. 189 "That was the horrible irony": Peter Bogdanovich, AI (e-mail), 9/24/13.

p. 190 "It's seven A.M.! Where are you!?": Cynthia Steinway, AI, 8/15/12.

p. 190 "It was like he pulled the wool over": Ibid.

p. 190 *"Do you think I want to live like this!?"*: Ibid.

p. 191 Peter promoted *At Long Last Love*: www.imdb.com/title /tt0072665.

p. 191 "I felt like, 'Wow, this is Hollywood'": Cameron Crowe, AI (e-mail), 6/29/11.

p. 192 "It has meant the most exquisitely torturous labor": Memo from Orson Welles to Dominique Antoine, April 12, 1975.

p. 193 "cash business": Howard Grossman, AI, 12/24/11.

p. 193 "never knew if we'd have film the next day": Steinway, AI, 8/15/12.

p. 193 "presently most embarrassed by lack of cash": Telex from Orson Welles to Dominique Antoine, 4/29/75.

p. 194 "He was taken in a state of coma": Shooting in Los Angeles: A General Report, undated memo from Orson Welles to Dominique Antoine, 5/75.

p. 195 "It was like a faucet got turned off": Epps, AI, 8/15/12.

p. 195 "If he agreed to his fee": Antoine, AI, 10/30/13.

p. 195 "Deeply worried about your departure": Telex from Orson Welles to Mehdi Boushehri, May 12, 1975.

p. 196 "There is no question to think of stopping your work": Telex from Mehdi Boushehri to Orson Welles (via Peter Bogdanovich's office), May 13, 1975.

p. 196 "Friday night massacre" . . . "*against me!!*": McBride, *Orson Welles*, p. 210.

p. 196 "Just having him look at me had been exciting": Epps, AI, 8/15/12.

p. 196 "Astrophore's indebtedness in Hollywood": Memo from Orson Welles to Dominique Antoine, June 1, 1975.

p. 197 "study the memo with some care": Letter from Orson Welles to Dominique Antoine, June 4, 1975.

p. 197 "So it occurs to me that I may have been missing": Letter from Orson Welles to Dominique Antoine, June 16, 1975.

p. 197 "He kept me waiting for weeks and weeks": Antoine, AI, 10/30/13.

p. 197 "We are waiting for you": Telex from Dominique Antoine to Orson Welles (via Peter Bogdanovich's office), June 24, 1975.

p. 198 "The moment my father thought,": Beatrice Welles, AI, 9/16/14

p. 198 "could have been an easy $125,000": Matthew Asprey Gear, "Orson Welles and the Death of Sirhan Sirhan" (Unpublished article, 2014).

p. 200 "[Orson] disappeared for forty days in the middle of the shoot": Bahman Farmanara, AI (e-mail), 3/6/12.

p. 201. Oja's age changed depending on the footage: Steve Ecclesine, AI, 1/18/12.

p. 201 "I remember thinking, 'This is so innovative'": Rick Shore, AI, 12/5/11.

p. 201 "To 99.99 percent of the audience": Ecclesine, AI, 1/18/12.

p. 202 "It was a psychological deficit on his part": Ibid.

p. 202 "I was suffering the most agonizing pain": Letter from Orson Welles to Mehdi Boushehri and Dominique Antoine, undated, September 1975.

p. 202 According to his then secretary Lynn Lewin: AI (Skype), 10/14/11.

p. 202 "Where do we go from here?": Letter from Orson Welles to Mehdi Boushehri and Dominique Antoine, undated, September 1975.

p. 203 "Clearly if we can't": Ibid.

p. 203 "He was escaping, you know": Antoine, AI, 10/30/13.

p. 203 "rather tough" . . . "date of delivery": Letter from Dominique Antoine to Orson Welles, September 19, 1975.

p. 204 "Mehdi and I . . . at any moment": Ibid.

p. 204 "Get up! . . . Wake up!": Bogdanovich, AI, 1/10/13.

p. 205 "Just go to Begelman": Ibid.

p. 205 "That's the end of my career": Ibid.

p. 205 "He had too much pride": Ibid.

p. 206 "At this moment": Letter from Orson Welles to Peter Bogdanovich, October 22, 1975.

p. 207 a breach in their relationship as evidenced by: Letter from Peter Bogdanovich to Orson Welles, November 23, 1975.

p. 207 "I cannot wait for payment any longer": Ibid.

p. 207 "Let me assure you that despite any disagreements": Letter from Peter Bogdanovich to Orson Welles, December 5, 1975.

p. 208 "As I warned you and Arnold Weissberger": Telex from Dominique Antoine to Orson Welles, October, 30, 1975.

p. 209 "Arnold, you must understand": Letter from Dominique Antoine to Arnold Weissberger, November 28, 1975.

p. 209 he was definitely in Paris on December 15: Telex from Dominique Antoine to Orson Welles, February 4, 1976.

p. 209 "He thought he was becoming a prisoner again": Antoine, AI, 7/5/12.

p. 209 "You choose the date" . . . "Put a date on it": Ibid.

p. 210 "In the moment": Ibid.

p. 210 "I'll have to find out where Orson is": Joseph McBride, "John Huston Finds That Slow Generation of *King* Has Made It a Richer Film," *Variety*, December 16, 1975.

p. 210 "You can't put an ultimatum": McBride, *Orson Welles*, p. 208.

p. 212 "Antoine sent Welles": Telegram from Dominique Antoine to Orson Welles, January 15, 1986.

p. 213 "He was a genius": Farmanara, AI, 3/6/12.

p. 213 "He'd already received": Ibid.

p. 213 Welles rejected several contracts from Astrophore: Letter from Arnold Weissberger to Orson Welles, March 22, 1976.

p. 213 Weissberger began pursuing options in which Welles could buy out Astrophore: Ibid.

p. 214 "We must never forget": Letter from Dominique Antoine to Orson Welles, June 24, 1976.

p. 214 "For the past six and a half years": Charles Higham, "The Film That Orson Welles Has Been Finishing for Six Years," *New York Times*, April 18, 1976, p. 45.

p. 214 "Orson's like a painter": Ibid.

p. 214 "Tragically self-destructive" . . . "to make pictures": Ibid.

p. 215 Welles wrote first: Letter from Orson Welles to Rich Little, April 22, 1976.

p. 215 "The plain truth": Ibid.

p. 215 "I'd told the story on a couple of talk shows": Little, AI, 5/22/12.

p. 216 "My three weeks with you": Letter from Rich Little to Orson Welles, May 13, 1976.

p. 216 "a man who possesses a great sense of humor": General letter of recommendation written by Rich Little, May 22, 1976.

p. 216 "a little wary": Letter from Claude Fielding to Werner Wolfen, June 2, 1976.

p. 216 "Astrophore is dead since June 13": Letter from Dominique Antoine to Orson Welles, June 24, 1976.

p. 217 "biggest wish would be to": Ibid.

p. 217 "I am ready to do anything": Ibid.

p. 217 "Is Orson Welles ever going to": *Boston Globe*, p. G18.

p. 218 Three days later, Norman Foster died: "Norman Foster, 72, Dies of Cancer; Services Tomorrow," *Variety*, July 9, 1976, p. 12.

p. 218 The report tracked: Coopers & Lybrand audit of Les Films de L'Astrophore, October 12, 1976.

p. 218 "Due to a complete lack of budgetary or accounting control": Ibid.

p. 218 "It's about as complicated": John Huston, *An Open Book* (New York: Alfred A. Knopf, 1980), p. 344.

p. 219 "There aren't any": Yule, p. 109.

p. 219 the loud crash of Bogdanovich falling back to earth may have had several causes: David Denby, "Bogdanovich—Will 'Nickelodeon' Be His 'Last Picture Show'? Peter Bogdanovich—What Went Wrong?" *New York Times*, January 30, 1977, D1.

p. 219 "It has the romance": Ibid.

p. 220 "My affair with Cybill": Ibid.

p. 220 "I've heard that since I was fifteen": Ibid.

p. 222 "Stradivarius took three years": Leaming, p. 490.

p. 222 "Come on, gentlemen": Ibid.

p. 222 "I won't set foot in that place" . . . "get any glovvier": Bogdanovich, AI, 1/10/13.

p. 223 "Orson thought I betrayed him": Ibid.

p. 223 "They both spent a few minutes putting": Ibid.

p. 223 "I've sent you two answers": Ibid.

p. 224 "It was a shorter note saying": Ibid.

p. 225 "It was just obvious what was going to happen": Michael Posner, "Severing Ties with Iran 'Stupid,' Canada's Envoy from the 1970s Says," *Globe and Mail*, September 13, 2012, www.theglobeand mail.com/news/world/severing-ties-with-iran-stupid-canadas -envoy-from-1970s-says/article4544100/.

p. 225 "It sounds like an interesting project" . . . "his subtlety and his brilliance": James George, AI, 11/17/11.

p. 226 George began negotiating a contract: Letter from James George to Mehdi Boushehri, May 30, 1978.

p. 226 Via Weissberger, Welles came back with a counteroffer: Letter from Arnold Weissberger to Orson Welles, June 7, 1978.

p. 227 "I am sorry": Letter from James George to Orson Welles, November 6, 1978.

p. 227 Under those agreements: Memorandum of agreement dated August 3, 1978, referenced in letter from James George to Avenel (via Arnold Weissberger's office), November 13, 1978.

p. 228 "My only concern": Letter from James George to Orson Welles, November 9, 1978.

p. 228 "Each day's news only": Letter from attorney Richard Kaplan to Arnold Weissberger, November 15, 1978.

p. 229 "I am not in this venture": Letter from James George to Orson Welles, November 22, 1978.

p. 229 "The resulting contract": George, AI, 11/17/11.

p. 230 "It's a tragic story": Paul G. Levine, "Going to the Welles Once Too Often," *Los Angeles Times,* p. H20.

p. 230 "makes up his mind": Ibid.

p. 231 "I'm the boy you could have had": McBride, *What Ever Happened,* p. 190.

p. 231 "Orson Welles's almost legendary": Charles Champlin, "Welles' 'Other Side of the Wind': Still Light on His Feet," *Los Angeles Times,* January 31, 1979, p. G16.

p. 231 "creatively as light on his feet": Ibid.

p. 231 "The end of it all": Ibid.

p. 232 "has only a few scenes": "Marilyn Beck's Hollywood: No 'Older Woman' Roles for Them," *The* (Springfield, MA) *Morning Union,* July 9, 1982.

p. 233 Françoise Widhoff . . . had received a letter from the French tax authority: Françoise Widhoff, AI (e-mail), 4/30/13.

p. 233 they petitioned the court to rule in their favor: Contained in procedural history of decision rendered by the Tribunal de Grande Instance de Paris, March 15, 1982.

p. 234 the French legal concept of *droit d'auteur*: www.sacem.fr/cms/home/la-sacem/definition_droit_auteur.

p. 234 "bear the stamp": www.theartnewspaper.com/articles/Art-and-copyright-whats-at-stake/17203.

p. 234 "If I ever get it again": McBride, *What Ever Happened*, p. 219.

p. 235 Welles had editor Jon Braun set up footage: Jon Braun, AI, 10/12/11.

p. 236 "There is this misunderstanding,": Beatrice Welles, AI, 9/15/14

p. 236 "captures our attention": www.youtube.com/watch?v=YZEWy—VsBQ.

p. 236 "I had a tremendous streak of luck": www.youtube.com/watch?v=YZEWy—VsBQ.

AFTERLIFE

p. 241 "Artists aim for something timeless": Jens Koethner Kaul, AI (Skype), 12/13/13.

p. 241 "a hot sheets motel": Feder, p. 4.

p. 242 "the trouble with movies": McBride, *What Ever Happened*, p. 299.

p. 242 "a genius of cinema": Ibid., p. 300.

p. 242 "I am sorry that Monsieur Mitterrand": Ibid., p. 300.

p. 243 "There are only two things": Ibid., p. 301.

p. 243 "Except as otherwise provided": Last Will and Testament of Orson Welles, January 15, 1982.

p. 244 Although long suspecting that he might be Welles's son: Alex Witchel, "Are You My Father, Orson Welles?" *New York Times*, September 30, 2011.

p. 244 leaving her his ownership rights: Confirmation of Ownership Rights, June 19, 1985.

p. 246 gruesome murder-suicide: Teresa Carpenter, "Death of a Playmate," *Village Voice*, November 5–11, 1980, www.teresacarpenter.com/voice_playmate.pdf.

p. 246. "only $21.37": David Crook, "Bogdanovich's Bankrupt Memorial," *Los Angeles Times*, December 19, 1985.

p. 247 she died a few hours later: "Paola Mori, Widow of Actor Orson Welles," *Los Angeles Times*, August 14, 1986, articles.latimes.com/1986-08-14/news/mn-6841_1_orson-welles.

p. 248 an agreement between Orson's family and his mistress was signed: In the Matter of the Estate of George Orson Welles, Deceased, District Court, Clark County, Nevada, Case No. P20544, November 7, 1986.

p. 248 Huston met the pair one morning in 1986: Norman Lear, AI, 3/13/12.

p. 248 "No, no, no" . . . "a little tequila,": Graver and Rausch, p. 135.

p. 249 "Pete? . . . It's Clint": Jason, AI, 1/22/13.

p. 249 "It's Orson Welles's last movie": Ibid.

p. 250 "Was all over the place": Tom Rooker, AI, 12/12/13.

p. 250 "He couldn't figure out": Jason, AI, 1/22/13.

p. 251 "You just knew it was a tragedy": Fred Zollo, AI, 6/9/11.

p. 251 "We had the money": Ibid.

p. 253 Fitzgerald wrote a letter to Boushehri: Letter from Michael Fitzgerald to Mehdi Boushehri, April 29, 1997.

p. 253 a "simple deal": Letter from Mehdi Boushehri to Michael Fitzgerald, May 25, 1997.

p. 253 He was surprised to find: Michael Fitzgerald, AI, 11/20/13.

p. 254 "I'm out": Ibid.

p. 254 filing for bankruptcy a second time: Ann W. O'Neill, "Director Bogdanovich Declares Bankruptcy," *Los Angeles Times,* June 4, 1997.

p. 255 "It's somewhat like riding a tiger": Ibid.

p. 255 "This is no artistic homage": "Welles' Daughter Blasts 'Touch'-Up," New York *Daily News,* August 30, 1998.

p. 255–56 "Beatrice Welles is not a filmmaker": Ibid.

p. 257 "ridiculous": McBride, *What Ever Happened,* pp. 210–11.

p. 257 "He was a very calm and lovely man": Matthew Duda, AI, 2/1/13.

p. 257 "Everyone wanted to shoot me,": Beatrice Welles, AI, 9/15/14

p. 258 "The last thing I ever wanted,": Beatrice Welles, AI, 9/15/14

p. 258 "Oja Kodar has nothing to do": Chris Hastings, "Daughter and Lover Fight over Unreleased Orson Welles Film," *Telegraph,* 8/18/2002, www.telegraph.co.uk/news/worldnews/europe/croatia/1404733/Daughter-and-lover-fight-over-unreleased-Orson-Welles-film.html.

p. 258 "should be shown": McBride, *What Ever Happened*, p. 214.

p. 259 "I'm still working with Orson": Ibid.

p. 260 "I used to think": Sean Graver, AI, 11/15/11.

p. 260 "Everyone was always in service of the project": Ibid.

p. 260 "To his death, I believe": Ibid.

p. 260 "the work of a genius": Tim Carroll, "Awesome Welles," *Sunday Times* (UK), February 13, 2005.

p. 260 "a creator at least twenty years": Ibid.

p. 260 "a Picasso in the attic": Duda, AI, 2/1/13.

p. 261 "The strangest, weirdest guy": Sean Graver, AI, 11/15/11.

p. 261 "I spoke to Orson on many occasions": Paul Hunt, AI (e-mail), 7/28/11.

p. 262 "it was a truly Orsonian deal structure": Duda, AI, 2/1/13.

p. 262 a deal was 99.9 percent done: Howard Swains, "Deal Near on a Lost Welles," *New York Sun*, April 2, 2007.

p. 262 "I think she's the problem": Letter from attorney Kenneth Sidle to attorney Patricia V. Mayer, April 23, 2007, quoting a March 3, 2006, e-mail to Paul Hunt and Sandy Horowitz.

p. 263 "No one could ever interpret": Letter from Kenneth Sidle to Patricia V. Mayer, October 19, 2007.

p. 263 "irreparable financial harm": Letter from attorney James P. Herzog to Patricia V. Mayer, February 15, 2008.

p. 264 "Just when you thought": Duda, AI, 2/1/13.

p. 265 "Her price just kept changing": Ibid.

p. 266 Widhoff signed over Astrophore's rights: Transfer of All Rights Held by Les Films de L'Astrophore to Orson Welles's "The Other Side of the Wind," to JKK Productions, dated September 25, 2012.

p. 266 "This could be the day we pull everything together": Marshall, 1/20/13.

p. 266 "Oja has given me her rights": Marshall, AI (e-mail), 12/22/13.

NOW WHAT?

p. 270 "Few men try for best ever": Richard Ben Cramer, "What Do You Think of Ted Williams Now?" *Esquire*, June 1986.

BIBLIOGRAPHY

NEWSPAPER AND MAGAZINE ARTICLES

"A Carefree Retreat." *Phoenix Magazine,* February 1973.

Aiken, Robert. "Citizen Welles." *North Shore News* (North Vancouver), February 8, 1999.

Alberge, Dalya. "Orson Welles Unseen Masterpiece Set for Release." *Guardian* (London), January 23, 2011.

"Anglo-Greek Pic Halts Prod." *Variety,* January 8, 1975.

Archerd, Army. "Just for Variety." *Variety,* July 3, 1970; March 25, 1974; February 13, 1975; April 23, 1975; May 19, 1975; April 11, 1975; May 29, 1975; October 23, 1975; November 6, 1975; February 2, 1978.

Associated Press. "Mercedes McCambridge, 87, Actress Known for Strong Roles." *New York Times,* March 18, 2004.

———. "DP Gary Graver Dies at 68; Worked for Welles, Corman." *Hollywood Reporter,* November 20, 2006.

———. "Welles Dead in Crash." *New York Times,* August 14, 1986.

Beck, Marilyn. "Hollywood Hotline." *Pasadena Star-News,* January 29, 1975.

———. "Coast to Coast." New York *Daily News,* December 6, 1986.

Beja, Morris. "Where You Can't Get at Him: Orson Welles and the Attempt to Escape from Father." *Film Quarterly,* January 1985.

Bergan, Ronald. "Suzanne Cloutier: French-Canadian Actor Most Celebrated as Desdemona." *Guardian* (London), December 11, 2003.

Berthomé, Jean-Pierre. "Two Open Doors to the Labyrinth; Interview: Dominique Antoine." *Positif,* July/August 1998.

Bogdanovich, Peter. "Is It True What They Say About Orson?" *New York Times*, August 30, 1970.

———. "Reply to Charles Higham Interview." *New York Times*, September 17, 1970.

———. "The Kane Mutiny." *Esquire*, October 1, 1972.

Brechner, Kevin. "Welles' Farewell, The Other Side of the Wind." *American Cinematographer,* July 1, 1986.

Brenner, Marie. "Is Sue Mengers Too Pushy for Hollywood?" *New York,* March 17, 1975.

Canby, Vincent. "The Undiminished Chutzpah of Orson Welles." *New York Times,* March 2, 1974.

Carpenter, Teresa. "Death of a Playmate." *Village Voice* (New York), November 5, 1980.

Carroll, Tim. "Awesome Welles." *Sunday Times* (London), February 13, 2005.

Champlin, Charles. "Falstaff in King Hollywood's Court." *Los Angeles Times,* May 12, 1974, sec. M.

———. "The Huston Magic: Before or Behind the Cameras." *Los Angeles Times,* August 4, 1974, sec. H.

———. "Welles' 'Other Side of the Wind': Still Light on His Feet." *Los Angeles Times,* January 31, 1979.

———. "Welles: The Very Voice of Genius." *Los Angeles Times*, October 11, 1985.

Conrad, Peter. "The Bard of Betrayal." *Observer* (London), September 27, 1992.

Coulouris, George, and Bernard Hermann. "The Citizen Kane Book." *Sight & Sound,* Spring 1972.

Cramer, Richard Ben. "What Do You Think of Ted Williams Now?" *Esquire,* June 1, 1986.

Crook, David. "Bogdanovich's Bankrupt Memorial." *Los Angeles Times,* December 19, 1985,

Daly, Maggie. "Maggie Daly's Column." *Chicago Tribune,* February 12, 1975; May 19, 1975.

"Deaths in the News." *Chicago Sun-Times,* August 17, 1986.

Denby, David. "Peter Bogdanovich—What Went Wrong?" *New York Times,* January 30, 1977.

Desowitz, Bill. "In Hollywood, Welles Seems to Be Having the Last Laugh." *Los Angeles Times,* January 24, 1999.

Dorsey, Helen. "Not the Last Show for Him." *Chicago Tribune,* December 12, 1971.

Ebert, Roger. "Welles' Legacy Honored at Hawaii Film Festival." *Chicago Sun-Times,* December 13, 1987.

Elvouri, Kari. "Oja Kodar Interview." *Filmihullu,* Fall 2003.

"F for Fake Cancels at Stratford Festival; Deny Iranian Slant." *Weekly Variety,* October 1, 1975.

Finch, Erika Ayn, and Joe McNeill. "Sedona's Citizen Welles." *Sedona Monthly,* January 2012.

Fleming, Michael. "All's Welles That Ends . . . " *Weekly Variety,* May 27, 1991.

Gagne, Nicole V. "Where Is The Other Side of the Wind, or *Quien Es Mas Macho:* Orson Welles, John Huston or Ernest Hemingway." *Cineaste,* Winter 2003.

Graham, Don. "Picture Perfect." *Texas Monthly,* February 1, 1999.

Greenberg, Peter. "Saints and Stinkers: The Rolling Stone Interview [with John Huston]." *Rolling Stone,* February 19, 1981.

Gussow, Mel. "Bogdanovich: Director Still Fan." *New York Times,* October 27, 1971.

Haber, Joyce. "Bogdanovich Starring in Welles Film." *Los Angeles Times,* March 19, 1974.

Hale, Norman. "Welles and the Logic of Death." *Film Heritage,* Fall 1974.

Harmetz, Aljean. "Peter Still Looks Forward to His 'Citizen Kane.'" *New York Times,* November 14, 1971.

Hastings, Christopher. "Daughter and Lover Fight over Unreleased Orson Welles Film." *Telegraph* (London), August 18, 2002.

Hattenstone, Simon. "Screen Diary." *Guardian,* June 6, 1991.

Higham, Charles. "And Now the War of the Welles." *New York Times,* September 13, 1970.

———. "Orson's Back and Marlene's Got Him." *New York Times,* January 31, 1971.

———. "The Film Orson Welles Has Been Finishing for Six years." *New York Times,* April 16, 1976.

Hitchens, Gordon. "Welles' Autobio-Pic 'Wind' Safely Outside Tehran, but Unfinished." *Variety,* January 10, 1980.

Holden, Stephen. "One Legacy of Welles: Tons of Unfinished Films." *New York Times,* December 11, 1996.

"Hollywood Salutes Its Maverick Genius—Orson Welles." *American Cinematographer* (special issue), April 1974.

Houston, Beverley. "Power and Dis-integration in the Films of Orson Welles." *Film Quarterly,* Summer 1982.

"International Soundtrack—Madrid." *Daily Variety,* March 27, 1974.

"Iran Moves into Int'l Film Scene with an 'Eastern H'wood' as Goal." *Variety,* February 5, 1975.

"Iranian Coin Enables Welles to Finish Suspended Features." *Weekly Variety* March 19, 1975.

"Iran Fetes F for Fake." *Weekly Variety,* October 15, 1975.

Iwata, Kiku. "An Obsession for Restoring Welles' Works." *Los Angeles Times,* June 30, 1992.

Johnson, Bob. "Orson Welles at Work on 'The Other Side of the Wind.'" *San Francisco Sunday Examiner and Chronicle,* May 25, 1975.

"Just for Variety." *Variety,* February 13, 1975.

Kael, Pauline. "Orson Welles, There Ain't No Way." *New Republic,* June 24, 1967.

———. "Raising Kane." *New Yorker,* February 20 and 27, 1971.

Kehr, Dave. "Obituary: Orson Welles." *Film Comment,* January–February 1985.

Kelly, Ray. "Film Historian and Author Joseph McBride on Spielberg, Welles and Screenwriting." *Republican* (Springfield, Mass.), October 2, 2011.

Leaming, Barbara. "The Genius Takes on Tinseltown." *Playboy*, December 1983.

"Life of Orson Welles and His Work Cited as 500 Mourn Loss." *New York Times*, November 3, 1985.

Levine, Paul G., "Going to the Welles Once Too Often." *Los Angeles Times*, November 10, 1978.

Lyons, Leonard. "Orson Welles Plans a Series of Projects." *Hollywood Citizen-News*, August 9, 1961.

MacNab, Geoffrey. "One of Our Classics Is Missing: Why Won't Beatrice Welles Let Audiences See Her Father's Greatest Movie?" *Guardian* (London), September 28, 2003.

MacNab, Geoffrey. "Orson Welles: Cinema's Lost Genius." *Independent* (London), September 16, 2005.

McBride, Joseph. "AFI Presents Orson Welles Its Third Life Achievement Award." *Daily Variety*, February 11, 1975.

———. "John Huston Finds That the Slow Generation of 'King' Has Made It a Richer Film." *Daily Variety*, December 16, 1975.

———. "Welles Before Kane." *Film Quarterly*, Spring 1970.

———. "Rough Sledding with Pauline Kael." *Film Heritage*, Fall 1971.

———. "Orson Welles Likes Himself." *Gallery*, December 1972.

———. "The Other Side of Orson Welles." *American Film*, July–August 1976.

———. "All's Welles." *Film Comment*, November–December 1978.

———. "Who Is John Huston?: The Riddle of Adaptation and Authorship." *Oxford American*, April 2007.

McCarthy, Todd. "Obituary: Orson Welles." *Variety*, October 16, 1985.

McGavin, Patrick Z. "The Late Genius Orson Welles: 13 Years After His Death, Hollywood Is Finally Taking His Calls." *Hollywood Reporter*, July 7, 1998.

Meyers, Jeffrey. "John Huston and Hemingway." *Antioch Review* 68, no. 1 (2010): 54.

Meyers, Robert. "Tribute to a Maverick." *Washington Post,* February 11, 1975, sec. B.

Moe, Doug. "Still Seeking 'The Other Side.'" *Capital Times* (Madison, Wis.). December 19, 2005.

Nashawaty, Chris. "The Film That Broke Orson Welles' Heart." *Entertainment Weekly,* April 14, 2006.

Nelson, Valerie J. "Obituary: Gary Graver, 68; Maverick Cinematographer, Tried to Complete Orson Welles' Final Film." *Los Angeles Times,* November 19, 2006.

"New York Soundtrack—Column." *Weekly Variety,* May 11, 1988.

"Norman Foster, 72, Dies of Cancer; Services Tomorrow." *Daily Variety,* July 9, 1976.

O'Brian, Jack. "The Voice of Broadway." *Bradford Era,* March 28, 1974.

O'Neill, Anne W. "Director Bogdanovich Declares Bankruptcy." *Los Angeles Times,* June 4, 1997.

"Orson Welles Plots H'wood 'Guess Who' Pic." *Daily Variety,* August 2, 1971.

"Orson Welles: Beacon and Exile." *Moviemaker,* April 2, 2004.

"Other Side of the Wind Negative." *Daily Variety,* February 13, 1980.

Paletz, Gabriel. "Orson Welles: Beacon and Exile." *Moviemaker,* April 1, 2004.

"Paloa Mori, Widow of Actor Orson Welles." *Los Angeles Times,* August 14, 1986.

Perlmutter, Ruth. "Working with Welles: An Interview with Henry Jaglom." *Film Quarterly,* Spring 1988.

Pollock, Dale. "Welles Says 'A' Budget Pic Not in Future." *Daily Variety,* January 30, 1979.

Posner, Michael. "Severing Ties with Iran Stupid, Canada's Envoy from the 1970s Says." *Globe and Mail* (Toronto), September 13, 2012.

"Print Ad—Orson Welles, His Latest Films." *Weekly Variety,* February 5, 1975.

Purtell, Tim. "Oscar Grouch." *Entertainment Weekly,* April 16, 1993.

———. "The Genius Nobody Wanted." *Entertainment Weekly,* October 8, 1993.

Richard, Combs. "Burning Masterwork: From Kane to F for Fake." *Film Comment,* January–February 1994.

Rodman, Howard. "The Last Days of Orson Welles." *American Film,* June 1987.

Rosenbaum, Jonathan. "The Invisible Orson Welles: A First Inventory." *Sight & Sound,* Summer 1986.

Rush, Geoff, Joanna Molloy, Marcus Baram, and K. C. Baker. "Welles' Daughter Blasts 'Touch'-Up." New York *Daily News,* August 30, 1998.

Sarris, Andrew. "Citizen Kael v. Citizen Kane." *Village Voice* (New York), April 15, 1971.

Shearer, Lloyd. "Welles Goes Porno." *Parade,* March 1, 1973.

Sokolov, Raymond. "Orsonology." *Newsweek,* August 3, 1970.

"Stafford Repp Obituary." *Daily Variety,* November 11, 1974.

Strassberg, Phil. "Film Venture Ferell's Aim." *Arizona Republic* (Phoenix), March 27, 1974.

Swains, Howard. "Deal Near on a Lost Welles." *New York Sun,* April 2, 2007.

Swisher, Viola Hegyi. "Orson Welles and Five Years of 'The Other Side of the Wind.'" *After Dark,* March 1976.

"Welles Making Directing Comeback." *Syracuse Herald American—Stars Magazine,* July 29, 1984.

"Television Review: The American Film Institute Salute to Orson Welles." *Daily Variety,* February 19, 1975.

Thomas, Kevin. "An Eye Trained on Welles." *Los Angeles Times,* February 8, 2004.

———. "Director Bogdanovich Knows What's Up, Doc!" *Los Angeles Times,* November 21, 1971.

Thomson, David. "Razing Kane." *Los Angeles Magazine,* April 1996.

———. "The Most Successful Person in Hollywood." *Movieline,* November 2002.

Tunison, Michael. "The Other Side of Orson Welles." *Moviemaker,* Winter 2002.

Tynan, Kenneth. "*Playboy* Interview: Orson Welles." *Playboy,* March 1967.

Welles, Beatrice. "And the Oscar Goes to . . . the Man in the Back Row for $1 Million." *Los Angeles Times,* March 17, 2004, sec. "Commentary."

Welles, Orson. "But Where Are We Going?" *Look,* November 3, 1970.

———. "Twilight in the Smog." *Esquire,* March 1959.

Whipp, Glenn. "Marshall Worked on Welles' 'Wind.'" *Variety,* February 17, 2009.

Wilson, Richard. "It's Not Quite All True." *Sight & Sound,* Fall 1970.

Wolcott, James. "The Big O." *Vanity Fair,* November 1999.

Wolf, William. "Going Back to Huston." *New York,* May 12, 1980.

CORRESPONDENCE

Antoine, Dominique. Dominique Antoine to Orson Welles. Paris, France, January 15, 1975.

———. Dominique Antoine to Orson Welles. Paris, France, June 24, 1975.

———. Dominique Antoine to Orson Welles. Paris, France, July 11, 1975.

———. Dominique Antoine to Orson Welles. Paris, France, September 19, 1975.

———. Dominique Antoine to Orson Welles. Paris, France, October 30, 1975.

———. Dominique Antoine to Orson Welles. Paris, France, February 4, 1976.

———. Dominique Antoine to Orson Welles. Paris, France, June 24, 1976.

———. Dominique Antoine to Arnold Weissberger. Paris, France, November 28, 1975.

———. Dominique Antoine to Peter Bogdanovich. Paris, France, December 4, 1975.

Bogdanovich, Peter. Peter Bogdanovich to Orson Welles. Beverly Hills, Calif., October 22, 1975.

———. Peter Bogdanovich to Orson Welles. Beverly Hills, Calif., November 23, 1975.

———. Peter Bogdanovich to Orson Welles. Beverly Hills, Calif., December 5, 1975.

———. Peter Bogdanovich to Orson Welles. Beverly Hills, Calif. December 18, 1975.

Boushehri, Mehdi. Mehdi Boushehri to Orson Welles. Paris, France, May 13, 1975.

———. Michael Fitzgerald to Mehdi Boushehri to Michael Fitzgerald. Paris, France, May 25, 1997.

Deschamps, Yves. Yves Deschamps to Orson Welles. Paris, France, October 7, 1974.

Ferre, Nadine. Nadine Ferre to Patricia V. Mayer. Saint-Cloud, France, July 25, 2006.

Fielding, Claude. Claude Fielding to Werner Wolfen. London, England, June 2, 1976.

Fitzgerald, Michael. Michael Fitzgerald to Mehdi Boushehri. Los Angeles, Calif., April 29, 1997.

George, James. James George to Mehdi Boushehri. Paris, France, May 30, 1978.

———. James George to Orson Welles, Beverly Hills, Calif., November 6, 1978; November 9, 1978.

———. James George to Arnold Weissberger/Avenel. [Location unspecified], November, 13, 1978.

———. James George to Orson Welles. Paris, France, November 22, 1978.

Herzog, James P. James P. Herzog to Patricia V. Mayer. Los Angeles, Calif., February 15, 2008.

Hines, Jim. Jim Hines to Frank Marshall. Carefree, Ariz., May 2, 1974.

Kaplan, Richard. Richard Kaplan to Arnold Weissberger. Beverly Hills, Calif., November 15, 1978.

Little, Rich. Rich Little to Orson Welles. Los Angeles, Calif., May 13, 1976.

———. General letter of recommendation for Orson Welles. Los Angeles, Calif., May 22, 1976.

McBride, Joseph. Joseph McBride to Ronald Gottesman. Madison, Wis., July 25, 1971.

McCarthy, Frank. Frank McCarthy to Charlton Heston and Howard Koch. Los Angeles, Calif., December 11, 1974.

Sidle, Kenneth. Kenneth Sidle to Victoria V. Mayer. Los Angeles, Calif., April 23, 2007; October 19, 2007.

Stevens, George Jr. George Stevens Jr. to Peter Bogdanovich. Los Angeles, Calif., January 22, 1975.

Weissberger, Arnold. Arnold Weissberger to Klaus Hellwig. New York, N.Y., May 6, 1974.

————. Arnold Weissberger to Orson Welles. New York, N.Y., March 22, 1976; June 7, 1978; November 6, 1978.

Welles, Orson. Orson Welles to Peter Bogdanovich. Beverly Hills, Calif., August 15, 1970; May 28, 1975; October 22, 1975.

————. Orson Welles to his Spanish producer. [Location unknown], [n.d.] 1973–1974.

————. Orson Welles to Dominique Antoine. Orvilliers, France, July 24, 1974; July 26, 1974; August 11, 1974; August 26, 1974; January 4, 1975.

————. Orson Welles to Yves Deschamps and editing staff. Orvilliers, France, July 30, 1974.

————. Orson Welles to Dominique Antoine and Mehdi Boushehri. Orvilliers, France, September 24, 1974.

————. Orson Welles to Mehdi Boushehri. Orvilliers, France, October 4, 1974.

————. Orson Welles to Tonio Selwart. Orvilliers, France, October 14, 1974.

————. Orson Welles to Norman Foster. Orvilliers, France, October 14, 1974.

————. Orson Welles to Paul Stewart. Orvilliers, France, October 14, 1974.

————. Orson Welles to Arnold Weissberger, Orvilliers, France, January 15, 1975.

————. Orson Welles to Mehdi Boushehri, Orvilliers, France, January 22, 1975.

————. Orson Welles to Dominique Antoine. Beverly Hills, Calif., April 12, 1975; April 29, 1975; [n.d.] May 1975; June 1, 1975; June 4, 1975; June 16, 1975; October 27, 1975; April 23, 1975; November 17, 1975.

————. Orson Welles to Mehdi Boushehri. Beverly Hills, Calif., May 12, 1975.

————. Orson Welles to Mehdi Boushehri and Dominique Antoine. [n.d.] September 1975.

————. Orson Welles to Rich Little, April 22, 1976.

————. Orson Welles to Mehdi Boushehri, [n.d.] 1977.

————. Orson Welles letter declaring Oja Kodar beneficiary of one-half of his pension plans. Los Angeles, Calif., October 4, 1985.

BOOKS

Abramowitz, Rachel. *Is That a Gun in Your Pocket?: Women's Experience of Power in Hollywood*. New York: Random House, 2000.

Bazin, André, and François Truffaut. *Orson Welles: A Critical View*. Rev. ed. Translated by Jonathan Rosenbaum. Venice, Calif.: Acrobat Books, 1992.

Berg, Chuck, and Thomas L. Erskine. *The Encyclopedia of Orson Welles*. New York: Facts on File, 2003.

Berthomé, Jean-Pierre, and François Thomas. *Orson Welles at Work*. English ed. London: Phaidon Press, 2008.

Bessy, Maurice. *Orson Welles: An Investigation into His Films and Philosophy*. 1963; repr., New York: Crown, 1971.

Biskind, Peter. *Easy Riders, Raging Bulls: How the Sex-Drugs-and-Rock 'n' Roll Generation Saved Hollywood*. New York: Simon & Schuster, 1998.

Bogdanovich, Peter, and Orson Welles. *This Is Orson Welles*. Edited by Jonathan Rosenbaum. New York: HarperCollins, 1992.

Bradbury, Ray. *Green Shadows, White Whale*. New York: Alfred A. Knopf, 1992.

Brady, Frank. *Citizen Welles: A Biography of Orson Welles*. New York: Scribner, 1989.

Brill, Lesley. *John Huston's Filmmaking*. Cambridge, UK: Cambridge University Press, 1997.

Browne, Nick, ed. *Francis Ford Coppola's* The Godfather *Trilogy*. Cambridge, UK: Cambridge University Press, 2000.

Callow, Simon. *Orson Welles, Volume 1: The Road to Xanadu*. London: Jonathan Cape, 1995.

———. *Orson Welles, Volume 2: Hello Americans*. New York: Viking Penguin, 2006.

Cobos, Juan. *Orson Welles:* España Como Obsesión. Valencia: Filmoteca Valenciana, 1993.

Cohen, Allen, and Harry Lawton. *John Huston: A Guide to References and Resources*. New York: G. K. Hall, 1997.

Conrad, Peter. *Orson Welles: The Stories of His Life*. London: Faber & Faber, 2003.

Dennis, Patrick. *Genius*. New York: Harcourt, Brace & World, 1962.

Estrin, Mark W., ed. *Orson Welles: Interviews*. Jackson: University Press of Mississippi, 2002.

Feder, Christopher Welles. *In My Father's Shadow: A Daughter Remembers Orson Welles*. Chapel Hill, N.C.: Algonquin Books of Chapel Hill, 2009.

Feeney, F. X. *Welles*. Edited by Paul Duncan. Köln: Taschen, 2006.

Garis, Robert. *The Films of Orson Welles*. Cambridge, UK: Cambridge University Press, 2004.

Gottesman, Ronald, ed. *Focus on Orson Welles*. Englewood Cliffs, N.J.: Prentice Hall, 1976.

Graver, Gary, and Andrew J. Rausch. *Making Movies with Orson Welles: A Memoir*. Lanham, Md.: Scarecrow Press, 2008.

Grobel, Lawrence. *The Hustons: The Life and Times of a Hollywood Dynasty*. Rev. ed. New York: Scribner, 1989.

Hamblett, Charles. *The Crazy Kill: A Fantasy*. London: Sidgwick & Jackson, 1965.

Harris, Thomas J. *Bogdanovich's Picture Shows*. Metuchen, N.J.: Scarecrow Press, 1990.

Hemingway, Ernest. *Death in the Afternoon*. New York: Charles Scribner's Sons, 1932.

Heylin, Clinton. *Despite the System: Orson Welles Versus the Hollywood Studios*. Chicago: Chicago Review Press, 2005.

Higham, Charles. *The Films of Orson Welles.* Berkeley: University of California Press, 1970.

———. *Orson Welles, The Rise and Fall of an American Genius.* New York: St. Martin's Press, 1985.

———. *In and Out of Hollywood: A Biographer's Memoir.* Madison, Wis.: Terrace Books, 2009.

Hogg, Michael. *Luck and Circumstance: A Coming of Age in Hollywood, New York, and Points Beyond.* New York: Alfred A. Knopf, 2011.

Houseman, John. *Run-Through: A Memoir.* New York: Simon & Schuster, 1972.

Howard, James. *The Complete Films of Orson Welles.* Secaucus, N.J.: Carol Publishing Group, 1991.

Huston, John. *An Open Book.* New York: Alfred A. Knopf, 1980.

———, and Robert Emmet Long. *John Huston: Interviews.* Jackson: University Press of Mississippi, 2001.

Jaglom, Henry, and Orson Welles. *My Lunches with Orson: Conversations Between Henry Jaglom and Orson Welles.* Edited by Peter Biskind. New York: Metropolitan Books, 2013.

Kael, Pauline, Herman J. Mankiewicz, and Orson Welles. *The Citizen Kane Book: Raising Kane.* 1st ed. Boston: Little, Brown, 1971.

Kellow, Brian. *Pauline Kael: A Life in the Dark.* New York: Viking, 2011.

Leaming, Barbara. *Orson Welles: A Biography.* New York: Limelight Editions, 1995.

Lewis, Jon. *Whom God Wishes to Destroy . . . : Francis Coppola and the New Hollywood.* Durham, N.C.: Duke University Press, 1995.

Lyons, Bridget Gellert, ed. *Chimes at Midnight: Orson Welles, Director.* New Brunswick, N.J.: Rutgers University Press, 1988.

Madsen, Axel. *John Huston.* Garden City, N.Y.: Doubleday, 1978.

Mazursky, Paul. *Show Me the Magic.* New York: Simon & Schuster, 1999.

McBride, Joseph. *Orson Welles.* New York: Viking Press, 1972.

———. *What Ever Happened to Orson Welles?: A Portrait of an Independent Career.* Lexington: University Press of Kentucky, 2006.

McCambridge, Mercedes. *The Quality of Mercy: An Autobiography*. New York: Times Books, 1981.

McCarty, John. *The Films of John Huston*. Secaucus, N.J.: Citadel Press, 1987.

Meyers, Jeffrey. *John Huston: Courage and Art*. New York: Crown Archetype, 2011.

Naficy, Hamid. *A Social History of Iranian Cinema, Volume 2: The Industrializing Years, 1941–1978*. Durham, N.C.: Duke University Press, 2011.

———. *A Social History of the Iranian Cinema, Volume 3: The Islamicate Period—1978–1984*. Durham, N.C.: Duke University Press, 2012.

Naremore, James. *The Magic World of Orson Welles*. New York: Oxford University Press, 1978.

Nolan, William F. *John Huston: King Rebel*. Los Angeles: Sherbourne Press, 1965.

Pahlavi, Ashraf. *Faces in a Mirror: Memoirs from Exile*. Englewood Cliffs, N.J.: Prentice Hall, 1980.

Pratley, Gerald. *The Cinema of John Huston*. South Brunswick, N.J.: A. S. Barnes, 1977.

Pye, Michael, and Lynda Myles. *The Movie Brats: How the Film Generation Took Over Hollywood*. New York: Henry Holt, 1984.

Riambeau, Esteve. *Orson Welles: Una España Inmortal*. 1st ed. Valencia: Filmoteca, Generalitat Valenciana, 1993.

Rosenbaum, Jonathan. *Discovering Orson Welles*. Berkeley: University of California Press, 2007.

Shepherd, Cybill, and Aimee Lee Ball. *Cybill Disobedience*. New York: HarperCollins, 2000.

Singer, Irving. *Three Philosophical Filmmakers: Hitchcock, Welles, Renoir*. Cambridge, Mass.: MIT Press, 2004.

Strasberg, Susan. *Bittersweet*. New York: G. P. Putnam's Sons, 1980.

Studlar, Gaylyn, David Desser, and John Huston. *Reflections in a Male Eye: John Huston and the American Experience*. Washington, D.C.: Smithsonian Institution Press, 1993.

Tarbox, Todd. *Orson Welles and Roger Hill: A Friendship in Three Acts.* Fort Worth, Tex.: BearManor Media, 2013.

Thomson, David. *Rosebud: The Story of Orson Welles.* New York: Alfred A. Knopf, 1996.

Tonguette, Peter Prescott. *Orson Welles Remembered: Interviews with His Actors, Editors, Cinematographers and Magicians.* Jefferson, N.C.: McFarland & Co., 2007.

Tozzi, Romano. *John Huston: Hollywood's Magic People.* New York: Falcon, 1971.

Viertel, Peter. *White Hunter Black Heart.* Garden City, N.Y.: Doubleday, 1953.

———. *Dangerous Friends: At Large with Huston and Hemingway in the Fifties.* New York: Nan A. Talese, 1992.

Walters, Ben. *Welles.* London: Haus, 2004.

Welles, Orson, and Oja Kodar. *The Other Side of the Wind: Screenplay.* Edited by Giorgio Gosetti. Paris: Cahiers du Cinéma, 2005.

Wood, Bret. *Orson Welles: A Bio-Bibliography.* New York: Greenwood Press, 1990.

Yule, Andrew. *Picture Shows: The Life and Films of Peter Bogdanovich.* New York: Limelight Editions, 1992.

FILM, TELEVISION, AND VIDEO

Arena: The Orson Welles Story. DVD. Directed by Leslie Megahey. London: BBC, 1982.

Behind the Curtain: Joseph McBride on Writing Film History. DVD. Directed by Hart Perez. Springville, Utah: Vervante, 2011.

Brunnen. Directed by Kristian Petri. Kbh.: Det Danske Filminstitut, 2005.

Orson Welles, interview by Dick Cavett. *The Dick Cavett Show.* New York: ABC-TV, July 22, 1970.

"Orson Welles Receiving an Honorary Oscar." Academy of Motion Picture Arts and Sciences. www.oscars.org/video/watch/43rd_Welles.html (accessed February 25, 2013).

Orson Welles: One Man Band. DVD. Directed by Vassili Silovic. New York: Criterion Collection, 2005.

Orson Welles: The Paris Interview. DVD. Directed by Allen King. West Long Branch, N.J.: Kultur, 1960.

Michael Parkinson, *Parkinson: The Orson Welles Interview.* London: BBC, 1974.

Prodigal Sons. DVD. Directed by Kimberly Reed. New York: First Run Features, 2008.

Remembering Orson. DVD. Directed by Frank Beacham. n.p.: Television Matrix, 1985.

The Other Side of the Wind: My Private Exercise. DVD. Directed by Kari Elvouri. Helsinki: Kari Elvouri, 2007.

Vies. DVD. Directed by Alain Cavalier. Paris: Les Films de L'Astrophore (prod.), 2000.

Who Is Henry Jaglom? DVD. Directed by Richard Lundun. New York: First Run Features, 1997.

Working with Orson Welles. DVD. Directed by Gary Graver. Chatsworth, Calif.: Image Entertainment, 1993.

WEB ARTICLES, WEB SITES, AND ONLINE RESOURCES

"AFI Tribute to Orson Welles." FilmmakerIQcom. filmmakeriq.com// 2011/09/afi-tribute-to-orson-welles (accessed June 24, 2012).

Andreeva, Nellie. "Showtime's Head of Acquisitions and Distribution Matthew Duda to Retire." Deadline.com. www.deadline.com/2012/03 /showtimes-head-of-acquisitions-and-distribution-matthew-duda-to -retire (accessed April 15, 2012).

At Long Last Love. IMDb.com. www.imdb.com/title/tt0072665 (accessed June 25, 2012).

Bartok. "Eric Sherman: 2 Weeks with Orson Welles." L.A. After Midnight. la-after-midnight-bartok.blogspot.com/2011/06/eric-sherman-2 -weeks-with-orson-welles.html (accessed May 24, 2013).

Brown, Phil. "Peter Bogdanovich." *Toro Magazine,* April 9, 2012. www .toromagazine.com/features/talking-to/6fdb4174-ebe9-e6d4-e5a6 -a19a65658c24/Peter-Bogdanovich (accessed March 25, 2013).

Cabrelli, Paolo. "Sunken Treasure: The Drowned World of Lost Movies." *Stylus,* May 22, 2006. www.stylusmagazine.com/articles/weekly_article

/sunken-treasure-the-drowned-world-of-lost-movies.htm (accessed May 19, 2011).

Clark, Brian. "Timeline: The Long, Tortured History of Orson Welles' Lost Film The Other Side of the Wind." *Movieline,* January 28, 2011. movieline.com/2011/01/28/timeline-the-long-tortured-history-of -orson-welles-lost-film-the-other-side-of-the-wind (accessed February 5, 2011).

Dargis, Manohla. "Go! Go! Go!" *LA Weekly,* December 20, 2000. www .laweekly.com/2000-12-28/news/go-go-go (accessed July 15, 2013).

Day, Chris. "Update: The (Possibly) Great Unfinished Films—The Other Side of the Wind." Febriblog, January 23, 2011. febriblog.wordpress .com/2011/01/23/update-the-possibly-great-unfinished-films-the -other-side-of-the-wind (accessed June 17, 2011).

Drees, Rich. "Welles's CITIZEN KANE Oscar Up for Auction." Film Buff Online, October 17, 2007. www.filmbuffonline/FBOLNewsreel/word press/2007/10/17/welless-citizen-kane-oscar-up-for-auction (accessed May 19, 2011).

Folsom, Tom. "Critic's Notebook: Why 'Easy Rider' Still Matters 45 Years Later." *Indiewire,* February 21, 2013. www.indiewire.com/article /critics-notebook-why-easy-rider-still-matters-45-years-later (accessed August 24, 2013).

French, Lawrence. "French/Rosenbaum Interview 1." Wellesnet. www .wellesnet.com/rosenbaum_interview.htm (accessed May 14, 2011).

———. "Is Showtime Near a Deal to Complete Orson Welles's THE OTHER SIDE OF THE WIND?" Wellesnet. www.wellesnet.com/ ?p=403 (accessed May 14, 2011).

Kehr, Dave. "The Lady from Shanghai." *Chicago Reader.* www.chicago reader.com/chicago/the-lady-from-shanghai/Film?oid=2552830 (accessed March 30, 2012).

Love, Damien. "Inherit the Wind." *Bright Lights Film Journal,* February 2007. brightlightsfilm.com/55/windiv.php (accessed May 19, 2011).

"Motion Picture Copyright for The Other Side of the Wind." Project Welles. www.projectwelles.com/wp-content/uploads/2011/02/Copyright-Mo tion-Picture.pdf (accessed September 25, 2011).

"News (See All . . .)." The Numbers. *Easy Rider.* www.the-numbers.com
/movies/1969/0ERID.php (accessed February 22, 2014).

———. *Bonnie and Clyde.* www.the-numbers.com/movies/1967/0BACL
.php (accessed February 24, 2014).

"Orson Welles AFI Speech—1975." Wellesnet. www.wellesnet.com/?p=46
(accessed June 24, 2012).

"Orson Welles' Partner Unsure About Showtime Completing His Movie."
Croatian Times, January 27, 2011. www.croatiantimes.com/news/Pan
orama/2011-01-27/16742 (accessed January 28, 2011).

Stokes, Simon. "Art and Copyright: What's at Stake." *Art Newspaper,* April
8, 2009. www.theartnewspaper.com/articles/Art%20and%20copy
right:%20what%E2%80%99s%20at%20stake/17203.

LEGAL DOCUMENTS

Certificate of Death for Orson Welles, State of California, October 15,
1985.

Contract Between Les Films de L'Astrophore and Avenel Inc., August 9,
1974.

Confirmation of Ownership Rights, June 19, 1985.

Coopers & Lybrand Audit of Les Films de L'Astrophore, October 12, 1976.

Decision of Tribunal de Grande Instance de Paris, March 15, 1982.

In the Matter of the Estate of George Orson Welles, Deceased, District
Court, Clark County Nevada, Case No. P20544, November 7, 1986.

Last Will and Testament of Orson Welles, January 15, 1982.

Memorandum of Agreement, August 3, 1978, James George to Avenel/
Orson Welles/Arnold Weissberger.

Transfer of All Rights Held by Les Films de L'Astrophore to Orson Welles's
"The Other Side of the Wind," to JKK Productions, September 25,
2012.

OTHER

Unpublished transcript of scene between Henry Jaglom and Paul Mazursky, filmed November 1970, Beverly Hills, Calif.

Unpublished transcript of Dennis Hopper monologue/interview, filmed November 1970, Beverly Hills, Calif.

Welles, Orson. Interview by Peter Bogdanovich. Tape recording. Los Angeles, Calif., February 2, 1970. Recordings courtesy of Cybill Shepherd.

———. Interview by Joseph McBride. Tape recording. Beverly Hills, Calif., August 23, 1970.

Audio recording of first day of shooting courtesy of Joseph McBride.

INDEX

Note: OW stands for Orson Welles. *Wind* stands for *The Other Side of the Wind*. Names of fictional characters are listed first name first, e.g. "Jack Simon (character)" under "J" not "S".